ARCTIC
PASSAGES

ARCTIC PASSAGES

A Unique Small-Boat Journey Through the Great Northern Waterway

John Bockstoce

QUILL

William Morrow

New York

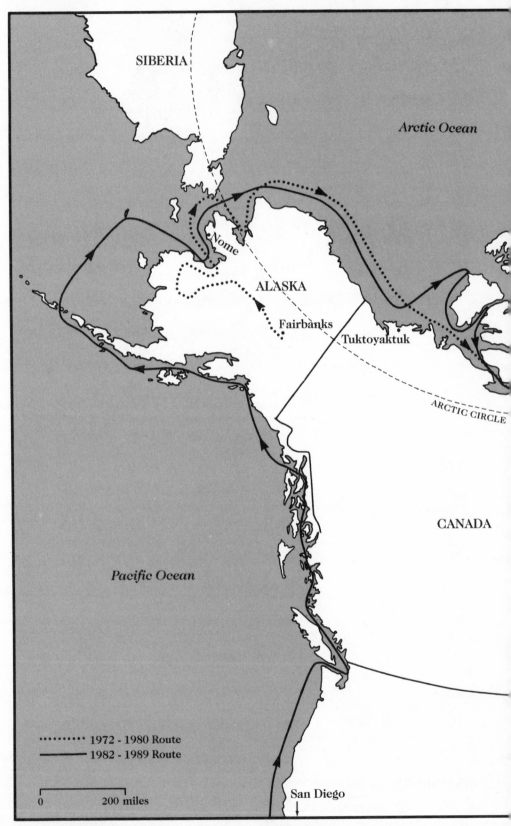

SIBERIA

Arctic Ocean

Nome

ALASKA

Fairbanks

Tuktoyaktuk

ARCTIC CIRCLE

Pacific Ocean

CANADA

•••••• 1972 - 1980 Route
———— 1982 - 1989 Route

0   200 miles

San Diego

Journey Through the Northwest Passage

North Pole

GREENLAND

Resolute

Holsteinsborg

Atlantic Ocean

Cambridge Bay

New York

UNITED STATES

Library of Congress Cataloging-in-Publication Data

Bockstoce, John R.
    Artic passages : a unique small-boat journey through the Great Northern Waterway / John Bockstoce.
        p. cm.
    Originally published: New York : Hearst Marine Books, 1991.
    ISBN 0-688-11606-X
    1. Alaska—Description and travel—1981- 2. Yukon Territory—Description and travel. 3. Northwest Passage. 4.Boats and boating—Alaska. 5. Boats and boating—Yukon Territory. 6. Boats and boating—Northwest Passage. 7. Bockstoce, John R.—Journeys.
I. Title.
F910.5.B624   1992
917.98'6045—dc20   92-6171
                                                                    CIP

Printed in the United States of America

First Quill Edition

1 2 3 4 5 6 7 8 9 10

BOOK DESIGN **AND MAPS** BY ARLENE GOLDBERG

Acknowledgments

Many hundreds of people have been generous and helpful to me on my northern journeys; some are mentioned in the text of this book, but most are not, and I regret that space and time do not permit me to mention them all. The best I can do is to say thank you, most sincerely, for enabling me to carry out my work. I am very grateful.

I must, nevertheless, identify a few whose assistance has been especially valuable. Those who have helped with logistics are Sheila Abendroth, Steve Braund, Dave Burnett, Nan Cooper, Tom Crowley, Vagn Dahl, Hiram Fuller, Elmer Groth, Jim Hamblin, George Hobson, Kurt Horlyk, George Jacobsen, Carl Jewell, Dan Kelly, Willie Ker, Willy Laserich, Lionel Montpetit, Bill O'Shea, Laddy Pathy, Paul Preville, Tom Pullen, Graham and Diana Rowley, Peter and Alma Semotiuk, Jim Smith, Carol Stephenson and the staff of Canadian Coast Guard Northern, Ray Tomsett, and Wally Trudeau.

The manuscript could not have been prepared without the aid of the following: Julian Bach, Rosalie Baker, Jan Kirshner and her assistants, Betty Kugler, Grace Olivera, Connie Roosevelt, the staff of the Southworth Library, and Nick Whitman. To Henry and Cathy Roberts I owe a special debt of thanks for their unfailing support and good humor at all times.

Lastly, my deep gratitude goes to the more than fifty people who have accompanied me, in three boats, on Arctic voyages of the last twenty years.

For John Grimston Bockstoce

Other Books by John Bockstoce

Eskimos of Northwest Alaska in the Early Nineteenth Century (1977)

Steam Whaling in the Western Arctic (1977)

The Archaeology of Cape Nome, Alaska (1979)

With William Gilkerson: *American Whalers in the Western Arctic* (1983)

Whales, Ice and Men. The History of Whaling in the Western Arctic (1986)

Editor: *The Voyage of the Schooner Polar Bear: Whaling and Trading in the North Pacific and Arctic, 1913–1914* by Bernhard Kilian (1983)

Editor: *The Journal of Rochfort Maguire, 1852–1854. Two Years at Point Barrow, Alaska, Aboard H.M.S. Plover in the Search for Sir John Franklin* (1988)

Contents

Introduction

The Arctic has meant many things to many people. Some find it thrilling. Some find it frightening. Some find it a mystical experience. Some find it repellent. Some find it lush and beautiful. Some find it a wasteland. Some exaggerate its hardships, while others overlook its dangers; but no one who has visited it can ignore its awesome power and elemental grandeur, and anyone who has visited it will bear its indelible tincture, however vivid or faint, for the rest of his or her life.

The Arctic has meant many things to me, but most of all the Arctic has meant great freedom: the freedom to strive, the freedom to fail, the freedom to learn, and the freedom to succeed. In essence it is the freedom to grow. That is why I have dedicated this book to my son—and in a larger sense, to all young people—in the hope that they will have the good fortune to find their own challenges, their own "Arctics," wherever they may be.

A view looking north of the western tip of North America, taken by the author in July 1969 from Cape Prince of Wales. The Chukchi Sea lies beyond Wales village.

Chapter 1

Umiaks

I flew out of Nome, Alaska, to the village of Wales on a dull and blustery day in July 1969. Approaching Bering Strait from the southeast, the plane rose over the lifeless and gray, almost lunar, landscape that is the massive headland of Cape Prince of Wales, the westernmost point of North America. When we reached twenty-five hundred feet, suddenly and precipitously the Cape receded below into the blue-black waters.

I was at the gates of the Arctic: ahead, the Chukchi Sea and Arctic Ocean; behind, the Bering Sea and Pacific, and fifty miles away, as massive as Cape Prince of Wales, was Cape Dezhnev— the easternmost point of Asia.

In the center of the strait the Diomede Islands, two black, flat-topped pillars of rock two miles apart, rose more than a thousand feet from the water. The nearer was Little Diomede, Alaska; the other, "Big Diomede," was Ostrov Ratmonova, U.S.S.R. Between them ran the International Date Line, which here is also the international frontier.

I was punch-drunk from jet lag that day, having just flown

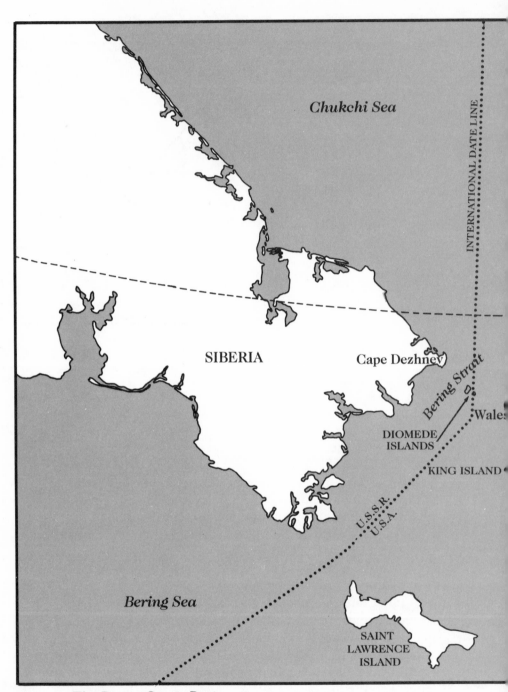

Chukchi Sea

INTERNATIONAL DATE LINE

SIBERIA

Cape Dezhnev

Bering Strait

Wales

DIOMEDE
ISLANDS

KING ISLAND

U.S.S.R.
U.S.A.

Bering Sea

SAINT
LAWRENCE
ISLAND

The Bering Strait Region

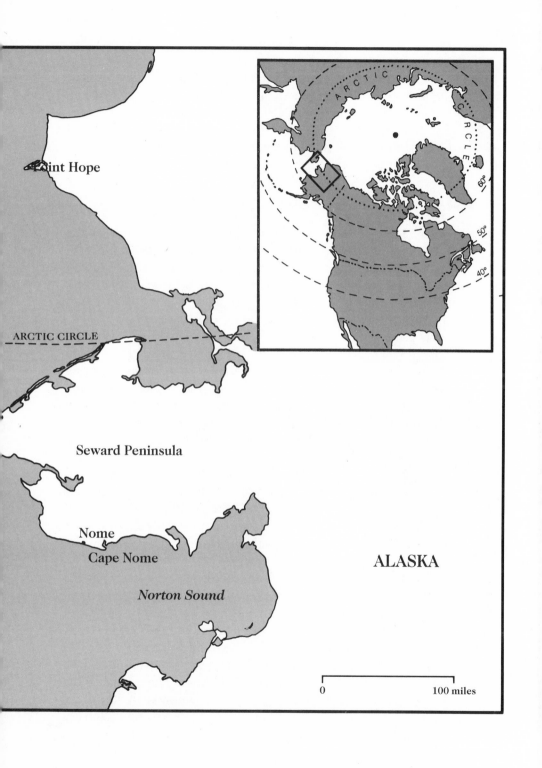

Point Hope

ARCTIC CIRCLE

Seward Peninsula

Nome
Cape Nome

Norton Sound

ALASKA

0   100 miles

halfway around the world at the orders of my boss, who wanted me to inspect the potential of a recently discovered archaeological midden on Diomede. I arrived with the same batch of trowels, cameras, notebooks, and measuring tapes that I had just been using on a dig in the deserts of eastern Iran.

The little plane bumped to a stop on the gray sand beach at Wales, a village of about three dozen huts. It seemed as if most of the village's one hundred forty Eskimos surrounded the aircraft, watching passively as the pilot heaved my kit out onto the beach. I dragged my bags a few yards to the sand dunes as the plane revved up with a roar, taxied a short way, and took off—and then the silence of the Arctic washed over me for the first time. Beyond the tree line, with no leaves to rustle, you hear only the whine of the wind, the ruffling of your own collar, and the rush of the surf. I felt I was on the moon.

My next task was to get to Little Diomede. A few hours earlier, when I got off the jet in Nome, I learned that I could only get to the island with the Eskimos in an open boat. During the summer it is impossible to fly there; Little Diomede is only about one and a half miles long, too small and steep to have an airstrip. In the winter, however, a bridge of ice, which can be used for landing, forms between the two islands. From December until late May small planes from Nome carry out regular passenger and mail service to the one hundred or so inhabitants of the island. After the ice melts away, the waters are either too ice-clogged or too boisterous for prudent pilots to land float-planes there. For the rest of the summer the only way to get to Diomede is by boat and the only boats making the crossing are those of the Diomeders themselves.

Someone, whose classical education must have gotten the better of him, described the Diomeders as the "Argonauts of Bering Strait." This is mostly hyperbole, but there is some truth in it. These men are mariners to a degree, and they are certainly freebooters par excellence—out of historical necessity.

In prehistoric times (well-documented history only began here in 1778, with the voyage of Captain James Cook) the Diomeders had only the sea to harvest: seals and fish during the winter, vast herds of walruses in the spring and autumn, and sea birds and some greens in the summer. Perforce the Diomeders became the middlemen in the extensive native trade between Asia and North America. For at least two millennia furs and walrus ivory flowed west to the markets of China and Europe, while metal goods followed the opposite course.

That day as I walked along the beach at Wales I saw the Diomeders' camp near the base of the Cape. It was about 3:00 P.M., and as I approached I could see that all seven or eight of them were just waking up. Closer, the men's rat-red eyes and shaky hands testified that they were all suffering from world-class hangovers. They had just returned from two weeks in Nome, 125 miles by boat to the southeast, where they had gone loaded with walrus ivory and returned awash in cheap whiskey.

But before their boozy breath hit me I was struck by their boat. It was tilted over on its side and propped up by two paddles. They were all camped under it and it looked enormous. It was an umiak, one of the most perfectly adapted watercraft ever devised by man. About thirty-five feet long, with graceful lines, it was a skeleton of thin wooden framing with five or six walrus hides sewn together edge-to-edge and stretched drumtight over it. The daylight passed through the skin with a wonderful caramel translucence. My fascination with umiaks began at that moment, and I couldn't have known it then, but it was also the beginning of my twenty-year challenge with the Northwest Passage.

One of the Diomeders asked me my business, and I told him I wanted to go to the island. His reply: "That'll be one hundred dollars. We leave this evening. You'll enjoy it."

With one eye on this painfully hungover "argonaut" and the other on the nasty swell that was running out there in Bering Strait, I didn't think I would enjoy it at all.

But I did enjoy it. We left around midnight, just as the swell was beginning to settle down somewhat. Bering Strait is only about thirty miles below the Arctic Circle, so there is plenty of twilight at midnight in July.

I was amazed at the amount of stuff that umiak held: seven or eight Eskimos, plus their baggage, plus me and my gear, a wall tent, a couple of gasoline campstoves (in use during the trip for coffee-making), two fifty-five-gallon drums of gasoline, a forty-horsepower outboard motor on the stern, a spare twenty-horsepower motor in the boat, and—acquired during the crossing—two large seals, about a dozen ducks, and a brace of geese.

The wind was from the north, and we could see only three or four miles as we began the twenty-mile crossing. This worried me—it wasn't hard to figure out that if we missed Little Diomede in the thick weather, one more mile would put us into Soviet waters, where we could expect a savage welcome from their border guards.

The helmsman knew his job. He kept his eyes on the box compass on the seat in front of him. I could see that the course he was steering would bring us to a point about four miles to the south of the island; this was to compensate for the strong north-flowing current that runs in the strait.

Soon Cape Prince of Wales vanished behind us under the low clouds and murk. The boat was immensely limber, its sides flexing as each swell passed under us. At first this made me nervous, but I learned that this very flexibility is the source of the umiak's great strength; that the entire framework is tied together, not screwed or bolted, thus allowing it to move slightly at every joint, bending but never breaking.

A few hours later we burst into a patch of clear air. With startling immediacy the gloomy dark side of Little Diomede rose vertically above us. Farther away Big Diomede was just visible in the mist.

Rounding the southern end of the island the helmsman guided the boat to a bouldery scrap of beach. The village was above us, two dozen small houses clustered on the steep hillside amid the large boulders. They looked tiny and vulnerable.

We were at once surrounded by about forty Eskimos, all who remained on the island. Dwight Milligrock, a sturdy, straight-forward man of about fifty years, introduced himself and offered to let me stay with him. I dragged my gear up the steep hill to his house and unrolled my sleeping bag on his floor. My day had begun in Anchorage more than twenty-four hours before, and I was dead tired.

I woke around noon to find that the sky was perfectly clear. With Dwight as my guide I huffed and puffed my way thirteen hundred feet up the steep hill to the flat top of the island. It was

The women of Little Diomede Island in the lee of a house, enjoying one of the rare sunny days. In the background, seal meat is drying on wooden racks. In the distance is Big Diomede Island, USSR, July 1969.

a beautiful day. Over the top of Big Diomede I could see Cape Dezhnev jutting out from Asia, massive and gray-black in the deep-blue of the strait. Behind me Cape Prince of Wales looked like its reciprocal. I suddenly realized that this was the only place on earth where you can see two oceans (the Pacific and Arctic), two seas (the Bering and Chukchi), two continents (Asia and America), two nations (the Soviet Union and the United States), and two days (today and tomorrow).

The Arctic may well have been in my blood before I knew it, for I had been reading books about travel and exploration since I was a boy. I grew up an only child in Hartford, Connecticut. After church on Sundays my parents and I often had lunch with my grandparents, who lived nearby. While these get-togethers were enjoyable, they seemed quite long to an energetic youngster, and I would frequently find myself in my grandfather's cavernous study, which was ringed in ancestral portraits, some of which dated from colonial times. As early as I can remember I was read-ing in his large collection of travel books, and he encouraged my foraging, allowing me free rein in his library. I remember vividly Howard Carter's description of the discovery of Tutankhamen's tomb, Roy Chapman Andrews's *On the Trail of Ancient Man*, and Richard Henry Dana's *Two Years Before the Mast*. A cousin of ours had married, first, General Billy Mitchell, and later, after his death, Admiral Richard Byrd's brother, and their exploits were prominently featured in the library as well. These, together with my grandfather's fascinating stories of his own travels to Japan at the turn of the century, all of which stood in such striking contrast to our relatively sedentary, city-oriented life, gave me an appetite for adventure and rough travel in wild areas.

During summer vacations my family usually stayed with my grandparents at their vacation house on the coast of Maine, and there my fascination with the ocean and sailing began—in fact for the better part of ten summers I was more or less constantly in and around boats and began to develop a sailor's skills.

The practice of medicine also fascinated me, and by the time high school arrived I began working as a volunteer orderly at a small regional hospital in Maine, entertaining some vague no-tions of becoming a doctor. But all that changed abruptly after my senior year. The Grenfell Mission, an organization that runs a number of nursing stations and hospitals in the isolated coastal communities of Newfoundland and Labrador, offered me a summer job as a general-duty worker. On arrival I fell in love with the area, forgetting any interest in medicine in the heady thrill of being on my own in a remote region. It was incredibly exciting to gaze across the Strait of Belle Isle at the Labrador coast, low and blue in the morning haze. With the voyages of the first European discoverers fresh in my mind, it seemed a heroic place. It wasn't very far north, but it felt like a frontier, and I was as happy as if I had been standing on the northern tip of Greenland. That day in July 1962 the North reached out and grabbed me, and to this day, I am glad to say, it has never released its grip.

From my freshman year at Yale I devoted myself to the dual goals of rowing and learning as much as possible about the Arctic. I eventually rowed on the varsity heavyweight crew, acquiring skills and stamina that were later very useful in paddling umiaks with the Eskimos. At the same time the best way to keep the North in my course of study was a "major" in anthropology.

All the while I was itching to get back to the Arctic and began writing letters to everyone who might help me find work there. A dozen or more people were the recipients of this appeal, which announced that I didn't mind what kind of job it was, but that I *had* to go north. Four or five people replied, and amazingly they all suggested getting in touch with James Houston, a Canadian artist who had just returned from fourteen years living with the Eskimos on Baffin Island and had just begun designing glass for Steuben in New York City.

Jim and I took to one another at once, and he kindly offered to help me; I think he saw in me the same sort of restless curiosity that had taken him to the North twenty years before. He suggested that I should spend the summer at the village of Resolute in Canada's high Arctic. Resolute village is located at nearly 75 degrees north latitude on the bleak and dreary limestone shore of Cornwallis Island. In those days it consisted of a couple of hundred Eskimos who had been relocated near the harbor and airstrip that served a joint United States–Canadian weather station.

I arrived there very green in July 1965 and found work as a laborer for a small bush aircraft company that ferried supplies and prospecting geologists all over Canada's Arctic islands. The job was perfect: When I wasn't working I could visit with the Eskimos, and occasionally I hitched a ride to one of the prospecting camps. I was awestruck by many things I had never seen—the twenty-four-hour sunlight, the barren island, seemingly devoid of vegetation, and the ice-choked seas. At midnight I often climbed to the top of one of the cliffs and in the gentle rosy light looked across Barrow Strait at other, distant islands, always wondering what was there.

Every evening, when the work was done, I walked to the Eskimo village and visited with two families, who welcomed me into their houses and into their lives. The more time I spent with the Eskimos at Resolute, the more I became fascinated by their language and society, their warmth and kindness, and by the time I graduated from Yale in 1966 I had made up my mind to try to earn a doctorate, studying some aspect of their culture. This was accomplished at Oxford University where I divided my time between rowing on the university crew and studying amid the immensely appealing litter and jumble of the Pitt Rivers Museum, one of the world's oldest ethnographical museums. In my second year I was elected president of the Oxford University Boat Club (the first American honored to be captain), and the time really flew; for when we weren't training for the grueling four-and-a-quarter mile boat race against Cambridge, I was undergoing one of the many rigorous tutorial sessions that are part of the curriculum. I received a Bachelor of Letters (B.Litt.) degree for a thesis on Eskimo culture change and was accepted into the Department of Ethnology and Prehistory's doctoral program. I knew by then, however, that I wanted to do my dissertation on some aspect of Eskimo prehistory. To do so I would have to carry out a series of excavations in the area and study under an Arctic specialist, and the faculty sensibly suggested that I should spend a few years in a journeyman's tour of several other institutions before returning to Oxford to finish my work.

One of the leading figures of Arctic archaeology was Froelich Rainey, the director of the University Museum in Philadelphia.

In the late 1930s Rainey, with his Danish colleague Helge Larsen, discovered the largest and most enigmatic archaeological site in the Arctic. Together these men excavated the great, two-thousand-year-old village of the Ipiutak culture at Point Hope, Alaska. Larsen and Rainey's site report remains an archaeological classic, and I suspect that this came about because of their complementary styles: Rainey's intuitively brilliant synthesis, and Larsen's careful, patient, and elegant mastery of details. To add depth and breadth to their understanding of the excavations Rainey, with his wife and little daughter, spent most of one winter at Point Hope, studying the Eskimos' whaling society, a project which resulted in an important monograph, and an association which allowed me to join a Point Hope whaling crew thirty years later.

For two years, while I worked as Rainey's assistant at the University Museum, I was the constant recipient of his generosity and insights, and he frequently suggested I should have some experience in other cultural areas as well. On one of his assignments I served as a technical consultant to NBC news in Moscow, Leningrad, and central Siberia for a program on early man. On another I spent two months in the deserts of eastern Iran carrying out an archaeological survey, work which gave me a profound dislike for heat, dust, and deserts. It was from there, in July 1969, that Rainey recalled me to go to Bering Strait and Diomede Island.

In 1969, after I had returned from Diomede to Nome, I was still in search of an appropriate site for my dissertation and decided to follow up a tip from a local amateur archaeologist. I managed to hitch a ride in a pickup truck thirteen miles east of town to the steep six-hundred foot bluff called Cape Nome. We drove out over a dusty dirt road that clung precariously to the face of the cliff. Rounding Cape Nome, a mile or two away I saw a series of parallel beach ridges, perhaps three hundred yards across, fanning out and enclosing the mouth of a couple of lazy rivers and a lagoon. It wasn't hard to figure out that this would be an excellent spot for summer fishing and winter seal hunting, both now and in the past.

Eager to explore, I unloaded my gear at the base of the cape and began walking back and forth over the beach ridges, which stretched more than two miles west to east. The entire beach was pockmarked here and there with more than three hundred shallow, squarish depressions which, I assumed, were the collapsed remains of ancient semisubterranean houses, most of which would have been part of a prehistoric Eskimo village. I estimated (correctly, as it turned out) that they must have been a couple of thousand years old, which put them squarely in the middle of a time of great change in Eskimo prehistory. My interest was whetted and right away I knew I had found the archaeological site to excavate for my doctoral dissertation.

I set up my tent on one of the moss-covered beach ridges, and, needing some food, walked a mile or so back down the road to a frame house where, I had noted, there was a small store. When I opened the door I found four or five kids of various ages wrestling over an antique cash register while their mother tried to restore order. Once things had quieted down I introduced myself, and telling them about the archaeological site, explained my hopes for working there. The kids' mother, Bonnie Hahn, a kindly and generous schoolteacher, at once offered to help in any way she could. It was the beginning of my friendship with the entire family, a friendship that continues to this day.

After some test excavations on Cape Nome's beaches, I returned to Philadelphia with a plan to come back the next summer and begin a full-scale project. When I started digging in earnest in 1970, in addition to the usual crowd of friends and student excavators, I had several of Bonnie's kids working for me as well. We camped on a beach ridge near the site but spent most of our evenings in front of the large stone fireplace in Bonnie's house, cataloging the artifacts, drawing excavation plans, and talking over the day's work. As we got to know the site better, it gradually became clear that several Eskimo cultures, both Asian and American, had inhabited those beaches, beginning about four thousand years ago and running more or less continuously right up to the present day; moreover there were indications that in the last five hundred years the Eskimos had hunted bowhead whales, the fifty-ton monsters that swim from the Bering Sea to the Beaufort Sea in the spring. This hunt

In a whale camp on the ice of the Chukchi Sea near Point Hope, Alaska, Luke Koonook (left) and I stand in front of a small windbreak. Luke is leaning on the stern of a whaling umiak.

became the core of the northwestern Alaska coastal Eskimo culture. Standing on the cape, looking west over the Bering Sea, I could imagine those prehistoric Eskimos paddling after the bowheads amid the ice floes in the opening water leads of spring.

When I got back to the University Museum in September 1970, Fro Rainey and I went over the summer's collections. He was fascinated by the whaling connection and immediately added, "John, to really get a feeling for the whaling component, you should spend some time with an Eskimo whaling crew. I went whaling thirty years ago, and it changed my whole perspective on the archaeology." Rainey wrote letters to his old friends at Point Hope, more than a hundred miles north of Bering Strait, and in April 1971 I arrived at that remote village of four hundred Eskimos. Located at the tip of a fourteen-mile sandspit jutting into the Chukchi Sea, it is right in the path of the spring migration of the bowhead whales. Laurie Kingik, a dignified and gentle elder of the community, and one of Rainey's good friends, offered to let me stay with his family and join their whaling crew. I was finally immersed in an Eskimo society, and I loved it.

The work was hard and tiring. First we had to cut a trail with pickaxes through the broken and jumbled ice ridges to the edge of shore-fast ice, then haul the umiak and tent and whaling gear out to the spot we had chosen for our camp. In those days we used dog teams, not snowmobiles, to help with the hauling, and in early April the temperature was regularly below zero Fahrenheit. By the end of April the light had improved enough to allow round-the-clock hunting—waiting at the ice edge for a bowhead's spout, then paddling after it, sometimes for hours, and usually without success. We were tired and cold a lot of the time, but when the village succeeded in capturing one of those huge animals, there was general rejoicing, as the twenty-four-hour job of butchering went on and tons of meat and blubber were stored away in ice cellars dug into the permafrost.

It didn't take me long to realize that at Point Hope I was among some of the most consummately skillful hunters on earth. Their entire lives were centered on whaling—and when they were not actively engaged in the hunt, they spent much of their time reflecting on it, preparing for it, or teaching their children about it. They understood full well the enormous achievement of capturing a fifty-ton animal and of providing the settlement with so much food. They knew that their lives depended on this exhausting and glorious adventure, for it provided them with food and fuel, a sense of community, and personal pride. And, having carried it out so successfully for more than a thousand years, they considered themselves to be superior people—and they wasted no time in telling me so.

I found the whale hunt utterly absorbing, but I was especially fascinated by its history and by its hybrid mechanics. The Eskimos were using tools and techniques that they had developed several millennia ago as well as manufactured harpoons and bomb-lance shoulder guns that had been invented in New England only a little more than a century before. How this mixture had come about puzzled me. I could see that it reflected the presence of the great Yankee whaling fleets in the nineteenth century, but beyond that I hadn't a clue. Then and there began a project to write the history of whaling in the western Arctic. Each spring for the next ten years I went to Point Hope to participate in the whale hunt. This work, plus an enormous amount of library and archival research, resulted in my book *Whales, Ice and Men*, which was published in 1986.

It was marvelous being at Point Hope. The whole Kingik family welcomed me warmly and made me feel at home, while Laurie took me under his wing, teaching me not only about their language and traditions, but also about their boats and sleds and tools and how they made them. In Eskimo tradition he became my *qumnaaluk*, or teacher. His son-in-law, Luke Koonook, a man of great stature in the community, was captain of the whaling crew, and Luke taught me the techniques of hunting whales, about the fickle and occasionally treacherous nature of the sea ice, and how to paddle their umiaks swiftly and silently. With me on the crew was a bunch of raucous, gung-ho young men: Laurie's two sons, George ("Blurr") and Earl; and Luke's three, Simon, Henry, and Lukie; as well as Norman Omnik, a close relation. We all received the same tutorials and on-the-job training.

Luke Koonook (left) *and two other Eskimo whalers tie a newly killed whale's flippers together in preparation for towing back to camp.*

I can't say that it was an entirely pleasant apprenticeship, for there is a lot of emotional testing among young men in Point Hope, and I assume elsewhere in the Eskimo world as well. These student hunters grow up and learn by observing, retaining, and studying their elders' ways—but only rarely by directly questioning them. I was fascinated by the hunt, and my curiosity frequently prompted me to ask my crew members about this or that, and occasionally my questions were answered with silence or, less frequently, by being told to shut up.

My approach was simply not theirs, nor were my credentials. The crew members cared not a hoot about my studies. They wanted to know whether they could count on me in the long, tiring, sometimes boring, sometimes frightening hunt—and most important to them was whether I was stable. This was tested, in their way, by teasing and subtle emotional pressures.

Just before I left Philadelphia for my first whaling season, Fro Rainey had warned me: "Remember, keep your mouth shut. At times it will be hell, but they'll be most concerned about whether you are steady." He was referring to the Eskimo practice of constant teasing of young children and newcomers who become the butt of nonstop jokes, none of them particularly clever. While it is relatively easy to ignore these when well-fed and rested, when you are tired, cold, depressed, and longing for some familiar company, it can be trying—at times almost unbearable. But I did remember Rainey's advice and never let my anger show, and I am glad I didn't because, of course, that is what they wanted to know: Was I steady under fire? Was I there for the long haul? Could they count on me when they found themselves in danger? Would I be a member of the team? They must have decided in the affirmative, because after three or four seasons of this everything changed and life on the whaling crew became really enjoyable.

In mid-April 1971 I was tagged with my Eskimo nickname. One night when it was too dark to hunt whales, we had hauled our umiak back to the tent and turned in for a few hours' sleep. When we woke my scratchy throat and dry mouth announced that I was cooking up a powerful head cold. We were all tired and chilly, and, to our grumbling dismay, we found that the

Bernard Nash, an Eskimo whaler, begins cutting up a large whale at Point Hope.

sheet-iron blubber stove had gone out. There were only a few pieces of *siqpan* (old blubber) in the bin in front of the stove, and with these we got the fire started again—leaving in the blubber bin only a foul scum of whale oil, cigarette butts, sputum, and other residue. To make things worse, we discovered that the only food in the grub box was a few biscuits. These we shared around, and I, feeling pretty terrible already, put mine on the edge of the blubber stove to warm up. As I was pulling on my *mukluks* (Eskimo seal-skin boots), the wind hit the tent with a big gust, shaking the stovepipe, which rattled the stove—and my biscuit fell into the foul goo left in the blubber bin. There were chuckles all round from the others, but I was so hungry and cold and generally miserable that I didn't see how I could feel any worse, so I pulled it out of the bin and ate it, causing most of the Eskimos to retch in disgust. The nickname surfaced shortly thereafter and was to stick with me for my remaining whaling days.

The whales weren't running all that day, so we began to practice snap shooting with our rifles at pieces of ice, which resembled vaguely the brief surfacing of a seal's head. Although I could hold my own with a shotgun, this type of shooting is fairly difficult. Once, when I had managed to miss an easy shot, my friend Norman Omnik blurted out in English, "Jesus, *Siqpan*, you couldn't hit a cow's ass with a banjo!"

Above all in my first whaling season, I was riveted by the umiaks—they were about ten feet shorter than the ones at Diomede, and they were covered with five or six *oogruk* (bearded seal) skins, making them lighter and more maneuverable than the Bering Strait boats. But like the Bering Strait boats, they were tough and flexible. During the lulls in the chase, as I sat beside the boat, waiting for the whales to pass, I thought about how, a thousand years ago, the Eskimos had spread from Alaska to Greenland with boats like these, and it gradually dawned on me that I wanted to travel in an umiak along the same route. I felt a powerful urge as I gazed across the ice at Cape Lisburne, low on the horizon, fifty miles to the northeast, and I found myself desperately wanting to visit it. But I also began to realize that each time I might reach one of these capes that had barely been discernible in the distance, there would be another far away beyond it, and another beyond that, and another. As my thoughts flew forward it suddenly dawned on me that I wanted to confront the greatest Arctic boating challenge of them all—the Northwest Passage. I knew that only a handful of vessels had ever made the transit of the northern waterway between the Atlantic and Pacific Oceans, and I wanted mine to be one of them.

Chapter 2

Preparations

In June 1971, when I headed south from Point Hope to continue my excavations at Cape Nome, I had my mind made up to build an umiak to pursue this dream of traversing the Northwest Passage. I had already figured out that the boat would have to be fairly large, bigger than the Point Hope whaling umiaks, like the Bering Strait–type I had traveled in to Diomede in 1969. To learn more about these boats I spent as much of my spare time as possible with the Eskimos in Nome who used their umiaks for walrus hunting. I was invited along on several of their hunts which were long and tiring—some lasted up to thirty-six hours. We were underway constantly, weaving in and out of the ice floes, the Eskimos always on watch for the brown heaps of sleeping walruses amid the beautiful whiteness of the sea ice.

When we spotted a group we would cut the outboard motor and paddle quietly toward them from downwind. Soon we would smell their peculiar odor ("Like a dead horse," said one of the hunters) and see their white tusks, their broad muzzles sprouting thick bristles, their small, bulbous, bloodshot eyes, and their huge, thick necks covered with warty, scarred skin. There were the magnificent old bulls carrying tusks nearly a yard long and weighing more than three thousand pounds, the cows with their thinner, more delicately curved tusks and the pudgy calves lying next to or on top of their mothers or woofing and scrambling along after them.

Sometimes groups of a hundred or more would lie asleep on the ice, jumbled on top of one another, occasionally grunting or bellowing, shifting slowly in their tight agglomerations, often waving flippers in the air to cool themselves, or rearing briefly to display their tusks in small territorial conflicts. From a distance these mounds of rumpled brown flesh seemed to be a part of a constantly fermenting mass. When they spotted us, as they often did, I was awed by their size and dense mass as they stampeded across the ice on their short flippers and tumbled pell-mell into the water.

More than two hundred fifty thousand of these animals spend their winter at the edge of the pack ice in the Bering Sea, and most migrate north through Bering Strait to the Chukchi Sea in the summer, feeding primarily on clams, snails, crabs, and even octopi that are found on the shallow and silty bottoms of the Chukchi and northern Bering Seas. The walruses apparently find their food by dragging their bristly muzzles along the sea floor. When they find a clam, they grab it with their mouth and quickly withdraw their strong, fat tongue, creating a vacuum that rips the soft part of the clam right out of its shell. A large adult male will eat up to one hundred fifty pounds of food a day, and the entire population has been estimated to eat more than a million tons of clams and other invertebrates per year. The Eskimo hunters often eat clams right out of the stomachs of freshly killed walruses.

When the animals had been shot, the back-breaking work of butchering them began. The skins had to be carefully stripped off in one piece so that they could be used for boat skins; then the meat and blubber were sectioned and the tusks and bacula (penis bones) were chopped out. The tusks were used for ivory carvings and the bacula (*oosiks* in the local jargon) would be either sold to tourists with a raunchy taste for the recherché or used in a variety of tools, particularly harpoons.

Once we were back on shore, the raw hides, weighing two hundred pounds or more, were stored in cool places until the end of the hunting season in June. The Eskimos would then scrape the remaining flesh and blubber from them and roll them up, leaving them in a warm place for a week or more. The hide would thus begin to rot a little and the hair could then be removed easily with a scraper.

The process of shaping the skins into an umiak requires extraordinary skill. The Eskimos almost invariably selected female hides for the boat skins because, although these were slightly smaller than the male hides, they were not warty or scarred from fighting. Walrus hide, which can be up to an inch-and-a-half thick, must be split in half to achieve a workable thickness for boat skins. The task is done by the Eskimo women who work with an *ulu* (a crescent-shaped blade) carefully opening the skin along its edge. The job of keeping both halves of equal thickness required skill, close attention, and a very sharp *ulu*.

Once the skins were split in half, they were laced at the edges on a ten-by-ten-foot wooden frame and stretched as tight as possible for drying. Depending on the weather it would take two to four weeks for the skin to dry. Then it could be stored in any dry place indefinitely, and at that point it was so hard that it was about as flexible as a very thick grade of linoleum. The dried skins are so tough that it is not difficult to understand why the Siberian Eskimos used them for armor. In fact, walrus hide is so strong that in the Middle Ages it was used as rope for lifting the massive stone blocks that were used to build the great gothic cathedrals of Europe.

While I was alternately excavating at Cape Nome and hunting with the Eskimos my mind was fixed on the problem of how I was going to build an umiak to travel in the Northwest Passage. My friend Dwight Milligrock had moved to Nome from Diomede, and I consulted him about my plans.

He was excited but added, "It'll be easier for you to repair an old umiak than to build one from scratch." He began to think out loud: "Let's see, the three umiaks at Diomede are all in use and so is the one at Wales. The boats on Saint Lawrence Island are too flimsy for your needs . . . Wait a minute! Harold Ah-

Bib Tevuk (left) *and I repair the umiak frame in August 1971 near Dwight Milligrock's house in Nome.*

mahsuk moved here from Wales quite a few years ago and brought his umiak with him. Let's go see him."

We hopped into my beat-up old van and bounced over Nome's dusty roads to the edge of town. There, in a rundown shack, I met a kindly white-haired Eskimo surrounded by his children and grandchildren. Dwight translated for me because this complicated interchange was beyond my abilities in Eskimo. "Yes," said Harold, "I'll sell you my umiak, but it's in bad shape. You see, I stored it behind my house here, and four or five years ago a snow plow hit it. Then last year the town pushed most of the snow on top of it." He told me that the boat, or what was left of it, had been built on Little Diomede in the 1930s and was used for walrus hunting and trading trips to Siberia. After the war, when the Soviets closed the border, Harold's father, who lived at Wales, bought the boat and used it for hunting expeditions and trips to Nome for wage employment.

Dwight and I walked around to the back of Harold's house, and we could see he wasn't joking. The umiak was propped up on gasoline drums in a marsh at the upper end of Nome harbor. It was partially covered with an old walrus hide that was black and rotting, and it was clear that when the town trucks had dumped the snow on top of it they had almost squashed it flat— the gunwales were splintered, the lashings were sprung, and several of the ribs were broken, but still, at close inspection we decided it looked reparable. A hundred dollars sealed the deal.

The next day I arrived with some of the archaeological crew—Mark Hollingsworth, Jim Jackson, and Earl Kingik. We cut away the remains of the skin and the broken parts and lifted the frame, now weighing less than two hundred pounds, onto the top of my van. Dwight had offered to show us how to rebuild the boat, so we put the frame in a dusty vacant lot next to his house. All that summer, whenever we weren't digging at Cape Nome, we worked on the umiak. It was a fascinating project, learning from Dwight while we rebuilt the boat, fueled in part by the mugs of coffee that his wife, Jesse, constantly carried out to us.

First we had to make a few new ribs. The boat was thirty-two feet long, with ribs spaced every foot of her length. She was also an evolved form of umiak, built with bent hardwood ribs. I asked Dwight about this. He said that this type was stronger and faster with an outboard motor than the traditional, "hard chine," flat-bottomed type of boat. The Eskimos had acquired outboards shortly after their invention, somewhere around the time of the First World War. "You've always used outboards?" I asked. "You didn't paddle these umiaks?" Dwight replied, "Do you think we were crazy? Would *you* want to paddle twenty miles across Bering Strait to the island?"

After I had sawed a piece of oak into individual ribs of the proper shape, Dwight helped me build a steam box. We took an old five-gallon fuel can and inserted several lengths of stovepipe

Bib Tevuk (under the umiak's frame) *and I relash the umiak's joints with sealskin line.*

in its side. A gallon or so of water was added and the whole thing went on a camp stove. When the water began to boil we put the ribs in the stovepipe and stopped up the openings with rags. After about twenty minutes, the wood was soft enough to be bent into the frame and fastened in place. When the ribs dried, they held their shape. New gunwales were installed and we strengthened the keel. Dwight then produced lengths of seal-skin rope, and over the next few days we relashed all the joints.

Now the boat was ready for the skins. Harold had sold me two good walrus skins along with the frame, but with a boat of that size I needed three more to complete the cover. Dwight and I managed to buy them from the King Island Eskimos in Nome. All five were stiff as boards, so before they could be cut and sewn together they had to be softened. We drove out past Cape Nome to Safety Inlet and weighted the skins down with rocks in the shallow lagoon. They became soft and rubbery after being sub-merged for five days. In this waterlogged state each weighed, I would guess, more than a hundred pounds. With some difficulty we hauled the squishy, slippery skins back into the van (which did not improve its odor) and returned to the boat frame at Dwight's house. We then draped the skins side by side on the overturned frame in the order in which they were to be sewn together, putting the toughest hides at the bow and stern.

Dwight had arranged for Stanislas Muktoyuk, an elder of the King Island Eskimos, to take on the tricky job of cutting the skins. He was now bent with great age, but as he whetted his knife it was clear that he was still skillful. He trimmed off the irregular and crenellated edges of the hides till the margin of each skin was exactly parallel with the next. Stan actually trimmed away so much from the edges that he left a gap the width of his hand between the hides as they lay on the over-turned frame. It looked as if the covering would be far too small to fit the boat frame when the skins were sewn together. But this was intentional: By making the covering a bit small Stan insured that the skins would fit tightly when we stretched them on the frame. We then carried the trimmed skins into Dwight's house, where seven or eight Diomede and King Island women were sitting on the floor, ready to begin sewing.

It took them all day to finish the job because each seam was

Women from Diomede and King Island sit on the floor, sewing together walrus hides that will later be stretched over and lashed to the umiak's frame.

eight feet long and had to be sewn twice—in a double or "blind" seam, with locking stitches. They used large thimbles and triangular-pointed glover's needles. It was hard work pulling the long strands of braided linen thread through that tough hide, as they had to take great care that no stitch went entirely through the skin. By not piercing the skin—that is, by leading the thread through only about half the thickness of the hide—they created a waterproof seam.

When the sewing was done, and the women got stiffly to their feet, we carried the cover outside and stretched it over the frame. We laced it drumtight, running heavy walrus-hide rope between the holes in the edge of the skins and the stringers on the inside of the frame. It was now evening and the cover dried slowly and evenly during the night. In the morning the cover was so tight that when I snapped my finger on the hide it gave off a deep reverberating boom.

Dwight then told me how to make a false keel, which is a

plank running along the keel outside the skin. It serves to raise the hull a few inches and thus protect the skins from abrasion when moving the boat over ice or gravel beaches. I bolted a two-by-four along the length of the keel, then, in Bonnie's fireplace, drew the temper on a piece of steel sled runner and hacksawed it into two pieces which I then bent to fit around the bottom curves of the bow and stern. This would give extra protection at the points that took the greatest punishment during landings and launchings.

It was nearly Labor Day before we had finished the work on the umiak. I borrowed a flatbed truck and took the boat, now weighing six hundred pounds or more, down to Cape Nome and stored it in Bonnie Hahn's barn for the winter.

While the umiak slowly took shape in Dwight's yard, I began to realize that this trip into the Northwest Passage might actually take place. As far as I can recall, up to that point my dream of a voyage had been merely that, and I suppose I hadn't truly believed it might become a reality. But, as we bent new ribs and replaced the gunwales and relashed the joints and, finally, put the skins on the umiak's frame, I began to think seriously about all the hundreds of details that had to be sorted out before we could get underway.

First, I knew I had to learn a lot more about the seas and coasts ahead of me. I spent the winter of 1971–1972 in England, working on my doctoral dissertation. In my spare time I roamed about in London's ship chandleries collecting charts and sailing directions, learned celestial navigation, and spent many hours burrowing through the Royal Geographical Society's magnificent library searching out all the firsthand accounts of trips in the Northwest Passage.

As the northern water route between the Atlantic and Pacific Oceans, the Northwest Passage lies between Davis Strait, where Greenland and Baffin Island most closely converge, and Bering Strait, where Asia and North America lie only about fifty miles apart. From the west the forty-five-hundred mile water course runs north from Bering Strait along the shallow and sandy shores of the Chukchi Sea coast of Alaska, then past Point Barrow, the northern tip of the state, then east through the Beaufort Sea and into Canada until it reaches the Arctic islands. Between the end of the Beaufort Sea and Davis Strait lies the vast Canadian Arctic Archipelago, comprising two dozen major islands, hundreds of minor ones, and thousands and thousands of inlets, shoals, and rocks. Although there are four potential shipping routes through this maze, only one, the southernmost, is feasible for a small boat—there is simply too much heavy ice clogging the others. I learned that this southern route through the archipelago hugs the northern shore of continental North America: Beginning at the waterlogged delta of the Mackenzie River, it eventually reaches Coronation Gulf, which is bounded on the north by Victoria Island's eighty-five thousand square miles of eroded limestone bluffs, then enters Queen Maud Gulf, a hideous congregation of shoals and glacial debris. Passing south of the monotonous plain of King William Island, the route turns north along the Boothia Peninsula with its rising shores and nobbly granitic hills, to Som-

The walrus hide cover lies on top of the frame, ready to be lashed on. Jim Jackson stands in the background; one of Dwight's sons in the foreground.

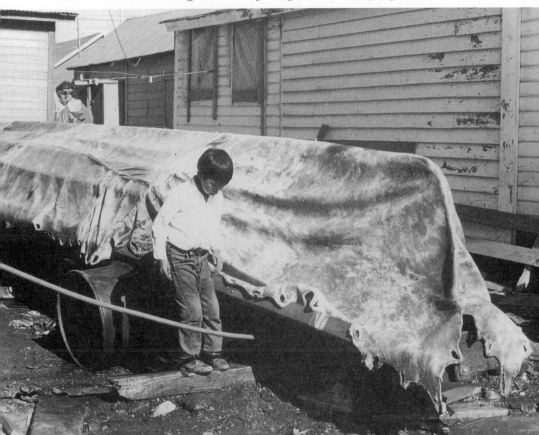

erset Island's steep limestone palisades—and I knew that if I made it that far, I would be in the eastern Arctic, and assumed that I would have at least another year or two before I would have to read up on *that* region.

I was surprised to find that in fact, the search for a passage began only a few years after Columbus's voyage of 1492, when adventurers in England realized that he had discovered, not the Indies, but a new continent. John Cabot was the first explorer to set out. He reached the New World, probably at Newfoundland, in 1497 and his report spurred several Elizabethan voyagers to follow him in search of a route to the riches of the East. Martin Frobisher was the next, in 1576, being, as one of his shipmates wrote, "persuaded of a new and nearer passage to Cataya, than by Cape d'bouna Speranza, which the Portugallas yeerley use." But Frobisher was sidetracked by a quixotic search for gold on Baffin Island; nevertheless, after him came John Davis, Henry Hudson, and many others searching for the eastern entrance to the then-hypothetical passage.

While these early attempts were fascinating, it was the Pacific voyages that held my interest even more, because I would be starting from the west. I learned that until the eighteenth century the west-to-east voyagers had either been searching for a mythical "Strait of Anian" as a western entrance to a passage or had been probing for a separation between the continents of Asia and America. Nevertheless, it was not until Captain James Cook's cruise in 1778 that Europeans began to have a clear idea of the waters northeast of Bering Strait. In the summer before his death Cook pushed his ships beyond 70 degrees north latitude and reached Icy Cape before being stopped by pack ice on the northwestern coast of Alaska. His was the first intentional penetration of the Passage from the west.

Although there were a couple of Russian voyages to the Bering Strait region in the years after Cook, the western search essentially ceased with him and was not resumed until after the end of the Napoleonic Wars. Then Britain and Russia, formerly allies, quickly became intense competitors, searching for a passage and the accompanying acquisition of new lands and riches.

The Russians got started first. In 1816 Otto von Kotzebue,

sailing for the czar, pushed through Bering Strait and along the north coast of the Seward Peninsula, searching waters that Cook had passed by. For a moment Kotzebue thought that he had discovered a route to Europe; soon, however, he was brought to a halt at the eastern end of the Sound that was later to bear his name, but this did not daunt the Russians—within four years other expeditions followed him.

At the same time John Barrow, the energetic second secretary of the Admiralty, was at work in England. Beginning in 1818, he dispatched six Arctic expeditions in the next ten years, four of them led by William Edward Parry. On his third expedition Parry was ordered to sail to the western Arctic via Davis Strait, while John Franklin was to descend the Mackenzie River in boats, and both were to meet Frederick William Beechey near Bering Strait in 1826 or, failing that, in 1827. The rendezvous never took place: Heavy ice stopped Parry, and he returned to England, but Beechey's and Franklin's expeditions succeeded in mapping large reaches and came within one hundred fifty miles of one another on the north coast of Alaska.

It was the Hudson's Bay Company that closed the gap. The company wanted to extend its trading activities and consequently sent Peter Dease and Thomas Simpson to complete the map of Alaska, by following Franklin's route. They had almost reached Point Barrow in 1837 when they found the pack ice hard on shore and the expedition came to a halt. But Simpson went ahead on foot and eventually reached the point, joining his surveys with Beechey's. Dease and Simpson then retraced their route up the Mackenzie and for the next two years carried out equally important explorations near Victoria and King William Islands, thereby filling in almost all of the gaps in the coastal chart of mainland North America.

The summer after Thomas Simpson reached Point Barrow, the Russian–American Company—the fur trading organization with a monopoly on Alaska—sent an expedition under Alexander Kashevarov to the same waters, with the same object in mind. Kashevarov was unaware of the Hudson's Bay Company expedition and was less successful than Dease and Simpson; for although he was able to round Point Barrow from the west, the

Eskimos were extremely hostile, forcing him to return south. For a few years things were relatively quiet on the western Arctic coast, but that was soon to change.

In 1845 Sir John Barrow sent Sir John Franklin (both had been knighted for their Arctic work) to complete the exploration of a northwest passage and thus to capitalize on England's efforts which had been underway since the fifteenth century. Franklin and his men were sent to win the prize for Great Britain by traversing the unknown region between Baffin Island and Victoria Island, and, as one nineteenth-century writer put it, "they forged the last link with their lives." The expedition was superbly outfitted with two stout auxiliary-powered ships and 128 able men, but when Franklin left England in 1845, he and his entire expedition vanished into the Arctic forever. In 1848 the first relief parties started out looking for him, and for the next six years dozens of expeditions searched throughout the North American Arctic. In the beginning no one knew where Franklin had gone, and at the end only one essential fact was confirmed: that Franklin and all his men had perished.

In 1848 a discovery of greater and far more long-lasting significance for the western Arctic was made. Captain Thomas Roys of Sag Harbor, Long Island steered the whaling bark *Superior* a thousand miles beyond the nearest whaleship and discovered the phenomenally rich bowhead whale population at Bering Strait. His catch of blubber and whalebone set off a whale-oil rush of such proportions that by 1852 more than two hundred whaling vessels were cruising in those waters. Whalemen were to scour the coasts of the western Arctic for the next seventy years and were to lose more than one hundred fifty whaleships there, most due to a combination of the fogs and shoals, the violent gales, and the crushing pack ice.

It was a Norwegian, Roald Amundsen, who finally won the prize in a little, forty-seven-ton herring sloop, the *Gjøa*. It had been Amundsen's lifelong desire to traverse the Passage, for, as he wrote:

> We knew there was a sea passage round Northern
> America, but we did not know whether this passage

was practicable for ships, and no one had ever yet navigated it throughout. This unsolved question agitated above all the minds of those who, from their childhood, had been impressed by the profound tragedy of the Franklin Expedition.

Assisted by only a thirteen-horsepower engine, he departed Norway in 1903 and sailed down the west coast of Somerset Island, then followed the coast of the Boothia Peninsula around King William Island. Amundsen spent the next two winters comfortably in Gjoa Haven, a snug harbor of the south coast of the island, while he took magnetic observations and explored by dog team.

In August 1905 he pushed on to the west, expecting to complete the passage that summer—but the Arctic was not through with him yet. Although the *Gjøa*'s men became the first to navigate through shoals and reefs of Queen Maud Gulf into the Beaufort Sea, as soon as they crossed the shallow and muddy waters off the Mackenzie River delta the crew found heavy pack ice blocking their way. They were finally brought to a halt near shore, opposite King Point, not far from the Alaskan border, and just short of the shelter of the whalers' harbor at Herschel Island. It was not until August 30, 1906, that they passed Bering Strait and were able to celebrate their historic achievement.

By the time I had finished my readings on the western Arctic voyages I had developed a very healthy respect for those waters: Cook had been stopped by the ice, Beechey had gone aground, Dease and Simpson, as well as Amundsen, were forced ashore by the pack ice, the Franklin search fleet had had trouble with the gales, and the whaling fleet had suffered all of these. But while my level of caution had risen considerably, I also began to realize that the umiak would be a very safe boat for the voyage, not only because of its flexible construction, but also because, when fully loaded with a ton or more of people and gear, it would draw only a little more than two feet. That way we would be able to stay close to shore in shallow water and we would often be able to work inside the grounded pack ice where it had come pressing down on the coast. Also, if a gale were to blow up, we would be able to land quickly and haul the boat up the beach, rolling it on sausage-shaped boat fenders as the Eskimos did, before the seas became too rough to get ashore.

There were a number of other Eskimo techniques that I intended to adopt as well. Once ashore we would camp under the umiak by turning it over and propping it up on its gunwhale, but it would also be sensible to carry a couple of sturdy tents so that we could keep the camp set up in case we might need the boat for a short trip. For mattresses we would use reindeer skins, which are far more comfortable than air mattresses and are soft and warm at even minus 50 degrees Fahrenheit. Each reindeer or caribou skin is a thicket of densely packed hairs, each of which is hollow, thereby retaining heat with great efficiency. I planned to do the cooking over the tried-and-true gasoline pressure stoves that Eskimos use throughout the Arctic. Because we would be above the Arctic Circle, in July it would be light for almost twenty-four hours a day. Toward the end of August, however, the days grow rapidly shorter, and I knew we would need longer-lasting light than flashlights could provide. Again I chose the Eskimo's choice: gasoline pressure lanterns.

Dwight Milligrock had told me emphatically that it would be necessary to carry two outboard motors—to take care of breakdown emergencies—and he suggested the usual Bering Strait umiak combination: a forty-horsepower and a backup twenty. I calculated that we could carry a little more than one hundred gallons of gasoline in the boat in five-gallon plastic jerry jugs and that this amount would weigh about eight hundred pounds. This would be enough to get us from one town to another, with plenty to spare in case we had to double back, but where the towns were more than a couple hundred miles apart we would either have to put out gasoline caches or buy supplies from the DEW Line (Distant Early Warning Line—military radar bases). The United States Air Force kindly gave me permission to purchase small quantities of gasoline from the DEW Line sites, thus making our fuel problems much simpler.

I also assumed that we could carry enough food to make it from town to town without hardship and that we could cover any tight spots with some extra freeze-dried rations. Dwight laughed at this: "Take Eskimo food. Just carry lots of dried salmon," he said. "It tastes good and is real oily—it'll keep you warm. That *Naulagmiut* [white men] food is no good when you're cold!" He was right. Somewhere on the north coast of Alaska we pitched that tasteless stuff overboard and never missed it.

My travels in Bering Strait had taught me that Arctic boat travel, even in the summer, can be very chilly indeed. When you sit motionless in a boat for hours on end, the wind just seems to suck the heat right out of your body. Summer temperatures near Bering Strait are likely to be in the low fifties, but at Point Barrow and along the north coast of Alaska and farther east they are often in the high thirties and low forties. I knew that although the umiak's canvas spray shield would cut the wind somewhat, in essence we would have to dress as if we were going to spend the entire day in a New England duck blind at Christmas: long underwear, heavy clothing, parkas, insulated boots, and hats and gloves. In addition we would also need hip waders for launchings and landings and tough foul-weather gear to cope with spray and rain.

My crew came together easily. Three members of my archaeological team wanted to come along: Jim Jackson, a friend from home, always cheerful and energetic; Bib Tevuk, an Eskimo from Nome who was fascinated by the cultural history of his people; and Earl Kingik, my good whaling friend from Point Hope. In England two friends from Oxford signed on: Mickey Astor, quiet and friendly, and one of the most mechanically capable people I have ever known, who offered to be our motor engineer, and Robin Lane Fox, a very witty, fox-hunting Oxford don who was, improbably, both a brilliant classical scholar and the gardening correspondent of the *Financial Times*. Mickey's reason for signing on was understandable—he loved travel—but Robin's baffled me. When asked, he replied, "I want to work in peace on the manuscript of my book about Alexander the Great." I doubted that he would find much peace with our crowd, but something must have gone right because his book did get finished and won great critical acclaim—as well as a number of literary awards. I later learned that he had carried the only copy of the manuscript with him in the umiak; it was the product of five years' nonstop work. Robin certainly trusted his luck. We wondered how his publisher liked those dirty and blubber-stained pages when they returned from the Arctic.

Later that winter I met a television producer friend in New York. When I told him of my plans for the umiak, he asked if he could film the adventure, and offered to send along a cameraman and a Boston Whaler as a camera boat. The motion picture photographer who showed up, Tony Mitchell, was a useful member of the crew, a burly, resourceful technician who had done a number of tours in Vietnam.

I knew that the month of June 1972 was going to be hectic, so I invited several friends to come to Nome to help with the fitting out. Victoria Waldron, a member of my archaeological crew, arrived, as did Hamish Leslie-Melville, an international banker from London, and Romayne Grimston, another friend. Robin Lane Fox and his wife, Louisa, reached Nome via the Asian route. They had come east from London and followed Alexander the Great's path from Greece to the Khyber Pass. Robin arrived for the start of the expedition looking as if he had just completed one, and a particularly rugged one at that. He already had a scruffy beard, and his total traveling clothing had been one gray double-breasted suit with wide chalk stripes. It had come from a thrift shop and was certainly vintage 1920. We all examined it closely for bullet holes, assuming that some gangster had met an ugly end in it.

In those long days of early summer we painted the umiak on Dwight Milligrock's orders: "It will absorb less water that way and the skins won't get baggy and slow you down. You won't have to dry it out so often." He added, "All Eskimos paint their umiaks now." He also helped us put an A-frame on the stern to hold an extra motor, if need be. He also had us put a yard-wide canvas spray shield completely around the boat and showed us how to keep it up by lashing it to the handles of our canoe paddles that we had jammed upright between the cargo and the side of the boat.

By the end of the month we were ready and only waiting for good weather to get started. We had no idea how far we would go that summer, nor did I have any idea that the adventure would consume the next seventeen years of my life.

Chapter 3

Trial and Error

My real education began on July 1, 1972. After several days of dirty weather, the sky was clear and the wind was calm. It was time to go.

We pulled on our hip boots, then rolled the umiak down the beach on sausage-shaped inflated boat fenders. Once we had it in the water we began a haphazard and disorganized assault on our small mountain of gear: tents, gasoline jugs, duffle bags, food boxes, reindeer skins (in place of air mattresses), and a couple of gunny sacks full of dried salmon were all heaped into the boat in random order. We then put the outboard motor on the stern, loaded the spare into the umiak and launched the sixteen-foot Boston Whaler. We were off at three-thirty in the afternoon.

By the time we had rounded Cape Nome—that is, by the time we had completed the first quarter-mile—we had discovered a major problem: It was clear that we would have to stop to repack this chaotic jumble, for no one could find a thing. A little more than an hour later we reached the narrow mouth of the

Snake River, Nome's harbor, and entered it to unload our whole mess on shore. After a lot of trial and error and head scratching we had things packed in a slightly more orderly fashion. As it turned out, this was the beginning of a long process of condensing our load, a process that would culminate nine years later in what we considered to be the "perfect pack."

We were off again at 7:00 P.M. Evening is usually a good time for boat travel in the Bering Strait region because the wind often dies down. It was thrilling to be racing along at last, the two boats slicing through the mirror-calm water. To our right the smooth sand beaches rolled past, while behind them the high rounded hills were backlit by a soft golden glow from the evening sun.

After five or six hours we reached Point Spencer, the ten-mile, curving sandspit that encloses Port Clarence, which is one of the largest and finest harbors in the Bering Sea. Once we had reached its tip, we steered northwest toward the steep gray eminence of Cape York. It was now 1:00 A.M. and in the half-light I could vaguely make out those cold, bold cliffs. Running along them is always tricky in a small boat, for it is extremely difficult to land there in the event of trouble. As luck would have it, just

The fully loaded umiak, under perfect traveling conditions, cruising at the beginning of the trip on July 1, 1972. Left to right: *Jim Jackson, Robin Lane Fox, and Bib Tevuk.*

as we drew abreast of the cliffs, the wind swung into the south-west and began to blow about fifteen to twenty knots, pushing in a steep sea. Now we were on a lee shore in an ugly patch of water with confused waves coming from two directions: The wind was sending them in from the southwest and they were reflecting back at us, off the cliffs, from the northwest. We were now bucking and rolling, but we had to keep on, for there was no place to land. At times we could only see the heads of the men in the Whaler, the seas were so steep.

We were now approaching Bering Strait, the beginning of the Northwest Passage, and as the light improved, the great outline of Cape Prince of Wales revealed itself far ahead. Rising abruptly to more than two thousand feet, it was an awesome sight even from ten miles away. The grandeur of the scene was exhilarating and made it "worth going through all this slop," as Mickey put it.

I was getting pretty anxious in that choppy sea, however, because our fuel was getting so low. I knew we would have to land at Wales village, just at the north side of the Cape, to get more gasoline and was worried. The beach there slopes out to sea very gently and evenly for several hundred yards, causing the waves to start breaking a long way from shore and making it a nasty place to land a boat when a sea is running. But even though we were then bouncing around in some fairly substantial southerly swells, I guessed that the bulwark of the Cape would block those rollers and give us some calmer water in front of the village. I was wrong.

At about 6:00 A.M. we were within a mile of the western tip of the Cape. I signaled to Mickey on the helm to begin our swing round the Cape. Rolling hard, we kept well off shore, and slowly the string of houses along the beach began to appear one at a time from behind the steep face of the cliffs—they looked tiny and forlorn amid the clinging patches of snow. But to our disgust the wind kept following us right around, so that we were *still* on a lee shore. From there I could easily see the outer line of surf on the beach, while inside that were two more lines of breakers.

As luck would have it, our outboard motor chose just that moment to cough and die. As we wallowed back and forth, Mickey and I hung over the stern and managed to pull the spark plugs. They were full of carbon, and when it was scraped off the motor sprang back to life. But I still had to figure how to land the boats through that cold surf. I shouted to the men in the Whaler to wait off shore until we had the umiak out on the beach—the last thing we needed was *two* boats foundering in the breakers at once.

As we turned the umiak to head in toward the beach the swells were behind us. We made it through the first line of breakers without a problem, touched the bottom lightly on the second, and grounded firmly in the midst of the third, about fifteen yards from dry sand. The umiak was bouncing up and down and threatening to broach, but by then we all had our hip boots on and jumped into the water simultaneously. The waves were slamming into the boat and two of us, up to our waists in the cold water, held it end-on to the surf while the other three pulled our gear out and raced up the gently sloping gray sand beach. When the boat was nearly empty we pushed it farther in and got the roller floats under the keel so that we could pull it up the beach. Then I signaled for the Boston Whaler to come in, and with much the same chaos got it out too.

Cold and wet and tired, we set up camp right away, first by

dragging the umiak high up the beach, turning it on its side and propping it up on canoe paddles to give some shelter to the cook. Tony Mitchell set to work cooking up a reindeer meat stew, while the rest of us put up the tents, made a good-sized fire from the driftwood lying about, and propped our wet clothes up on sticks near it. *Any* hot food would have tasted great at that point, but the stew was delicious and we wolfed it down, then turned in for our first sleep in twenty-four hours.

I woke late that afternoon to the dull roar of surf on the beach and to the thwack of the wind pummeling our tent. As I un-zipped the tent door a cold, damp blast blew in. The wind had swung fully into the northwest, roaring out of Siberia and push-ing a strong surge onto Wales's beach. Above us the low gray clouds thundered by, dappled with small spots of clear sky, through which the pale sunlight spread outward in sheets of striated gold. It was a thrilling scene. The Diomede Islands stood out black against the dull gray sky, and far away, low on the horizon I could just make out Cape Dezhnev, Siberia.

One small thing tarnished this Arctic sublime—when the wind changed direction while we slept, it blew smoke and sparks from the fire down onto our drying clothes, and Tony Mitchell's blue jeans had completely burned up. All we could find of them were the metal studs and the teeth of his metal zipper, lying in perfect alignment on the sand. They looked like a child's connect-the-dots drawing.

Wales was then a village of about one hundred forty Eskimos who lived along the beach in cozy homemade houses amid the sand dunes at the base of the Cape. Among the houses were a few larger buildings: a school, a mission, and a small store. A lot of the people were away, working on summer construction jobs, but those who remained were curious and welcoming, and we were constantly invited into their houses for coffee and conver-sation. It was a peaceful, friendly little village.

But things had not always been so in Wales. Until well after the middle of the nineteenth century the settlement actually consisted of two groups, only about a half mile apart, which were mutually antagonistic and deeply involved in the cross–Bering Strait native trade that linked the aboriginal peoples in America and Asia. There may have been as many as six hundred fifty people there, exploiting the vast richness of the area: whales, walruses, ducks, and geese in the spring and fall; fish and greens in the summer; seals in the winter; and caribou at many times of the year. They were known throughout the region as tough, aggressive traders and skillful hunters. This boldness, which was generally a part of native life throughout northwestern Alaska, contributed to a village tragedy in 1877. At that time the maritime whiskey trade was in full swing out of San Francisco and Hawaii, and each year schooners made their way to Bering Strait, loaded with rotgut booze and contraband firearms to trade for furs and ivory. The Wales people had had considerable success in bullying and even holding up some of the ships—until July 5, 1877, when a rough crowd of Hawaiians arrived there. The Wales people boarded the schooner *William H. Allen* and tried to force the captain to give them whiskey. The leader, who was probably drunk, stabbed one of the sailors and soon a gun fight broke out. When it was over thirteen natives and one Hawaiian lay dead.

Incidents such as these brought the United States Revenue Cutter Service to Bering Strait to suppress the whiskey trade, but for many years the Eskimos harbored a desire for revenge, and it was likely the factor in the murder, in 1893, of Harrison Thornton, the first missionary to the settlement, who was shot by a deranged man with a whaling gun. A small marble obelisk marks his grave high on the flanks of the cape behind the village.

A quarter-century later another scourge of civilization arrived to ravage the community. The great worldwide influenza epidemic of 1918 finally reached Wales, killing almost all of the adult population. Only a small and broken village was left—one that lacked the benefit of guidance from its elders, all of whom had died.

The wind stayed high for a couple of days and we spent the time exploring the ancient archaeological sites near the town and climbing over the steep slopes of the cape to gaze across Bering Strait. But July 5 dawned clear and calm, so we quickly loaded up and set off in the Chukchi Sea along the north shore of the Seward Peninsula.

We ran easily for about seven hours along the even sand beaches and gently contoured grass-covered dunes, until we reached the village of Shishmaref, a small hunting and reindeer-herding community. We paused there long enough to buy a hundred gallons of gasoline and to tinker with one of the motors, then pushed ahead in a perfect evening, the northern sky a uniform orange above a light scattering of sea ice. After traveling in the half-light of the Arctic summer night, we went ashore at 9:00 A.M. to cook breakfast at Cape Espenberg. Here the northern tip of the Seward Peninsula touches that imaginary line, the Arctic Circle, the point in the Northern Hemisphere where the sun is above or below the horizon for one day each year, but in fact the twilight lingers from mid-May to mid-August throughout the night, giving effectively twenty-four hours of light.

I took my binoculars and climbed the high, moss-covered dunes to look into Kotzebue Sound. When Otto von Kotzebue reached these waters in 1816, he found the Eskimos of the region with a rich supply of furs. The natives were numerous, physically large, aggressive, and well-armed, sophisticated traders—definitely not our present-day stereotype of the smiling, gentle dwellers of the North. The report about the Eskimos' furs prompted the Russian–American Company, which held a monopoly for the fur trade in Russian America (present-day Alaska), to send an American, Captain Gray, to check on the accuracy of Kotzebue's information. We have only a sketchy account of Gray's voyage, but it seems that he anchored his ship somewhere on the north shore of the Seward Peninsula and pushed into Kotzebue Sound in a small boat. Gray must have been highly enterprising, for he went far beyond his orders (and against company policy) by trading the first firearms to the Eskimos and appears to have shared his findings with more than the Russians, facts that became apparent the following year, 1820, when another Russian Northwest Passage expedition reached these waters. When one of the two ships arrived in Kotzebue Sound the Eskimos caught them by surprise and shot at them with guns. But soon, when the other Russian ship entered the sound, the Russians realized that they were being followed by one of John Jacob Astor's brigs, the *Pedler*. Its captain, William Pigott, announced that he was there to trade firearms for furs. Clearly, from the Russian point of view, Gray's voyage had been a mixed blessing at best. These inroads on the Russian monopoly would

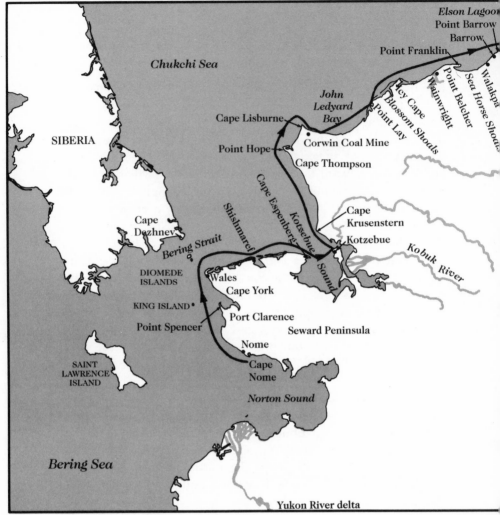

The Umiak's Route, 1972–1974

continue all over Alaska for nearly the next half-century, and this, combined with the inefficiency of the Russian-American Company, would lead to the czar's decision in 1867 to sell the vast land to the United States.

The mosquitoes and the surprisingly hot sun snapped me out of my historical daydream. Oddly enough, the temperature in inner Kotzebue Sound in July has been measured as high as 85 degrees, although it is usually in the fifties. I walked back down to the boats to head toward the town of Kotzebue on the eastern

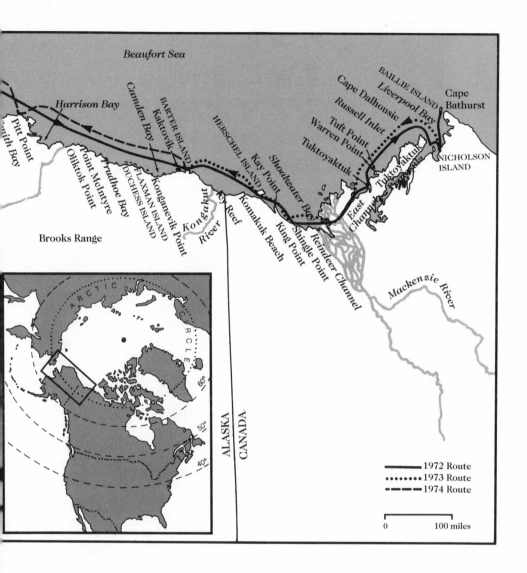

Beaufort Sea

Harrison Bay

Pitt Point
ith Bay

Point McIntyre
Oliktok Point
Prudhoe Bay
DUCHESS ISLAND
FLAXMAN ISLAND
Konganevik Point
Camden Bay
Kaktovik
BARTER ISLAND

HERSCHEL ISLAND

Kongakut River
Icy Reef
Kay Point
Komakuk Beach
Shoalwater Bay
King Point
Shingle Point
Reindeer Channel

Brooks Range

BAILLIE ISLAND
Liverpool Bay
Cape Dalhousie
Russell Inlet
Tuft Point
Warren Point
Tuktoyaktuk

Cape Bathurst

NICHOLSON ISLAND

East Channel
Tuktoyaktuk

Mackenzie River

ARCTIC CIRCLE

60°

50°

40°

ALASKA
CANADA

————— 1972 Route
•••••••• 1973 Route
– – – – 1974 Route

0   100 miles

shore. It seemed odd to be wearing only T-shirts while we were winding in and out of the scattered ice floes.

After several hours Kotzebue's white radar dome began swimming in the mirage, and by 6:30 P.M. we were within a mile or two of the town. Racing toward it, we began counting on buying a good meal at the little restaurant there. In our haste, however, we ran smack aground on the shoals formed from the outflow of the Noatak, Kobuk, and Selawik Rivers. We had not seen them in the muddy water, but learned the hard way that when our stern wash began to break over itself, that meant we were in three feet of water or less. It took four and a half hours of wading around in those shallows to find our way into the channel and it wasn't until 11:00 P.M. that we finally reached the shore, sunburned and tired.

The town of Kotzebue came into being in 1900 during a bogus gold rush to the Kobuk River. Once a small foreign population was established there, it remained as a trading post and missionary station, later becoming a regional transportation hub and administrative center. In 1972 it was a town of about eighteen hundred people, most of whom were Eskimos on welfare, living in a bunch of rundown shacks. There were also a couple of general stores, and a latticework of dirt roads, over which teenaged Eskimos buzzed incessantly on small motorbikes. The comparison with the peace and beauty we had just left was unpleasant. To make matters worse, that evening the mosquitoes were particularly fierce and a horde of motorbikes churned the roads into clouds of dust.

None of us wanted to stay here long, and most of us slept in the boats right on shore. With all the clatter and mosquitoes we didn't get to sleep until about 3:00 A.M. I woke several hours later with the gritty feel of dust in my mouth. It took awhile to chase up seventy-five gallons of gasoline and to collect some provisions, so we weren't able to shove off again until evening.

Once outside the shallows we headed directly for Cape Krusenstern, about thirty miles away to the northwest. By now we had begun to develop a traveling routine, procedures that would serve us for the next nine years. Two of the crew manned the Boston Whaler, dividing the work as they chose. The rest of us were in the umiak: Two were on watch, one in the bow, keeping an eye out for unexpected shoals or drift logs, and one on the helm, while the other two rested; I was the navigator and, being constantly on duty, served no watch. The watches lasted for two hours, and the men on duty served in the bow or stern every other watch. I sat on a piece of walrus hide on top of the gasoline jugs, just forward of the helmsman. From there it was easy to keep track of our position and order course changes, in addition to refilling the motor tanks and mixing in the engine oil. I could also pump out the water in the stern if we were taking spray.

The boat was loaded so that forward of the jerry jugs there were plenty of soft reindeer skins on top of our grub boxes and tents. We covered these with a large canvas tarp, so that it would be a comfortable place to get some sleep when not on watch.

Off duty, when they were not asleep, each crew member had his own pastime: Bib frequently played his harmonica, Mickey took photographs, Jim and I endlessly discussed navigation and Arctic history, Tony kept us all laughing with one ribald story after another, and Robin rarely lifted his head from a Latin or Greek text—and I think it was this diversity of interests that made for an easygoing and cooperative crew.

On shore we had begun to develop a routine as well. Bib and Jim often fished for our supper. Mickey worked on the motors, Robin took over the commissary details of portioning our food supplies, and everyone took a hand in cooking and washing up. There was nearly universal praise for the reliability of our Coleman camp stoves, but Robin never seemed to master them completely; instead of a low blue blaze like a Bunsen burner, they often produced for him something that looked more like a flamethrower. Suspecting a dark, nationalistic plot in the whole thing, he announced one day: "If I ever meet that Yank Coleman, I'll roast him slowly over one of our good British AGA stoves."

Shortly we rounded Cape Krusenstern, where the temperature dropped to the forties and we pulled on our parkas, glad to be out of Kotzebue's heat. We ran along the even gravel beaches in a nearly straight line toward Cape Thompson's rocky cliffs ninety miles to the northwest. Halfway there the headland rose, low on the horizon, just visible far ahead in the velvet haze. Passing it, the Arctic's stillness was disturbed by the cries of nearly half a million sea birds. Cormorants, gulls, kittiwakes, murres, guillemots, and puffins were diving out of their refuges in the cliffs to feed on the fish and rich plankton blooms in the waters nearby.

We then continued on for more than thirty miles along the great gentle arc of the Point Hope Peninsula, which is in fact a giant sandspit, stretching fourteen miles into the Chukchi Sea, formed in the slack water created by the bulwark of Cape Thompson. At noon on July 8 we reached the village near the tip

Under way north of Point Hope with the spray shield up. I am in the foreground. Jim Jackson (right) *and Bib Tevuk* (left) *are pulling on their boots. Earl Kingik is on watch in the bow.* MICHAEL ASTOR

of the peninsula and gladly shut down the motors, anticipating our first rest since leaving Wales three days before.

As I explained earlier, it was here that I had spent the last two springs, serving on an Eskimo whaling crew, a job I would continue for the next eight years. I immediately went over to the Kingik house and had a wonderful reunion with my newly adopted surrogate family. Laurie Kingik came back with me to the beach, where the crew had set up camp on one of the strands. He walked around the umiak, inspecting the seams and lashings in a way that bespoke his years of knowledge, then turned and said, "You are a real Eskimo, Sonny. I am proud of you." The praise came from one of the men I most respected. I slept well that night.

The sun was already high enough to warm the tent the next day when I was awakened by a great *WHOOOOSH*ing sound, then another and another outside the tent. I fought my way out of the bag and tore open the tent zipper while the rest of the crew snored away. In the blue ocean in front of me, only twenty yards from shore was a pod of gray whales blowing great jets of vapor into the air.

These brownish, mottled, somewhat scabrous creatures were traveling purposefully along, migrating to the northern Chukchi Sea from their winter range five thousand miles to the south in the lagoons of Baja California. Among other names (mostly pejorative), the nineteenth-century Yankee whalemen called these thirty-foot whales "mud diggers." The men had noticed that these whales often came to the surface trailing great plumes of mud from their mouths, and they assumed the whales were digging for mussels on the bottom; hence another name, "mussel diggers."

Only in the last decade have scientists come to understand this behavior. While towing side-scan sonars over the sea floor near Bering Strait, two geologists, Hans Nelson and Kirk Johnson, noted a number of oblong pits on the bottom in waters one hundred to one hundred fifty feet deep. It became clear that these were the scars left by gray whales that, as the whalemen had surmised, were diving to the bottom to feed. Scientists now believe that the whales roll the side of their mouths onto the bottom, then retract their huge tongues, creating a powerful suction that takes in great volumes of mud and water. The whales then squirt the muck out of the sides of their mouths, straining out the amphipods (small bottom-dwelling, shrimplike crustaceans) on the plates of baleen that hang from their upper jaw. The geologists also discovered that this harrowing of the sediments actually creates a more favorable habitat for the amphipods. So the whales' very feeding activity creates more of their food supply.

In the nineteenth century and again in the 1930s these whales were hunted close to extinction by commercial hunters. Today, however, there are about sixteen thousand of them—approximately the size of the population before commercial hunting began. The Eskimos of northern Alaska have never hunted these whales: Their name for them is *agviluak* (wrong whale) because of the gray's well-deserved reputation for pugnacity. For the same reason the Yankee whalemen also called them "devil fish"—they knew them to be ugly opponents. As one wrote: "Chasing devil fish, the . . . boat struck and got the head of the boat knocked off."

As aggressive as these whales are when attacked, they are still preyed upon by killer whales. In 1975 the Point Hopers watched from shore as a school of killer whales surrounded a lone gray. It sensed the killers and tried to head in shore where it would be protected by the shallower water, but two of the larger killers sank their teeth into its fins and forced it back into deeper water. Time after time the gray fought its way free and headed toward shore, but each time the killers caught it and steered it back out. After two and half hours the gray whale was dead.

Strong northerly winds held us at Point Hope for several days but on the morning of July 11 we woke to find a rare flat calm. The others hurriedly packed their things while I trotted over to the Kingik house to say good-bye and to corral Laurie's son, my friend Earl Kingik, who would be coming with us.

Rounding the tip of the point and heading back toward the mainland, we could see the entire range of low mountains from Cape Thompson in the south to Cape Lisburne in the north, a span of fifty miles, all blue and jagged in the morning light. This stretch of jumbled rock is the terminus of the Rocky Mountains. Here the great mountain chain that begins at Tierra del Fuego finally completes its ten-thousand-mile meander as the backbone of the Americas.

We motored along the even, monotonous beaches for a couple of hours, heading toward the mountains and driving small flocks of sandpipers ahead of us. At the base of the peninsula marshes and wet meadows rose above the low beaches. We stopped for coffee at the first higher land, Kotuk Point, where Earl spotted a mammoth's tusk protruding from a thawing muck bank. Remains of the Pleistocene epoch such as this are found over much of Alaska, remnants of a time when giant mammals roamed the land and so much of the earth's water was frozen in the great Ice Age glaciers that the sea level had fallen three hundred feet. At that time all of the Chukchi Sea, as well as Bering Strait and the northeastern third of the Bering Sea, had become a vast, cold and dry rolling tundra meadow connecting Asia and America. In fact the continents were still joined as recently as ten thousand years ago, close to the time when the ancestors of the Eskimos and Aleuts wandered along the coast, out of Asia and into the New World. Their migration took place many thousands of years after the American Indian population had traveled the same route across the Bering Land Bridge.

Remains of mammoths and other extinct fauna have occasionally provided the Eskimos with convenient quarries of ivory and bone for their tools and weapons. Earl and Bib tried to pull the tusk from the bank, but one end was still firmly frozen in, and even after taking an axe to its icy matrix it would not budge; so after half an hour we pushed on north along the rising hills and past the bold bluffs of Cape Dyer to Cape Lisburne, a massive gray cliff leaping vertically to twelve hundred feet.

This was an unsettling place. Laurie had often told me how Eskimo hunters traveling in the winter always gave the cape a wide berth, going far inland, although it would have been much simpler to traverse its right-angled corner by going around on the flat sea ice. But the cape is so high and steep, and the winds coming off it are so severe that they seem to blow directly downward, rolling and billowing off the top in great williwaws, forcing loose rocks right off the cliff face and blowing the ice offshore. But that afternoon the wind was still, and we rounded the cape accompanied only by the cries of hundreds of thousands of sea birds. Ahead of us a mile away was the single, cubic building of the Cape Lisburne Air Force Station.

The village store at Point Hope had been out of gasoline, and the only combustible in stock had been "white gas"—pressure appliance fuel—which has a very high burning temperature. We knew that it would make the motors run very hot, but there was no choice, so we had mixed it half and half with our remaining motor gasoline (which was itself actually 80/87 aircraft fuel) and added a lot of motor oil to the brew. The motors smoked quite a bit and they certainly overheated, but they got us to Cape Lisburne without a hitch.

The commanding officer came down to the beach when we

pulled up in front of the station, and he generously offered to help us with whatever we needed. What we needed was one hundred eighty gallons of gasoline to take us to Point Barrow. This he gave us as well as a hot meal and a few beers. While we ate he explained that his station, with its huge white radar dome at the top of the Cape, anchored one end of the DEW (Distant Early Warning) Line, a close picket of radar bases stretching from there to East Greenland, with stations approximately every hundred miles. The DEW Line was built hurriedly in the mid 1950s in response to the threat of Soviet bombers coming over the North Pole, a massive construction project that took only three years, and one that, for a time, secured our northern approaches. We would have liked to stay but the weather was holding. We had already learned that in the Arctic every minute of good weather must be used to the maximum effectiveness—there simply isn't that much of it.

We pushed off and headed east along the great curving sweep of coast that would eventually lead us to Point Lay and Icy Cape. After only an hour or so Earl, in the other boat, began signaling to us and pointing to shore. Dotted on the sloping hillside were thousands of caribou. They were part of the western Brooks Range herd that each spring migrates north through the mountains from the Noatak and Kobuk river valleys. They had reached their calving grounds on the Arctic Slope in May and June and were now slowly grazing their way back south.

A true hunter, Earl was eager to get us some fresh meat. We landed and he quickly killed two young bulls about half a mile from the boats. A couple of us towed the boats along shore on a line while the others cleaned the carcasses and dragged them back to the beach. With our larder full of precious meat we pushed off again. Earl and Bib were now much happier; for both understandably preferred their native foods to ours. The rest of us were not unhappy either: Caribou has a light and delicate flavor which many find far more appealing than beef.

We hadn't gone much farther when the motor on the umiak began to cough and snort. When it finally gave out, Mickey and Jim worked to solve the problem, while my thoughts turned to the great bight where my umiak was now bobbing gently.

This ninety-mile-long body of water was still unnamed. The

first American to see these waters was John Ledyard of Connect-icut, a petty officer on one of Captain James Cook's ships when they passed here in 1778. Ledyard was also the United States's first explorer, a restless, curious man who kept moving all his life and who, among other adventures, traveled on foot almost the whole way across Siberia before he was arrested and deported by Catherine the Great's agents. (He died in Cairo in 1789 at the beginning of an overland trek to southern Africa.) In 1783 in Con-necticut, Ledyard published his memoirs of Cook's voyage, and this account helped to set off the American scramble for the rich trade in sea otter pelts with the Indians of the Northwest Coast.[1]

Once the outboard had come back to life we pushed on in near-calm conditions. As we moved east of Cape Lisburne, grad-ually the jagged mountains grew lower and farther from the coast, and finally at Cape Beaufort, a weathered limestone hill, they vanished altogether. Soon we were left with a low, monot-onous gravel beach. We had reached the Arctic Coastal Plain, a vast waterlogged wilderness stretching more than five hundred miles to the east.

After stopping for half an hour at the then-deserted village of Point Lay to cook a meal and grab a catnap, we pushed ahead in perfect, cloudless weather, crossing the seventieth parallel and reaching Icy Cape, the low spur of beach that marked Captain Cook's farthest northern point, the place where he found the pack ice hard on shore. We found, however, only open water, and with fatigue closing over us we continued on along the featurelsss shore until we reached the village of Wainwright, more than twenty-four hours and two hundred fifty miles after leaving Point Hope.

The particular ice conditions in any summer in the Chukchi Sea depend on a combination of ocean currents and weather. In the late spring, as the sea's ice cover begins to break up and drift about, two warm currents, flowing north out of Bering Strait, shape its character. One of the currents flows more or less north-northwest directly into the Arctic Ocean, while the other follows the coast of Alaska. Together they clear the ice away in their

[1]A few years later, because no place in Alaska bore his name, I was able, with the assistance of a colleague at the University of Alaska, to have the Board of Geographic Names designate this water as John Ledyard Bay.

paths as the summer progresses. But between the currents a great wedge of pack ice hangs down from the Arctic Ocean. In the nineteenth century the whalemen called its southern tip "Post Office Point," because as they cruised along its edge it was here that they paused to exchange information and letters from home. This wedge of ice is in fact like a huge tongue, hanging in the center of the sea, which can wag back and forth, depending on the wind direction. It seems likely that Captain Cook arrived at Icy Cape after a period of northwesterly wind, but we, in 1972, had been more lucky and had run up the open path of water while the pack hung in the middle of the sea.

As we set up camp on the beach in front of the village I could see that out on the horizon was a thin line of white, the southeastern edge of polar pack ice in the Chukchi Sea. Earl, whose hunter's eyes were far sharper than ours, spotted a small red dot out there too. It was clearly a large ocean-going vessel. We all wondered who could be up here at this time, so despite our need for sleep we pushed off in the Boston Whaler to go out to the ship. Drawing closer, we could see that she was a light icebreaker of the Canadian Coast Guard, the *Camsell*, a well-known Arctic veteran that alternated her duties between winter buoytending in British Columbia and summer convoy duty, resupplying the many small settlements of Canada's western Arctic.

One of the officers hailed us and invited us aboard for a tour of the spotless vessel. After we had a chat with her captain, John Lennie, one of the officers mentioned that they had not had any fresh meat since leaving Victoria, British Columbia. It was a simple matter to hoist one of our caribou carcasses out of the Boston Whaler. It would be six years before the favor was repaid, but when it was, we were very grateful.

During the night a light northwesterly pushed the pack ice close to shore. When we woke it was calm again, but it was certain that we would not be able to make any progress until an easterly opened a shore lead (a narrow path of icefree water) for us. The temperature rose to a surprising and unpleasant 80 degrees and the mosquitoes, enjoying "their" weather, nearly drove us mad. In our enforced idleness Earl and Bib spent the time with their friends from town hunting walruses at the fringe of the pack ice. Earl took two young bulls, which he gave to some of his cousins in the village, while Robin worked on the proofs of his book on Alexander the Great and Mickey and the others worked on the motors. I spent the time talking with the old people, particularly with Waldo Bodfish, the son of a whaling captain from Martha's Vineyard. A number of Arctic families have one or two ancestors from the whaling fleet; Waldo's father, Captain Hartson Bodfish, was an exceptionally skilled whaler and mariner. Over endless cups of coffee he told me about the early days of whaling and trading on this coast. The whole town was extremely friendly and interested in our voyage, especially the members of the enormous Bodfish clan, and time passed quickly.

It was not until July 19 that the wind finally swung into the east and pushed the pack ice far enough off shore to allow us to travel on. Near Point Belcher, we noticed that the shore was littered with huge timbers, sticking out of the sand at odd angles. It was a mass of frayed and splintered wood interspersed by long, twisted iron bolts. Some were whole slabs of planks joined together for twenty yards or more. I later learned that these were the remains of the thirty-one whaleships from New England and Hawaii that were driven ashore by the ice in 1871.

The whaleships, like us, had run up a lane of water between the land and the pack ice. Whalemen had only discovered the western Arctic bowheads in 1848, but by 1871 they had taken so many whales that the population was less than half its former size. So to make paying catches the captains had to take greater and greater risks with their ships. They had run en masse up this cul-de-sac. The fleet then reached the end of open water between Wainwright and Point Belcher, and the ships simply dropped anchor, assuming that the ice would retreat, as it usually did, to allow them to push ahead to the whaling grounds at Point Barrow. But instead of the southeasterly they expected, the wind swung into the southwest and pushed the ice toward shore, trapping the ships.

One may wonder why a southwest wind would push the ice toward the shore when the coastline runs in the same direction. It would seem that the ice ought to move along parallel to shore, but not closer to it. The fact is that sea ice does not move in the same direction as the wind, but rather at about 30 degrees to the right of it—because of the force of the earth's spin, the Coriolis

effect. Here, paradoxically, a southwest wind will torque the pack ice right onto shore, while a northeast wind will lift it off.

The whaling fleet waited in this shore lead in August 1871, while the ice slowly crept toward the ships. By mid-September the captains realized that they could wait no longer for a favorable wind to free them. They ordered the ships abandoned and took to their whaleboats. It is astonishing that no lives were lost: Twelve hundred fifty men, women, and children sailed down the narrow water lead to Icy Cape, where the rest of the fleet, six

Stopped by the pack ice hard onshore near Walakpa Bay, Bib Tevuk walks out to inspect its thickness while Earl Kingik (right) *and I stand at the bow of the umiak.* MICHAEL ASTOR

ships, the "timid" ones, were waiting to take the crews to San Francisco and Hawaii. The crush of humanity on board was such on the way that, with so many mouths to feed, a few of the ships had to cook their meals in the blubber pots.

But it was the natives who suffered a real tragedy. When the ships were abandoned, large numbers of Eskimos went out to them and pillaged the vessels. Among other things, they were looking for the alcohol supplies, most of which had been destroyed before abandonment. Instead, the Eskimos found the ships' medicine chests, and, assuming that everything in glass bottles was hooch, drank the medicine, and many died as the result.

We moved on past this gloomy place and out along the low sand islands that form Point Franklin. On a map the Point Franklin spit resembles Icy Cape, and as at Icy Cape, the alongshore current shoots by the point, then eddies back in a swirl. Here we found the edge of the pack ice again and we could see the current pulling bits of ice off its edge and spiraling them around the point.

The sky had been getting darker and darker all the way up from Wainwright, and just as we were confronting this swirling ice, it began to rain, a steady, soaking rain that lasted for a couple of hours. Fortunately it was not driven in by a strong wind, but the extra moisture in the air raised a low, miasmic fog from the ice, making it hard to keep our bearings. It was important to know where we were because we had to get around Sea Horse Shoal off the tip of the point. When I judged we had gone far enough, we turned east a bit, toward shore—and promptly ran aground.

Feeling damp and depressed we grumpily pulled on our hip boots and pushed the umiak off the shoal. Just as the rain stopped we broke into clear water. It was then an easy matter to keep going east until we reached the high mud bluffs of Skull Cliff and, we thought, to follow their graceful arc all the way to Point Barrow, the northernmost point in Alaska.

But as we approached the cliff, the edge of the pack ice began angling closer and closer to shore, and we were running in a narrowing shore lead. Finally it forced us right to the beach, and we had to use our axes and ice chisels to chop our way through small pieces that were jammed between the floating ice and the shore. After a few more miles of very shallow water, eventually it grew so shoal that we had to walk along the beach, towing the boats by lines. We arrived this way in Walakpa Bay, which is a little more than twenty miles south of Point Barrow.

Walakpa Bay is a short but deep gash, scored by the erosion of a small stream, in the otherwise monotonous mud cliff, which is here about forty feet high. When we got there the tide was milling into the small embayment, and it pulled the umiak right in with it and over a small sandbar. I should have asked myself what was causing this sudden rise in the water. I was overlooking the fact that the tidal range in northern Alaska is only about six inches and that it is the winds that noticeably raise or lower the water level there: An easterly will lower it and a westerly will raise it, and changes in the water level are often felt well before a change in the wind. This rising water foretold a westerly.

We spent an hour or so there, cooking breakfast in the twilight of midnight under those dark mud cliffs. Above us at the top of the cliff was a small granite obelisk which seemed painfully out of place here, where little evidence of man's intrusion could be seen. It was dedicated to the memory of Will Rogers, the great humorist, and Wiley Post, the famous aviator, who died in a plane crash here on August 15, 1935. The cenotaph was now thoroughly pockmarked by bullet scars. Being the only vertical feature for miles, it had become a convenient target for Eskimos who were sighting in their rifles. It was sad to see the monument so badly defaced.

A fog had risen off the ice while we were breakfasting, so we waited a little longer for better visibility, then moved on, zigzagging through the floes that I noticed were now being driven along by a two-knot northerly current. The floes also seemed to be consolidating somewhat, and this should have set off alarm bells in my head.

When we were only two miles from the town of Barrow, just as were moving around a large grounded piece of ice, all the open water seemed suddenly to vanish. The ice floes simply closed in on the umiak. Trapped, Earl and I knew that they would crush the boat within minutes. No one panicked, but everyone was pretty scared as the five of us leaped out onto the nearest floe, and straining every muscle, with veins standing out on our faces, managed to pull the umiak, fully loaded, right up onto the ice, just as our pool of open water disappeared. The boat must have weighed at least twenty-five hundred pounds; it shows what five men with their adrenaline flowing can do in a pinch.

The Boston Whaler had been trailing us and was safe in a pool of water next to the beach. Frantic, we slid the loaded umiak across this piece of ice to the open water and then to the beach. We immediately hauled both boats out of the water as even that last pool was closed. Then all at once the current suddenly went slack, the pack went motionless, and there was nothing but the Arctic's awesome silence all around us.

I climbed to the top of the bank and saw nothing but tightly packed ice as far as the horizon, with no open water at all. It was clear that we weren't going anywhere until the ice slacked off. In retrospect I realize that we should not have pushed off from Walakpa Bay; the rising water foretold a west wind, and a west wind would push the pack ice hard onto the shore.

I wish we had stayed at Walakpa for another reason as well: Our camp was now only two miles from the town of Barrow and we were frequently visited by Eskimos who at all times of the day and night asked to buy drugs or alcohol from us. We had neither.

In 1972 there were more than two thousand Eskimos living in the town of Barrow, an area where less than five hundred had lived a century before. They had been drawn there by the lure of employment and town life, but at that time there was little employment and, as far as I could see, little town life either. Barrow had the feel of a down-at-the-heels town on an Indian reservation. The dirt streets were filthy and the town itself was mostly a ghastly accumulation of shanty-style plywood shacks. Things have changed greatly for the better in recent years, but in 1972 these conditions contributed to the palpable tension and an ugly atmosphere. Our walks into the town gave us a feeling that none had ever felt before in an Arctic settlement—of being entirely unwelcome and loathed.

It was only when we visited Earl Kingik's relations that the feeling passed. He had a number of cousins in town, and many of them gave us meals or coffee and offered advice on how to cope with the waters ahead of us. Mickey and Robin were amazed at the breadth of Earl's far-flung family. "I've got cousins from Nome to Coppermine in Canada," said Earl. I explained that this situation was less than a century old and that it reflected the turmoil through which all of northern Alaska's Eskimo societies had gone.

Until well after the middle of the nineteenth century there were relatively few extended kinship networks in the region. In those days all of northwestern Alaska was divided into about twenty-five discrete Eskimo societies that occupied territories with clearly defined boundaries. These groups lost little love on one another and usually considered themselves to be under the threat of war. Strangers were always greeted with hostility; hence the Eskimos' routine aggressiveness against foreign expeditions.

There were, however, two ways of gaining safe passage through another territory. One was during the general truce that existed in the height of the summer, allowing people to travel to the annual trade fairs at Kotzebue Sound, in the Colville River delta, and near Barter Island in northeastern Alaska. At each trade rendezvous goods that originated from as far away as Siberia or central Arctic Canada flowed back and forth in a well-integrated network that supplied, among other things, the needs for soapstone (from the east) and metals (from the west). Furs and sea mammal oils were often the medium of exchange.

The other type of safe passage through alien territory could

Two crew members stand alongside the umiak which has been dragged up onto the ice only moments before the floes closed in, threatening to crush the boat.

be obtained by a trading partnership with a man in another society. This was established by a temporary exchange of spouses between the partners and the result was the creation of an extended kinship network that provided protection for its members.

All of this changed at the end of the nineteenth century when the whaling industry began hiring large numbers of Eskimos from all over Alaska to work aboard the ships at Herschel Island in Canada or in whaling stations at Point Barrow or Point Hope. This great mixing of peoples coincided with a period of famine and epidemic disease, and by 1910, when the whaling industry was moribund, the old territorial order had completely broken down. The mixed and fragmented remnants of the old societies reformed in scattered trapping camps and in a few small villages, and one result was the wide kinship networks that now span the entire northern part of the state.

We were very glad to leave our campsite several days later, and even more so to be approaching Point Barrow. At 71° 23′ N it is the northernmost point in Alaska, and, except for the Boothia Peninsula in the eastern Arctic (which is only about thirty miles closer to the Pole), it is the northernmost point on the continent. We approached within five miles of the point, surging along on the strong current, but this time without the pack ice nearby. As the low, gray sandspit slipped by, we drew abreast of a small hillock—and suddenly there was no land to the north, east, or west. Behind us was the Chukchi Sea, ahead was the Arctic Ocean, and to our right was the Beaufort Sea. We were alone on a vast gray sea. It was both exhilarating and frightening. Thomas Elson, the first European to see the point, was similarly struck by the utter loneliness of the place, tentatively naming it "World's End."

A few days later, we were two hundred miles east of Point Barrow, and a thousand from Cape Nome, and running well when we arrived at Point McIntyre at the western end of Prudhoe Bay. The oil work was quiet that summer: The discovery phase had ended and the recovery phase had not yet begun, so we camped in a deserted building on the shore.

Mickey Astor went exploring in one of the empty drilling

camps nearby and came upon a particularly dirty and oily pair of driller's coveralls. He returned with these as a joke for Robin, who recently had been complaining of the cold. We all expected Robin to put them promptly into the camp fire. On the contrary, he took to them like a puppy takes to a dirty blanket and spent the rest of the summer in them. They were so smelly that dogs growled at him wherever we were.

When we woke at Point McIntyre we found the skies clear for the first time in more than a week, and for the first time we saw the outline of the Brooks Range—a hundred miles away, low and jagged in the rosy morning sky. These rugged mountains somehow seemed very friendly compared with the monotonous sand islands. We ran along on sparkling water while flocks of eider ducks flew westward in low skeins along the edge of the pack ice. Farther on, the ice was closer in shore and very loose, giving us a mirror-smooth surface as we ran through the scattered floes.

That evening Earl, in the bow, was studying the horizon intently with binoculars. I asked him what he was looking at, and after a couple of minutes he turned and said, "I can see a blinking light on the horizon!" It was the tall aircraft beacon at Barter Island. We cut right across part of Camden Bay and heading directly for it, and at two-thirty on the morning of August 5, reached Kaktovik, a tiny village of two dozen small houses and one very large DEW Line station.

There we had a wonderful surprise. Victoria Waldron, one of the archaeological team from Cape Nome, who had helped us load the umiak more than a month before, was waiting for us— with the two items that had been most missed from our larder, rum and fresh vegetables. She was standing on the beach surrounded by her provisions when we pulled in. I shouted over the engine's racket: "You're a sight for sore eyes." It coughed to a halt as our bow grated onto the shore, and she replied, "You certainly aren't!"

I looked down at myself and saw that she was right. I hadn't bathed or shaved for more than a month, and my clothes, with oil, dirt, and bloodstains all over them, were appalling. This, plus my red eyes from lack of sleep, would have given children nightmares. The other six of us looked about the same. Victoria thought that we were lucky that we weren't arrested on the spot. Fortunately the station chief at the DEW Line station let us use his showers and washing machines.

Kaktovik was a friendly place, especially in contrast to our last town, Barrow. Walt Audi, a gregarious and self-reliant bush pilot, offered us the use of his house, and other people invited us to their houses for meals. It was sad to leave, but on August 7 we were rested and the weather was good. In eight hours we reached the 141st meridian and entered Canadian waters. On shore was only a single small white obelisk indicating the international boundary. The border here was established by treaty between Russia and Great Britain in 1825 (before any European had seen it) as a way of preventing the two countries from encroaching on each other's territorial claims and poaching each other's furs. A line was drawn north from Mount Saint Elias on the Pacific Ocean. More than six hundred fifty miles north, after crossing three mountain ranges, it entered the Arctic Ocean on a low, eroding bit of mud bank. Guarding it as we passed was a lone, majestic bull caribou. It raised its magnificent rack of antlers, then cantered off inland.

The conditions were perfect—a beautiful, clear day, with a light tail wind. We continued along the coast, with the mountains, here called the British Mountains, coming ever closer to the water. The deep snow-filled gorges stood out brilliantly against the dull gray of the jagged peaks. Soon Herschel Island began to rise from the sea, its gentle outline a wide brown lens on the horizon. We ran through the narrow passage between the island and the mainland, and then into Mackenzie Bay, our first encounter with the muddy waters of that great river.

As soon as we came out from the shelter of Herschel Island we began to pitch and roll in a confused short chop that seemed to be put up by a current running over shallows and against the wind. It grew worse as we rounded the spur of a mud bluff called Kay Point and crossed the shoals that run off it. "Why the hell did I ask to come on this trip?" said Bib, looking slightly green.

Suddenly in the midst of this bouncing I heard a dull thud and a cracking noise. I turned to see the outboard hanging over the stern at a drunken and precarious angle. The torque from the motor had pulled the top of the transom off, and it was now only being held on with several sealskin lashings. There was no way we could repair it out there and, because there were vertical mud banks all along the shore, there was no place to land either. Our only choice was to slog along at low power until we could find a good place to carry out the repairs.

The best alternative seemed to be to roll along for another twenty-five miles, and go ashore on the nice gravel beach at Shingle Point. We had been underway fourteen hours since leaving Barter Island, and it was good to stretch our legs on shore. Hauling the umiak's stern out onto the beach, Bib Tevuk and I got right to the repairs, while the others cooked a meal and napped in the warm sunshine. It took us about ten hours to undo all the lashings, to reinforce them and to adze a block from a piece of driftwood to support the lower unit of the outboard, but once everything was back together, we pushed off right away. Earl and Tony, preferring the Whaler, took that while the rest of us piled into the umiak.

Our next planned stop was to be the village of Tuktoyaktuk on the other side of the Mackenzie delta, and the shortest route was to cut right through the delta, going in one of the western mouths and coming out the east side. This route had the added advantage of giving us some protection from the rising wind.

It was twilight and a bit choppy as we pushed off into the muddy delta waters. As the light grew fainter it was increasingly difficult to tell where we were amid those low and featureless, willow-covered mud banks, and of course it was impossible to see the shoals. After about an hour we ran aground in Shoalwater Bay, having mistaken it for the western entrance to the delta. To make matters worse, it started to rain, and my chart, which was printed on thin paper, began to disintegrate (after that I learned to carry my charts in waterproof see-through packets), but we groped along into Shallow Bay and finally found the entrance to the delta at Reindeer Channel.

The waters now were sheltered, but piloting had become very difficult in the dim light—the riverbanks had become a single black mass. We were tired and disoriented, and several times we lost the meandering channel and ran aground.

Finally we reached the deeper waters of the Mackenzie's middle channel, and just as the light began to improve, found the small, winding slough that took us into the wide east channel. As the sun rose it found us charging along toward Kugmallit Bay at the eastern edge of the delta.

At last the white dome of Tuktoyaktuk's DEW Line station floated up in the mirage on the horizon. We reached the town near midday on August 9. Having come directly from Barter Island in a little more than thirty-six hours, we were all very tired, but one thing remained: to make a formal entry into Canada. We pulled ashore in front of the Royal Canadian Mounted Police buildings, then straggled groggily up the bank to check in. We assumed that the authorities would be fascinated by the length of our voyage and by the umiak.

Dirty and red-eyed from the trip, the seven of us probably looked like a bunch of pirates coming over the rail, but we were well behaved and polite. In twenty-five years of traveling in northern Canada I have always found the RCMP force to be the soul of professionalism, skill, and helpfulness, but as we entered the station, it was clear that this was not going to be an easy interview.

We were faced by a very large man, with a rather small head and a belligerent countenance. He made it clear right away that he didn't give a damn about how far we had come or what we had come in, and if it were his decision he would send all of us right back to Alaska. He wanted names, passports, and the serial numbers of our guns and cameras and motors—and fast. He made me fill out a very long form that was used for the entry of oceangoing ships: name, tonnage, propulsion, home port, cargo, crew list, intended destination, etc. He muttered that he wanted me to post a bond on the outfit, but that he could not find a regulation to cover our expedition. As a tour de force he lined us up and began to read us a long list of what we were and what we were not allowed to do while in Canada.

During this homily I noticed that Robin, who was next to me in line, appeared to be mumbling something. He was looking at the sign on the wall and repeating, *Royal-Canadian-Mounted-Police-Royal-Canadian-Mounted-Police* over and over, like a mantric chant. When the litany of laws was complete the policeman barked, "Any questions?" Robin then muttered under his breath, "Why don't you get stuffed as well as mounted?" We kept a low profile in Tuktoyaktuk for several days.

The run east of Tuktoyaktuk was marred principally by strong northwest winds, which kept us on shore for a few days. Finally we reached Cape Dalhousie, another one of those ugly, low, eroding mud banks. As we turned into Liverpool Bay it became foggy, and we only found the DEW Line station at Nicholson Island after thrashing around in the fog for several hours, then using my transistor radio to home it on its radio beacon. We camped on the beach at Nicholson for a day or so,

The crew at Nicholson Island, N.W.T., at the end of the trip in August 1972. Left to right: *Robin Lane Fox, Jim Jackson, Bib Tevuk, Tony Mitchell, and Mickey Astor.* Seated: *Earl Kingik.*

but, just as we were ready to leave, the main bearing froze on the umiak's motor. There was no way to repair it, and we knew that the twenty-horsepower spare would push the boat very slowly at best, so we decided to leave the Boston Whaler there and use its motor on the umiak and put the whole crew in it. We were off again the next day.

For five hours we slogged through thick fog and a heavy ground swell. I was hoping to push on toward Cape Parry, which was two hundred miles ahead by our coastal course. But that leg involved some very exposed and difficult stretches, and because it looked as if the wind might rise, we decided to go ashore to cook a meal and see how the weather turned out.

We made the mistake of landing on the smaller of the two Baillie Islands. Once ashore, the wind came up hard from the southeast, holding us on that islet, which was only a few hundred yards in any direction. The wind then swung into the northwest and it began raining and blowing twenty-five to thirty knots, trapping us on our little grass-covered island. The temperature ranged between thirty-five and forty-one degrees Fahrenheit, keeping us in our tents for more than a week. It was uncomfortable and it soon became clear that our food supply would not hold out for more than about two weeks.

As we lay in our tents we had plenty of time to talk over our progress, our plans, and our situation. There was no doubt the best of the summer's weather was past us. We could now look forward to gales of increasing frequency—and several of us had to be back at work in early September. The conclusion was inescapable: We would cache the boats near an airstrip and fly home for the winter.

When the wind finally went down a bit, we packed up and started back to Nicholson, where we arrived on August 25. Jim Bodena, the capable and efficient station chief at the DEW Line site, was very helpful, and made our stay pleasant as we winterized motors and cached the boats. We took a DEW Line supply plane to Cambridge Bay and then a commercial flight to Edmonton.

It had been a good summer. We had covered fifteen hundred miles, coped with the Arctic, and learned a tremendous amount from our mistakes.

Chapter 4

Return to Bering Strait

For me, the year 1973 was a turning point in many ways—a good year, and the best part of it was that I married Romayne.

When I returned to Oxford in October 1972, the first thing I did was to telephone Romayne Grimston. I had met her a year before when we caught one another sneaking out of an appallingly boring cocktail party. By chance we met again soon at a dinner party, and we went out together for the rest of the winter and spring. It did not take me long to fall in love with her, for she was very attractive, with a fine sense of humor, and as Bill Gilkerson, an artist friend, put it, she has a voice "like birdsong." Also, being sweet and gentle, she was, and is, a fine counterpoint to my somewhat feisty character.

To my great delight she came to Nome, Alaska, for a few weeks in June 1972 with a group of my friends, while we made preparations for the maiden voyage of the umiak. Romayne proved to be a good sport and very adaptable, and she seemed to enjoy those long, warm summer days at Bonnie Hahn's house at the foot of Cape Nome.

I knew right away that I wanted to marry her, but when I proposed to her in November, I was concerned that my odd career, as well as my peripatetic life and occasionally dangerous travels might not appeal to her. Lithe and delicate, she did not look at all like someone who might seek out wild and rugged places, for she was then working for Moët et Chandon, running their château in the Champagne region of France.

I needn't have worried. Quite the contrary to her looks and demeanor, I learned that she was used to rough travel, and as a young girl had covered most of Africa and the Middle East with her parents. When I somewhat apologetically asked if she was apprehensive about the dangers of my travels, she replied, "Not a bit. It all sounds fascinating. I want to come along with you— though I must admit that a summer in France, with lots of champagne, sounds more to my taste."

We became engaged in December and were married only a month later—very quickly because her father was dying of cancer. At such short notice the only suitable church we could find was the chapel of St. Stephen in the Palace of Westminster, near the Houses of Parliament. We were allowed to use this private chapel because Romayne's father, an earl, was a member of the House of Lords.

We were married on a cold and gray day in January 1973. It was at once a very happy and a very sad occasion; for we had so much to look forward to, yet her father was so terribly ill. One bright spot was our wedding cake. Romayne's mother, instead of ordering the usual frothy cliché of icing, bells and filigrees, produced a cake in the shape of an enormous igloo.

We spent the spring in England while I worked on the final draft of my doctoral dissertation about my excavations at Cape Nome. I returned to Alaska in April to continue my whaling studies, and Romayne joined me there in June at Cape Nome, while I carried out some brief archaeological surveys on the Seward Peninsula. Then Jim Jackson, who had been with me for the past two summers and was taking another break from his anthropological studies at the University of New Mexico, arrived, as did Mark Hollingsworth, an old friend from home and

A view of the abandoned whalers' village at Pauline Cove, Herschel Island, July 1973. Here, far beyond the tree line, the shore is littered with driftwood from the outflow of the Mackenzie River.

a veteran of the Cape Nome excavations. Wally Otton, a quiet, thoughtful Eskimo from Elim on the Seward Peninsula, joined us later. Like me, he had become an extra member of Bonnie Hahn's family.

I had been hired that summer to do some exploratory archaeological work at Herschel Island which is about fifty miles east of the Alaska-Canada border and a little more than two hundred east of Prudhoe Bay. The job would only take a couple of weeks at most; then we planned to go to Nicholson Island, where I had left the umiak the year before. It is usually very difficult to fly laterally across the Arctic: Most routes run north–south. In our case reaching Herschel was no exception. We flew from Nome to Fairbanks, to Whitehorse in the Yukon, to Inuvik in the Northwest Territories—all on commercial airline flights—then hitched a ride on a helicopter to Herschel, in the Yukon, a journey of two thousand miles to cover the eight hundred air miles from Nome.

We landed at Pauline Cove on the east side of the island at the abandoned settlement on the sandspit. It was a handful of weathered wooden buildings, some of them a century old, the relics of the whaling and fur trading era in the western Arctic.

When the helicopter's noise finally died away, we were suddenly swept over by the silence of the Arctic and we immediately felt much closer to the early part of the century. Instead of the noise of traffic or the roar of that helicopter, now all we could hear was the twitter of one or two songbirds, the ripple of water on the half-dozen bits of ice in the cove, and the intermittent creak of an ancient door swinging in the wind.

In the evening I took a walk alone up on the hills above Pauline Cove. The temperature was about 40 degrees, but it was so still that a shirt was all I wore. Below me the water was a mirror and the hillsides a velvety green, contrasting with a few pieces of white ice floating in the cove. The perfect surface of the water was broken only by a small chevron of ripples as a gaggle of ducklings purposefully followed their mother as she moved slowly across the harbor.

I looked south, past the sandspit, toward the mainland shore and the British Mountains beyond. A white line of ice scribed the far shore, while a single, wispy rain cloud hung above Kay Point—and to the west the end of a rainbow was stationary for nearly an hour. The sun touched the northern horizon at midnight. I walked back down the green valleys, gently sloping from the erosion of hundreds of rivulets over thousands of years. The only sounds were the occasional cries of a long-tailed jaeger, the cackle of a loon, and the gutteral and sharp rumble of a lone raven. The place seemed timeless.

Back on the sandspit, the litter of the whaling industry surrounded us: rusty old drums, bits of rotting cordage, and—on the hillside—the white picket fences surrounding a cluster of graves. In the silence we could sense the times when nearly a thousand people—Eskimos, Whites, Blacks, American Indians, and Polynesians—and more than a dozen ships, had wintered over in the little harbor, waiting for the ice to melt and release them for ten weeks to chase the bowhead whales that were then worth ten thousand dollars apiece for the baleen (whalebone) in their mouths.

We wanted to learn more about the changes that had overwhelmed the Eskimos when the American whaling fleet began wintering at the island in 1889, and planned to excavate two houses, one from just before the time the whaleships arrived, and one from just after. Grassy mounds covered the remains of collapsed houses, and there were few clues as to which was which. They all looked about the same—roughly rectangular, with a low entrance passage facing south. But in the nearly horizontal light of early morning we were able to see more details in the shadows cast by the old house walls, and it became clear that some were more gently rounded than others, hence presumably older.

We were lucky. The first house we excavated had been inhabited in the 1880s, a time when few of the Eskimos had had more than minimal contact with Whites. We were able to get a relative date for the house by the one cartridge case we found: It was intended for use in a Winchester rifle made first in 1876. Apart from that, and a small blob of lead, which was presumably the overflow from a bullet mold, the hunting implements were all traditional arrowheads and other gear.

The other house had been used in the 1890s, and the contrast was dramatic. We found very few traditional Eskimo tools; the horn, bone, and ivory implements had been replaced by manufactured tools which the Eskimos could suddenly obtain very cheaply by trading meat to the whalemen—or by renting their wives to them. The place was littered with broken china and glass, cartridge cases, and many other things which the whalemen carried north from San Francisco and sold without markup. The Eskimos readily accepted these things: Some were more durable and effective than their tools, and everything could be obtained for far less labor than before. In the stark contrast between those two houses we witnessed the passing of a culture. It was a powerful and sad message.

There is also an unfortunate footnote to the story of our excavations at Herschel. When the helicopter arrived to take us back to Tuktoyaktuk, I had planned to bring the artifacts along for shipment to the south, where we could conserve and analyze them, but the contractor inexplicably refused to allow us to remove them from the island. I pointed out to him that it would be very difficult to write an intelligent site report without the artifacts. Instead he placed them in one of the whaling-era warehouses on the beach, a house which also contained about twenty drums of helicopter fuel. A month or so later some Eskimo children, playing there with matches, set the place on fire. It burned for several hours, with the red-hot fuel drums exploding and going up like roman candles. When I returned to the site there was nothing left but some charred wood and scorched earth.[1]

We reached Nicholson Island in mid-July 1973 and were met on the airstrip by my friend Jim Bodena, the station chief at the DEW Line site. He immediately told me how my umiak had narrowly missed being destroyed that winter when a heavily loaded DC-3 had overshot the runway. We found the equipment in good shape, and we spent the next few days painting and repairing the boat and checking the motor and food supplies.

I had decided during the winter that it would be necessary to return to Bering Strait; for we had only been able to make jury repairs to the damage the stern suffered in 1972 at Kay Point. To repair it properly required complete dismantling. Furthermore, because walrus skins are only fit for heavy boat use for two, or stretching it, three, seasons, it seemed best to rebuild the frame and to put new skins on the boat under the practiced eye of Dwight Milligrock or another of the Bering Strait Eskimos. There was simply no one nearer who understood the intricacies of large umiaks; nor was there a supply of well-cured walrus hides outside the Bering Strait region. Once the umiak had been rebuilt and reskinned I could then return to the Northwest Passage.

So, when we shoved off from the beach at Nicholson, we steered, not northeast, toward Cape Bathurst and the inner part of the Passage, but northwest toward Cape Dalhousie and Alaska. And, we shoved off in the umiak alone, leaving the Boston Whaler to be picked up on our return.[2]

In the following weeks we were to encounter every one of the challenges that we confronted in 1972, in reverse order.

---

[1]Fortunately I had not surrendered any field notes or photographs. Recently the government of the Yukon has declared the site a territorial park and my records have helped their archaeologists to write a thorough history of the island.

[2]We never recovered it. A year later I had a report that it had vanished, and another that it was being operated by an Eskimo, somewhere on the Mackenzie River.

Rounding the depressing mud headland of Cape Dalhousie we spent several hours in a steep rolling chop that gave the boat an unpleasant gait. Then, running in Russell Inlet we became confused in the fog and ran aground before finding our way out across the sandbars. When we reached the mouth of McKinley Bay, I decided to catch a catnap, and while I was asleep the helmsman made the easy mistake of steering too close to shore and therefore taking us inside the northeast-running sandspit and shoals. When we discovered the error, it took us a couple of hours to work back around them; once we had gone a few more miles, to Warren Point, the wind came up to nearly twenty knots, so we decided to make camp and wait it out.

We set up our tents behind the sandy bluff in a small field rippling with thousands of tufts of cotton grass. Their white flowers stood out beautifully against the green of the tundra meadow. There was also a team of biologists camped nearby studying the Canada geese in the area. It was a pleasant place to wait a few days for the wind to die down, and we should have stayed there a lot longer than we did.

Just as soon as the boat was underway, under a clear sky, the wind came up from a near calm to about fifteen knots from the northwest. I realized that a storm must be brewing for in the quarter of an hour it took to reach the nearest cove, at Tuft Point, the wind came up another five or ten knots and began to build a steep sea in those shallow waters. The situation was rapidly becoming dangerous. Waves were already breaking on the shoal between us and shore and I decided the best way to cross was to ride a wave over it into the cove.

We started to roll heavily as we came around broadside to the waves, positioning ourselves for the run in. I climbed into the stern cockpit, with Mark Hollingsworth on the helm, so that I could work the pump in case we took on water and provide some extra weight to hold the stern down, because in those swells we had begun to hobbyhorse badly, and on the crests the propeller was coming out of the water and racing free with a scream.

Approaching the breaking shoal, now only fifty yards away, the brown muddy seas seemed enormous, although I would guess they were only about five feet high. Suddenly a wave caught us, throwing us forward faster and faster. When we reached the bar there was a dull thud as the false keel touched the bottom and the boat nearly stopped, throwing us all forward as the waves surged past us. I was afraid we would slide crosswise to the seas and broach and fill, but with a long pole I kept the stern into the waves. The next breaker came and partially filled us, drenching Mark and me, but with a shudder the boat moved forward and then slid across into the cove.

We went right to shore and began unloading, but our troubles were far from over. The boat was now on a narrow beach at the foot of a fourteen-foot sand bluff that was topped with long-rooted beach grass. The sea was clearly rising, and it didn't require a genius to see that there soon would be no beach left to camp on. The only thing to do was to lug the entire outfit up to the top. About twenty-five yards back from the face of the bluff were the remains of a trapper's log cabin, perhaps fifty years old. Two of the walls were still standing, so we put the tents up behind them to get a bit of shelter from the wind, which was by then blowing forty knots.

It wasn't easy getting the tents up. We all had to work on one tent at a time to keep it from blowing away. The wind was now so strong that shouting was the only way to be heard. We staked and guyed the tents and put Romayne and some gear in one so that she could hold it down with her weight on the integral floor. These tents proved incredibly strong and resilient—they had been designed in a wind tunnel to withstand the storms on Mount Everest—but the wind was now so fierce that I grew worried that they might blow away, including the one with Romayne in it, so Mark and I dragged heavy driftwood logs and put them in each tent.

We then turned to the umiak. When we came across the bar we had noticed a fifty-seven-foot schooner at anchor in the little cove—the first vessel we had seen all summer. She was now bucking hard, with two anchors out on heavy chain. Amazingly, the wind had kept rising and by then had put the water level up so far that the shoal and sandbar were completely under water and identifiable only by a wild mass of breakers. It was clear that the beach where the umiak was would soon disappear as well.

The wind was now so strong that everyone had to walk bent double toward the boat, turning their faces from the blast which was now driving the sand so hard that the grains felt like needle pricks. The rising water had almost reached the umiak, and I wondered how five of us were going to get that heavy boat vertically up that sand bluff—and quickly.

I needn't have worried. We decided to try to roll the umiak, side over side, up the incline. Each time we lifted the upwind gunwhale, the wind surged under the boat, lifting it up and turning it on its own axis, thus rolling it up the sand cliff nearly one whole rotation—where it was slammed against the cliff face. We only had to lift the lower gunwhale three or four times and the wind did the rest.

When we (or rather the wind) had the boat just below the top of the bluff, we lifted the lower gunwhale once again. The wind hit the boat so hard this time that, lacking any more of the cliff to stop it, it simply spun in its own diameter. The other gunwhale came whipping round and caught me right in the gut, throwing me up in the air, while the boat, with three of the crew hanging on, rolled over the top onto the flat tundra. I fell halfway down the bluff and made a soft landing right on Mark.

We quickly cut some driftwood stakes, drove them into the ground, and, using the anchor line, lashed the umiak down—for it showed every indication that it would keep on rolling. It was now impossible to be heard over the shrieking wind: We had to cup our hands over one another's ears and shout to be understood.

At this point, thoroughly unnerved by the ferocity of the storm, I made my way over to our tent to try to comfort Romayne, who, I assumed, must by then have been wild with fright. With tendons standing out on my neck, white knuckles, and eyes which must have been the size of saucers, I cannot have looked very collected or soothing, especially when I screamed at her, "NOW DEAR, THERE'S ABSOLUTELY NOTHING TO WORRY ABOUT! WE'RE SAFE ON SHORE!" At that moment the wind hit with a particularly vicious gust, forcing the tent wall down and rolling me off my hands and knees onto my side. It was not the posture of a man confidently in charge of things.

I found Romayne quite the opposite of a figure of ashen fear: She was deep in her sleeping bag on top of a pile of reindeer skins, reading a gothic novel. She slowly looked up at me with a countenance of perfect peace, and replied, "That's all right, dear." Thinking that her travels in Africa must have toughened her for crises such as these, I backed out of the tent muttering, "What a woman! What a woman!"

It was a year later that I learned the whole story. On our wedding day in January 1973, as Romayne and I were leaving for our honeymoon, her mother, who was not at all certain that Romayne hadn't just made a big mistake, pressed a small vial into her hand, saying something like, "If things get bad, dear, these will help you cope." The bottle contained a number of valium tablets, the ten-milligram series—the proverbial "blue bombers." The gift was only six months old when the storm hit us at Tuft Point, and Romayne who, I would guess, was probably beginning to think that her mother's doubts had some validity, gulped one down. And, yes, she said it did make things seem better. Certainly it gave her a Madonna-like serenity, while I was jumping around like a rat on a stove. She claims to this day that she has never breached that bottle since.

The next day the wind died somewhat. After another twenty-four hours it was heading toward fifteen knots, and we began to dig ourselves out. The tents were gnarled and mashed down drunkenly on one side, but amazingly, they had not torn. Sand had been blown everywhere and into everything. We found handfuls of it inside the outboard motor cover; it was in all the food boxes, in the rifles, and even in the compass box. It had blown so hard that it had sandblasted my glasses, and for the rest of the summer I viewed life through somewhat frosty lenses.

We eventually rolled the boat back down the bank and onto the beach which had reemerged from the water. The barrier bar was visible again, and inside her the schooner was now riding peacefully. Jim and Mark and I launched the umiak and went out to her. On her stern in handsome letters was NORTH STAR OF HERSCHEL ISLAND. It was a sturdy and seaworthy wooden boat. From her lines we judged that she had been made quite a few years before, for she had a handsome bow that is seldom seen today. She carried a pilot house aft and had the look of a small North Sea trawler.

We pulled alongside and one of the crew asked us to come

into the pilot house for coffee. He then looked down into the umiak, with the sealskin lashings and dirty, sand-covered walrus hides, and said, "I can see that you didn't buy that from Sears."

North Star was immensely strong and well cared for. As we sat sipping coffee (and shedding our halo of caribou hairs, picked up from our sleeping skins), we learned that she had been built in San Francisco in 1935 and been brought north on the deck of a fur trade vessel to Herschel Island, where she was sold to Eskimo trappers who lived on Banks Island. The new owner and captain, a Swede named Sven Johansson, who was asleep below decks, had bought her in the mid-1960s on Banks Island after she had been ashore for nearly a decade. He used her in the summers, primarily on charter to the Geological Survey of Canada, and spent winters in the Arctic mountains west of the Mackenzie, trapping and guiding.

The geologist, Jim Shearer, and I immediately began talking about the storm. I said that it must have blown harder than fifty knots. The reply: "You're right, it was more than fifty knots" (smiles on all faces). "How much more?" I asked. "We don't know" (winks and a pause). "The cups blew off our anemometer when it gusted to seventy-five knots!" Seventy-five knots is a little more than eighty-six miles per hour. When I reported this to Romayne, her comment was, "You sure know how to show a girl a good time."

Late in the day the wind dropped and the swell went down with it. We all left our storm refuge; the *North Star* to continue her surveys, and we to keep on toward Alaska. We reached Tuktoyaktuk in less than a day. The people there confirmed the strength of the storm, though incredibly all remembered an even more violent event in 1971, when it had blown nearly one hundred miles per hour, and the sea, driven by the wind, had risen eight feet, flooding the town and drowning most of its dogs. The seas swept most of the large boats, some sitting in cradles, right off the beach and across the harbor, dragging their anchors all the way. The rotting wrecks of barges and schooners on the far side of the bay made the point most effectively.

Armed now with an even greater respect for the Arctic's power, we pushed off westward in a flat clam. In retracing our path of 1972 by entering the East Channel of the Mackenzie delta and then crossing over to Reindeer Channel our luck improved; for the calm weather held, and the temperature was seventy degrees as we raced along. But the calm had one drawback in that it allowed all the various insects of the delta to come after us. Even several hundred yards from shore black flies were homing in on us like bees. In fact, the Mackenzie delta's heat and bogs are a homestead for billions and billions of flies and mosquitoes in the short summer. The river valley seems to act as a conduit to allow the heat of the continental interior to flow northward. Occasionally the temperature goes above 90 degrees in the delta, but the frozen ground thaws only a foot or so, providing thousands of square miles of soggy breeding grounds for the bugs.

After eight hours or so we were all hungry and stiff, so we pulled ashore in mirror calm and 75-degree heat on one of the bends of the Reindeer Channel. As we pushed our way through

Mosquitoes on Romayne's parka in the Mackenzie delta, 1973.

the thick willows on the bank we were immediately jumped by thousands of mosquitoes and black flies. Romayne quickly put on a headnet and the rest of us merely sprayed gobs of insect repellent all over our faces and hair, and everyone kept their parkas on in the muggy heat to keep the bugs from biting right through our shirts.

Two or three hundred mosquitoes slowly buzzed about each of us in a sort of logey halo. But it was the black flies that drove us crazy, crawling up our sleeves and inside our socks and leaving bloody welts where they bit us. Mosquitoes seem to bore into skin with a needlelike pricking sensation; black flies, as all northern travelers know, seem to attack with fangs.

About this time I had to relieve myself, so I disappeared deep into the willow thickets, followed by my personal mosquito horde, as well as the black flies, and I assume, a cloud of midges. When I fought my way back into the little clearing on the riverbank, I found that Romayne had fried a batch of bacon and eggs. They smelled delicious. She said, "I've already put some pepper on them. Do you want salt?" "No, thanks," I said, thinking to myself that she had been pretty liberal with the pepper. (Snickers all around from the rest of the crew.) It was only then that I realized that the "pepper" flakes were in fact dead mosquitoes that had been unlucky enough to fly into the pan.

No one was sorry to leave that buggy place and to break out of Reindeer Channel into Mackenzie Bay. With the temperature in the low sixties, the boat seemed to fly for seven or eight hours, eventually reaching the mud cliffs, one hundred to two hundred feet high, that march along the shore toward Herschel Island. We reached Pauline Cove at Herschel nearly twenty-four hours after leaving Tuktoyaktuk and decided to camp there for a night's rest.

The wonderful, calm weather was still holding when we woke, so I decided to shove off right away, heading toward the Alaskan border. After two or three hours of running, we noticed large pieces of ice on the horizon. These did not look like pack ice: Pack ice appears first as an irregular string of white beads on the horizon; as one draws closer, more and more "beads" appear until they become a solid line of white. These, however, were huge hummocks, the immense grounded remnants of pressure

The author plots the next leg of the course through the Mackenzie delta while Jim Jackson inspects the motor. MARK HOLLINGSWORTH

ridges that had been built during the winter when the polar pack was driving inexorably against shore by gale-force winds, causing it to fracture and pile upon itself into great sinuous heaps. Grounded pressure ridges are found in the shallow water all across the Arctic. Here, a quarter mile from shore, the moving ice first touched bottom and slowed, while the pack continued moving in, buckling and rafting up upon itself. It was now July 26, and after a couple of months of melting, the ridges were still thirty or more feet high. We wondered how tall they had been when they were formed.

Our water supply was low because we hadn't been able to fill our jugs since leaving Tuktoyaktuk. These big pressure ridges were likely to have fresh melt-water pools near their tops. One of the pleasanter aspects of sea ice is that it loses its salt during the winter and becomes almost entirely drinkable by late spring.

The salt percolates downward, leaving the upper part completely fresh, giving it a beautiful azure-blue translucence. We pulled up next to one of the ridges and threw our grappling hook out to get a hold on it. Then Jim and Mark, with ice cleats on their hip boots, ran up to the top, where they found a pool of marvelously sweet water. No one wanted to stay on that precarious ice perch for long, however, because grounded pressure ridges, when they are melting in the summer, gradually lose mass and eventually become afloat. When they do, they often roll over abruptly.

Almost as soon as we were underway again, we began to notice the white beads of ice on the horizon, and it wasn't long before we found the ragged edge of the pack ice. We followed it along, closer and closer to shore, and within an hour we had run out of open water. Fortunately we were brought to a halt at Komakuk Beach, right in front of the last DEW Line station in Canada, only twenty miles from the Alaskan border. The crew of that isolated station, starved for company, wandered down to chat with us as we pitched our tents on the beach.

A tidal current must have started to run, because soon the ice in front of our camp began to mill around and loosen somewhat, and it looked as if even a light wind might lift it off the shore. I doubted that we would have to wait very long to get going again. In fact it only took about thirty-six hours before there was enough open water to allow us to move on. In the meantime we spent the hours continuing to pick the Tuft Point sand out of our equipment.

The temperature was in the low fifties, with a flat calm and a high overcast sky when we set off again. But after an hour or so the pack ice once again began to force us closer to the shore, which was now a six-foot-high eroding mud bank. By the time we reached the international boundary the ice had forced us within three feet of the bluff. We threaded in and out of the floes at dead low speed, using long poles to help make the tight turns. Above us on the beach was Boundary Marker Number One, a four-foot, white obelisk that had been in place only since 1912, when the first survey party accurately determined the location of this imaginary line, 141 degrees west of Greenwich.

After ten or twenty miles of very close work the ice began to slack off the coast and allow us a little more freedom to choose

Romayne wearing a head net to protect her from the mosquitoes (one of which is approaching the camera upper right) during a stop on a ground ice pressure ridge a quarter of a mile offshore in the Beaufort Sea.

our path. The temperature stayed in the high thirties while we moved through intermittent fog and light rain on our way to Barter Island. We were very cold and wet when we finally reached the town, eleven hours from Komakuk Beach. Walt Audi, my bush-pilot friend, gave us another warm and hearty welcome. A large glass of scotch tasted very good that evening.

I decided that Barter Island would be a good place to leave the umiak for the winter (not a wise decision as it later turned out), and Walt offered to keep an eye on the outfit for me. Behind his house we built four pyramids of empty oil drums, turned the boat over on top of these and lashed it down, then cached our gear under it. We placed the boat heading to the northeast so that the prevailing winter wind would blow the snow clear of it.

Several days later we piled into the Barter Island airport limousine (a twenty-five-year-old Air Force surplus jeep, without doors, shock absorbers, or brakes) and rocketed down the hillside to the military airstrip, where a flight left for Fairbanks. Mark and Jim agreed that the scariest event of the summer had not been the storm at Tuft Point, but the ride in that jeep.

In April 1974 I returned to Point Hope for another six weeks' whaling, then went to Nome for a month of archaeological surveys and excavations. One day I drove to the town of Teller at Port Clarence and to my surprise saw the *North Star of Herschel Island* in a cradle on the beach there. I hadn't seen her since that awful storm in 1973, and I finally had a chance to meet her owner, Sven Johansson, who had been asleep when we first visited. He was on his way from the Canadian Arctic because his little daughter, Silva, was to begin school in the South, but the autumn passage from the Mackenzie delta to Bering Strait proved to be unusually stormy and difficult, and when they reached Port Clarence, he decided to winter there, renting a small house near his boat. Later in the spring Romayne and I traveled on *North Star* to King Island in Bering Strait and then to Nome, where we collected our crew and then left for Barter Island.

We arrived in Barter Island in July 1974. What we found was not encouraging: The sea ice was nearly solid, meaning that it would be several weeks before we would be able to leave, and we discovered that the starboard gunwhale of the umiak had been broken in two. I had placed the boat too close to one of Walt Audi's buildings, and a snow drift had built up over both of them. Then, in the spring, the snow became so heavy from melt water and rain that its weight snapped the gunwhale where it was resting on one of the oil drums.

Fortunately, I had a very capable crew that year: In addition to Romayne were Ungsi Long, an Eskimo whaler friend from Point Hope and one of Laurie Kingik's grandsons; Bill Baker from home, an avid boatman and rower; Don Robinson, a cousin who had just returned from Bangladesh and yearned for some cool weather; and Pat Hahn, Bonnie's son, a quiet, capable young man with a wonderful sense of humor who was to help me on all my subsequent open-boat journeys. They were cheerful, energetic, and self-reliant, setting to work at once to get the boat into shape. In no time we had taken the skin cover partly off, spliced in a new piece of gunwhale, and relashed the skin.

The work of getting the outfit ready for the trip went quickly—the only problem was that there was still little movement in the ice off shore, and suddenly the prospect of taking the boat all the way to Nome that summer seemed remote.

With all that time on our hands, we stretched out what jobs remained to be done and were able to contemplate the scene around us. Before us was the vast rubbly whiteness of the Arctic Ocean, and behind, twenty miles away, gray and jagged, were the Romanzof Mountains of the Brooks Range. To the east and west were the sandy barrier beaches that extend from the Canadian border to beyond Point Lay in the Chukchi Sea, and the island itself, under a lush tundra cover, was one of the few pieces of higher land on the same six-hundred-mile stretch of coast.

This island, or one near it, was named in 1826 by John Franklin (later Sir John Franklin), who was then in command of his second Arctic expedition. He and his men were the first Europeans to reach these parts, and among their important observations they noted a large group of Mackenzie Eskimos camped near Barter Island for a trade rendezvous with the Point Barrow Eskimos.

To this rendezvous the Alaskans brought copper pots and

beads, and later tobacco, all of which had originated in Siberia, and which had passed through a number of native trade fairs before reaching them. The Mackenzie Eskimos brought English manufactured goods that they had obtained from the Hudson's Bay Company trading posts on the Mackenzie River, and equally important, they brought an essential artifact, soapstone lamps, a material which was unavailable in Alaska and which probably had been quarried a thousand miles to the east, in Coronation Gulf. Although this part of the coast had never been densely inhabited, for a short time each year Barter Island was the lynch-pin in a native trade network that extended several thousand miles east to west.

After 1890 whaling vessels began to travel these shores regularly, and Barter Island ceased to be used as a trade rendezvous, for the whalemen could supply almost all the natives' needs. But twenty years later, when the whaling industry was almost dead, most of the ships stopped coming north and the Eskimos dispersed into small camps and a few villages along the coast, earning their living by trapping. They were then supplied by small native-owned boats that met trading ships at Point Barrow. This was the state of things more or less until the 1950s, when the Cold War swept across the Arctic. Then the large DEW Line station was built high on the bluff, relatively regular air service began, and eventually a school was built. The little village took its native name for the island, Kaktovik.

As we worked slowly through those long, quiet days at Barter Island, the only other activity seemed to be in the harbor. Two small, rusty tugboats (actually converted landing craft) and a couple of small barges were the core equipment of the Adams Brothers Tug and Barge Company. This modest outfit generated more than its share of noise night and day, as the three Adams brothers—raw-boned, industrious, self-reliant Texans, who were immensely likeable and very generous—whipped their craft into shape for contract work at the nascent Prudhoe Bay oil fields. Twenty-four hours a day there was the constant clang of hammers, the chug of generators and compressors, and the blue flashes of arc welders.

It was almost the beginning of August before the ice eased off enough to let us head west. We left Barter Island around midnight with clear skies and a near calm. We made good time, working through scattered ice across Camden Bay, but after thirteen hours we were brought to a halt by densely packed, milling ice floes at Konganevik Point.

Happily, we shortly met up with one of the Adams Brothers' tugs pushing a barge, and Tom Adams asked if we would like to put our boat on the barge for a few miles while they forced their way through this difficult ice. I knew that otherwise we might wait at Konganevik for a week, so I jumped at the offer.

As soon as the fog lifted a little they started up those screaming diesels and pushed ahead, bashing along steadily, shouldering large chunks of ice out of the way. Bill Baker and I sat in a large bulldozer stationed on the front of the barge, and it seemed as if we were driving right through the pack ice. At Flaxman Island we entered the lagoon behind the barrier islands and moved on in perfectly flat, icefree water.

The tug pulled up at Duchess Island, which is not much more than a low sandbar. We unloaded the boat and gear from the barge while Romayne cooked a meal on shore. Not wanting to waste the wonderful traveling conditions, as soon as we had eaten and said our thank-yous and good-byes to the Adams brothers, we were off again, racing along in the flat water behind the barrier islands.

Shortly after midnight we were off Prudhoe Bay. In 1972 there had been little to see, but now, with the advent of oil drilling, the scene was dramatically changed. In the twilight of midnight, cranes stood out from the horizon and everywhere were the orange beacons of the oil wells' gas flares. It was depressing to think that now that a road had been built from Fairbanks to Prudhoe, it would be possible to drive right to the shore of the Arctic Ocean. If a person hopped into a taxi in New York City with enough money he could now be carried to this wonderful wilderness without any of the problems or logistical difficulties that all previous travelers, including myself, had had to endure. (Only a few years later a cruise ship would traverse the same coasts.)

We reached the DEW Line station at Oliktok Point, just to the east of the Colville River delta, at about 6:30 A.M., and waited for a couple of hours—swatting mosquitoes—for the personnel to wake up and allow me to buy forty gallons of gasoline.

Then we were off again, running deep into Harrison Bay to avoid the encroaching ice.

Reaching Pitt Point, where there is another DEW Line site, about twenty-four hours after leaving the Adams brothers at Duchess Island, I was unsure about the reception we might get there; some sites wholeheartedly welcome visitors, others turn them away. In general I have found that the warmth of the reception is inversely proportional to the proximity of the stations to population centers—the closer they are, the more they are visited by people hoping to cadge free drinks. The nickname of the Pitt Point station is "Lonely"—and they were glad to see us. I was sent back to the crew with two six-packs of Budweiser and an invitation to take showers at the station.

The next day we woke to find that the wind had risen, driving in a steep chop. I had no choice but to wait, so we welcomed an invitation to the DEW Line station bar after dinner. This small cubicle was named the Pussy Cat Lounge and had been decorated by the all-male staff with dozens of *Playboy* centerfolds. As at every DEW Line base the crew (radar technicians and support personnel) lived indoors year round with virtually no interest in, or contact with, the world just outside their walls. Almost everyone at this station (and the other Alaskan stations too) wanted to quit their jobs to get work at Prudhoe, where the pay was roughly double what they were earning.

We pushed off in the afternoon and rounded Point Barrow shortly after midnight. Then we ran south a few miles to where I had permission to stay at the Naval Arctic Research Laboratory. We went ashore, pitched our tents on the gray gravel beach, and were soon asleep.

When I rose in the morning I had to face the fact that summer would shortly be over and that we still had about eight hundred shore miles to go to reach Nome—with no really suitable spot to leave the boat in between. There just wasn't enough time to complete the trip. I accepted my friend Tom Crowley's offer to carry my outfit to Nome on one of his barges and spent the next couple of days packing our gear before taking a plane south to begin my new job as a curator at the Whaling Museum in New Bedford, Massachusetts.

That should have been the end of the story of my first long umiak trip, but it wasn't—quite. The umiak reached Nome

After our return in June 1975, I had to dig the remains of the umiak out of the ice and wreckage of Nome Harbor, which had been hit by a severe storm in November 1974.

safely and was placed for temporary storage on a second-story balcony at the Crowley Maritime Company's harborside warehouse. From there it was supposed to be carried by truck down to Bonnie Hahn's camp at Cape Nome, where it would stay for the winter.

But the truckers forgot about the order, and then on November 11 and 12, 1974, Nome was hit by one of the worst storms in a century. Seventy-mile-per-hour winds drove in heavy seas, raising the sea level ten to twelve feet and flooding the low-lying areas of town. My umiak was blown right off its balcony perch, then rolled along the causeway and into the harbor. There, a number of the steel barges that were up on their winter skids had floated free and were crashing around, along with a number of houses, boats, and whatever other debris had been swept in. The umiak took a terrible pounding, but amazingly it stayed afloat until freeze-up. I think the only thing that kept it up was the thirty empty five-gallon gasoline jugs that I had packed inside and lashed to the ribs for shipment south from Point Barrow.

When I returned to Nome in April 1975, I began to look for the umiak but I had to walk across the harbor ice for an hour before I spotted the tip of the gunwhale protruding through the snow. The boat had washed up in the marsh less than fifty yards from where I originally found her in 1971.

She was solidly frozen in, and the next question was how to get her out of there. I scraped up some gravel and dumped a couple of wheelbarrow loads around the umiak because the dark stones would absorb the sun's heat and help to melt the ice quicker.

When the whaling season at Point Hope was over in June I went back to Nome and found that the melting had gone quite well. After another few days of on-and-off work with a pickax I finally got the boat out of her ice cradle. The skin covering was torn and punctured everywhere and both gunwhales were smashed and splintered, but, considering the pounding it had taken, the rest of the framework was relatively sound. I borrowed a trailer and hauled the wreck down to Cape Nome, where I stripped off the rotting walrus hide cover and began to consider my return to the Northwest Passage.

Chapter 5

The Yukon

In 1975, after I had stored my wrecked umiak at Cape Nome, I spent several weeks with biologists from the Alaska Department of Fish and Game, counting walruses in Bering Strait, driving a twenty-one foot boat between Nome, Wales, Diomede Island, and King Island in the long summer days. Then, after more excavations at Cape Nome, I used a small dinghy to carry out some archaeological surveys in the Imuruk Basin, the inland salt water lake near Port Clarence. All the while I was thinking about how best to rebuild the umiak and approach a long trip in the Northwest Passage, and I discussed virtually every aspect of the boat and outfit with my Eskimo friends.

Then, in 1976, I spent three weeks in the town of Gambell on Saint Lawrence Island. I was there primarily to buy two historical American whaleboats for the Whaling Museum in New Bedford, but just after concluding the deal, I was stormbound for nearly two weeks. I passed the days learning about the Saint Lawrence Islanders' skinboats and talking with them about their traveling techniques. At the same time I was able to buy enough walrus hides to put a new cover on my umiak.

Also stormbound on the island was a group of bird watchers from New England, who soon ran afoul of the natives. They had not brought along enough food for their stay, and because the village store had virtually empty shelves (a normal condition in remote villages in the weeks before resupply), they had been barging into houses, offering to buy, among other things, canned goods and toilet paper.

I gave them what I could spare, but was pretty low myself, having existed for the past few days on an interesting diet of walrus heart and Mars Bars. But when I asked them for a little coffee from their ample supply I was turned down flat. The next morning, a foggy one, as I sat picking my teeth on the high gravel beach, one of the birders, who was approaching six hundred species on his "life list," asked if I had seen a particularly interesting species of dovekie, hoping to add it to his total. I replied with a soft belch and some satisfaction that Herbert Appossingok and I had just shared a few for breakfast.

Later the same day I was inspecting an ancient midden when another of the birders came stomping along. I was somewhere near the nest of a long-tailed jaeger, a bird which is a particularly fierce defender of its territory, diving and screaming and occasionally defecating on intruders. The birder, a somewhat haughty Boston Brahmin female, was trying to win the hearts and minds of the people by showing an interest in their native names for all variety of things. Seeing the jaeger she asked, "Ahnd wot do yew call that buhd?" addressing a particularly scruffy teenager nearby.

"Uh, lady, we call dem *shit hawks*."

I left Saint Lawrence Island with my walrus hides and returned to Nome to arrange for the whaleboats to be collected by Tom Crowley's resupply barge. The rest of the summer was spent hiking and surveying around a number of lakes and the ancient lava beds in the interior of the Seward Peninsula.

In the autumn of 1976 I turned to the logistical and financial planning for my trip in the Northwest Passage. My friend Bill Graves, then the senior assistant editor at the National Geo-

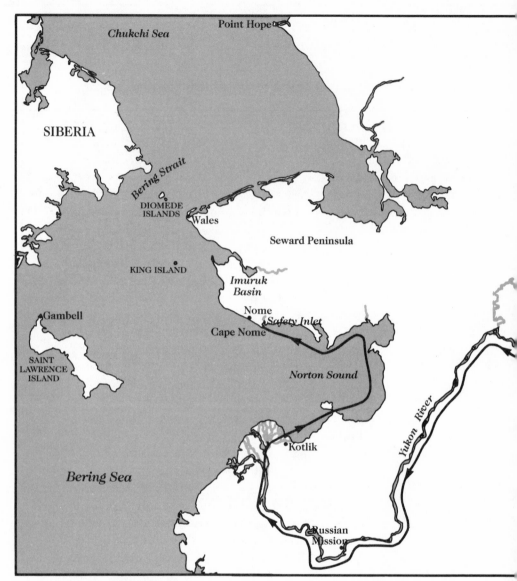

Canoe's Route, 1977

graphic Society, invited me to Washington to describe my plans to the editorial board. He and I had met a year earlier at a symposium where I had been lecturing on Eskimo whaling. At that time he was beginning to work on an article on the same subject, and asked if he might accompany me on one of my springtime trips to Point Hope. He and I took to one another immediately, and it didn't take me long to figure out that he would be a wonderful traveling companion. In early May 1976

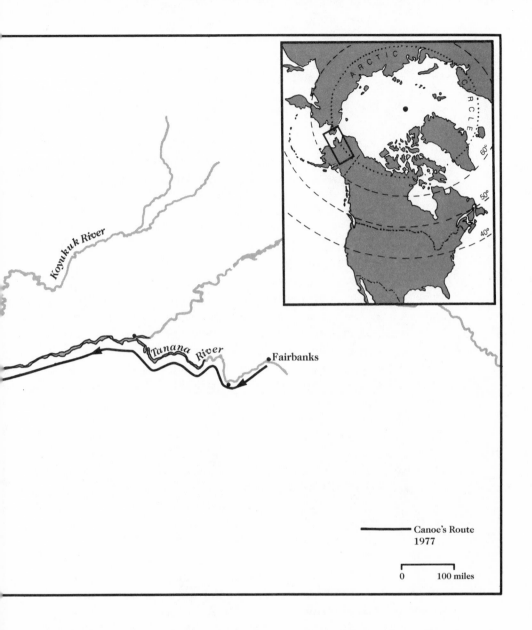

Koyukuk River

Tanana River

•Fairbanks

—— Canoe's Route
1977

0   100 miles

we spent a week with the Koonook family's whaling crew on the
ice at Point Hope, and chased whales almost constantly. Bill was
always willing to take on even the smallest, most basic camp
chores and proved himself to be a strong and resilient paddler, a
fact that greatly impressed the Eskimos. I later learned that at
least part of his adaptibility and adventurous spirit had come
early: As the fourteen-year-old stepson of Francis Sayre, the
High Commissioner in the Philippines, he had spent six months

on Corregidor in 1942 and had escaped with his family in a submarine.

During our week on the Chukchi Sea's ice, Bill and I became good friends. In preparation for his article he asked me about the history of Eskimo whaling and then about the great migration of a thousand years ago in which the whale-hunting Eskimos had spread across the Arctic from Alaska to Greenland. At some point I told him of my plan to use an Eskimo umiak to follow much of the same route in the Northwest Passage. At once Bill said he thought it would make a great story for the *National Geographic*. I explained to him that from what I had learned on the 1972–1974 trip, it would be best to leave from the Mackenzie delta and, for a resupply point, to aim for the town of Resolute in the high Arctic, at the other end of the Inner Northwest Passage— and that this trip might take anywhere from one to three summers, depending on the variables of weather and ice. I added that another season or two would be needed to reach the far end of the Passage at Davis Strait.

So, by the time I had returned to Nome in late May 1977 I was ready to push ahead in earnest. I wanted to use two boats with identical outboard motors, thereby simplifying repairs and spare parts. The long-shaft thirty-five-horsepower motor proved to be the best choice because it fit well on the high stern of the umiak and was the largest motor that could be hand started easily. It was also relatively uncomplicated mechanically and, at one hundred ten pounds, could be carried by one man in a pinch.

For a backup boat I wanted a twenty-foot, flat-stern freighter canoe. A big, stable craft with a good cargo capacity, it was widely used throughout the Canadian Arctic. It is also about the largest boat that two people could handle together, and drag up on a beach to unload. I found one for sale in Fairbanks, Alaska— but the only problem was getting it to Nome. Air freighting it to Nome would have been enormously expensive. I welcomed the only alternative: taking it down the Yukon on its own hull.

Next I had to find someone to help me take it down the river. During the summer I had spent a lot of time working with the Hahns at Cape Nome and had become almost an extra member of the family. Bonnie Hahn had done everything she could to help me with my archaeological projects—and all of her five kids had worked for me at one time or another. I immensely enjoyed living with the Hahn family, fitting in somewhere between Bonnie's strong, stable leadership on the one hand and her rambunctious, intelligent, and self-reliant passel of kids on the other.

That year Pat Hahn, Bonnie's youngest son, was about to graduate from high school in Nome. He wanted badly to go on the Northwest Passage trip and offered to help me to get the canoe to Nome. I couldn't have asked for a better traveling companion. He had been on the 1974 trip, was good with machinery, knew something about boats, and, being a northerner, cold weather did not bother him at all. It was the beginning of an important friendship for me.

I prepare to set out in the canoe in perfect conditions on the Tanana River near Fairbanks in June 1977.

We set out for Fairbanks the day after his graduation and collected the canoe the same day. We also picked up some lumber for rebuilding the umiak, some food, and two of the outboards. Our first job was to get the canoe ready for the trip. The Chestnut Canoe Company of Oromocto, New Brunswick, was well known for making fine, sturdy craft in the traditional way, from cedar and canvas. But I knew that the twin challenges of the Yukon and the Northwest Passage would indeed be hard on this boat. We put a heavy layer of fiberglass around the bow and stern, places where it would take a lot of wear in ice and groundings. We also added four oak runners along the bottom, parallel to the keel—to prevent damage to the hull on landing. Inside we installed a two-by-four-inch keelson running the length of the keel for extra strength and inserted four vertical two-by-twos between the keelson and the thwarts to prevent the bottom from flexing when pounding into rough seas. Then we put on a spray shield along the entire length of both gunwhales. This yard-wide canvas dodger was held up by lines through grommet holes in its edge; these in turn were tied to the handles of canoe paddles that were stuck upright between the cargo and the sides of the canoe. When the spray shield was up, the canoe looked a bit like a telephone booth moving through the water on its side, but it made the boat much dryer, and by cutting the wind, quite a bit warmer as well.

On May 29, 1977, Pat and I trailered the canoe to the banks of the Tanana River, just outside Fairbanks. We loaded in the lumber, our grub box, a Coleman campstove, the outboards, as well as spare parts and propellers, a tent and sleeping bags, a couple of reindeer skins for mattresses, ten five-gallon gasoline jugs and three fuel tanks, a shovel, an axe, and a handful of tools, and shoved off for Nome and the Northwest Passage.

The next day, more than two hundred miles below Fairbanks we entered the Yukon. This ancient river was wide and impressive, rolling along with an awesome, seemingly unstoppable force. It surged ahead at about seven miles per hour, and, with the twelve-to-fourteen miles per hour from our outboard, we were moving at close to twenty miles per hour past dense dark-green stands of spruce which were interspersed with the lime-green of the young leaves of birch, aspen, poplar, and

Pat Hahn stands in front of a trapper's cabin at Blackburn Landing on the Yukon River.

cottonwood—all this contrasting with the rugged outline of the snow-capped mountains to our right.

It didn't take long to settle into our traveling routine. Dividing our time in watches, one of us stood in the stern steering, while the other sat or slept in the bow. Between us was the cargo. Whenever a six-gallon tank of gasoline was empty (it took about two and a quarter hours), we would change places. When hunger overtook us we simply stopped the motor and drifted along while we rummaged through the grub box, but Pat and I soon discovered that we were perfectly happy just opening a couple of cans of sardines and drinking some coffee from the thermos, so our lunch breaks never lasted long. We went on this way till about nine or ten o'clock when the light began to get too poor to travel, and by then we were usually stiff and tired anyway, and it was never difficult to spot a good place to pitch our tent for the night.

These long days passed very quickly. The scenery was constantly changing and the topographical maps we were using made the landforms doubly interesting by showing abandoned settlements, and other features as well. There were always tanks of gasoline to mix with motor oil or small repairs to carry out while underway. The riverbanks just seemed to roll past us in a fascinating panorama.

A few more days brought us to the settlement called Russian Mission, and as soon as our bow was on shore, a group of friendly people, young and old, came down to welcome us, saying that we were the first boat down the river that year and inviting us to their houses for coffee or a meal. The town was a charming log-cabin village of about two hundred Eskimos, dominated, on a bluff above, by a tin-roofed Russian Orthodox church dotted with eastern crosses. We asked where we could pitch our tent, and one of the men pointed to the little grass airstrip right at the edge of town saying, "You can camp here. Planes hardly ever land." It was the only level and relatively clean place around, so we followed his advice, hoping that we wouldn't feel the hot breath of a prop wash.

The next morning was sunny and calm and few people seemed to be stirring in town. In the silence I walked up to the church and through the dusty glass of the window saw an Eskimo priest in full ecclesiastical vestments saying Mass accompanied by only an acolyte. I could feel the warm, embracing hand of Mother Russia reaching out from more than a century before.

This church, the first in interior Alaska, was built in 1851, but an Eskimo settlement had been on this bluff for, presumably, thousands of years. It was some of the only dry ground at the head of the Yukon-Kuskokwim delta, a vast diamond-shaped, lake-covered swamp, approximately two hundred miles on each axis, phenomenally productive in fish and wildfowl.

We were underway shortly before noon, and after another day's travel I began to feel that we were nearing the Bering Sea. The temperature was in the low forties, with a brisk westerly, giving us a tedious, sloppy run. The river was now as wide as two miles in places, and it was often impossible to keep dry by getting in close to the windward shore—because the only deep water was usually in the center.

The river finally swung to the north, and after another fifty miles we reached the "Head of Passes," the beginning of the Yukon delta. The current had been weakening for some time, and now it had become positively sluggish. It was increasingly difficult to tell where the channel was, but we pushed on care-

Services in progress in the Russian Orthodox church that gave the name to the settlement called "Russian Mission."

fully and only touched bottom once. Entering Apoon Pass, the eastern branch of the delta, we found we were back in the late spring in the Bering Sea. There were snowbanks all along the river and masses of ice blocks three feet thick, five or six feet up on the banks, the remnants of the breakup's surge. We had passed out of the spruce forests and now there were only dense thickets of alders and willows and large drift logs lining the banks. Pat and I found it depressing: The sky was a low overcast; the temperature in the high thirties; and the land was low, flat, and wet—with mud everywhere.

We reached the last town in the delta after ten hours of very cold and wet traveling. As we pulled the bow of the canoe up onto the mud of Kotlik, a village of about two hundred people, we learned that the sea ice in Norton Sound, six miles farther on, was plugging everything up and that it would be impossible to proceed. After wandering around the town for a while, searching in vain for a dry spot of ground to pitch our tent, we were fortunate to meet Jim Shulz, the local minister, who offered us the use of his "guest house," a warm and dry converted twenty-foot cargo container. To us it was luxurious.

We woke the next morning to find snow flying and the temperature in the mid-thirties. Thinking fondly of how we had pushed off from Fairbanks only one week and one thousand miles ago, we remembered we had been in our shirtsleeves, with the temperature in the seventies.

It took a couple of days to break out of the delta and skirt the shore of Norton Sound to Cape Nome, which we calculated by our route was fourteen hundred miles from Fairbanks. It had been a very useful trip, for Pat and I had learned how to use the canoe effectively, and we now had confidence in its performance. My hunch about it had proved right: It would complement the umiak perfectly; the lighter and faster freighter canoe could be used for any scouting expeditions or quick trips while the more capacious umiak could haul the bulk of the supplies and function as our cooking shelter while we were on shore.

After a day's rest I began repairing the boats. We had cracked a couple of the canoe's ribs when trying to squeeze between two pieces of ice in Norton Sound, which is a standard procedure in the more flexible and durable umiak. I had these patched up in no time and then returned to the umiak frame which had been so badly damaged in the storm of November 1974. I spent a fortnight replacing all the broken parts and reinforcing and relashing the entire structure. Finally I scraped and sanded all the accumulated dirt and oil from the timbers and then gave them two coats of linseed oil for added water repellancy.

Next the new skins had to be put on the frame. Dwight Milligrock had moved back to Diomede Island, but Frank and Ursula Ellanna, two elders of the King Island Eskimo community in Nome, offered to help me. By 1977, most of the King Island Eskimos had lived in Nome for about ten years, having moved there from their island, a tiny vertical-sided rock, forty miles south of Cape Prince of Wales, when the Bureau of Indian Affairs closed their school. Without an airstrip, or even a beach, King Island was even more remote than Diomede. The island could only be reached in the summer by umiaks, which had to be hauled out of the surf onto the great boulders at the base of the cliff. For a few thousand years the island provided a living for these people, who built their houses on stilts attached to the cliff face and harvested the abundant seals and great herds of walruses in Bering Strait. The King Islanders were as skillful boatmen as the Diomeders, and the best of the King Islanders was Frank Ellanna.

He and I took the skins to Safety Inlet for soaking, and five days later we brought them, and the umiak frame, to his house at the east end of Nome. The skins were a particularly fine set, and Frank cut them beautifully. Ursula organized the King Island women to do the sewing, and when we had the skins lashed on the frame, it was a perfect job—a fast, tight boat cover.

When I was planning the trip with Bill Graves, we decided that it would be pointless to retrace the route of my trips of 1972, 1973, and 1974. It made sense to leave from a point near our farthest eastward advance of 1972. The town of Tuktoyaktuk, at the mouth of the Mackenzie River, became our point of departure. To get my outfit to Tuktoyaktuk I arranged with the Crowley Maritime Corporation to haul it on one of their barges going to Prudhoe Bay, where the Northern Transportation Company, the principal carrier on the Mackenzie, would collect it on their backhaul from Prudhoe. I packed the canoe and gear into a twenty-foot cargo container and strapped the freshly painted umiak on top of it, then left Nome for the south, to continue my work at the Whaling Museum and library research on the history of whaling in the western Arctic.

Just before Labor Day the phone rang at my house in Massachusetts. Over the crackle of static a voice identified itself as belonging to the Crowley Maritime port manager at Prudhoe Bay. A storm had disrupted all the schedules up there, and they had been unable to transfer my outfit before the Northern Transportation Company tug left for Tuktoyaktuk. Furthermore, their boats were about to leave for Seattle. Did I want them to leave the shipment in Prudhoe for the winter?

This was bad news—Prudhoe was the worst possible place to leave the umiak because the ice opens very late there. The only choice was to have them carry the container to Seattle, more than three thousand ocean miles from Tuktoyaktuk!

I flew to Seattle in mid-October and found the outfit in good shape. Because I was now going to have to ship it overland to the Mackenzie, I bought a condemned forty-foot shipping container and repacked everything with the help of the Crowley yard crew. A trucking company hauled the container a thousand miles to Hay River, Northwest Territories, on Great Slave Lake. There my friend Lionel Montpetit, the president of Northern Transportation Company, arranged to have it stored in their yard. In the spring they would haul it on one of their barges a thousand miles down the Mackenzie to Tuktoyaktuk.

It was not an auspicious beginning to my second long umiak trip.

Chapter 6

Cold Progress
Eastward

Even before I reached Tuktoyaktuk in 1978 I knew that we were in for an icy summer. Flying down the Mackenzie valley, five hundred miles from the Arctic coast, I saw to my dismay that Great Bear Lake was still full of ice. Northerners use it to predict summer ice conditions in the eastern Beaufort Sea. When I reached Inuvik, at the head of the Mackenzie delta (and the last stop before Tuktoyaktuk) I spent a few days with my friend Mark Fraker, a marine biologist, helping with aerial counts of beluga whales in the sea north of the delta. We found the pack ice almost right onshore despite the great warmth of the Mackenzie's muddy outflow. Worse still, when I reached Tuktoyaktuk a few days later, the harbor was frozen solid, and I knew I was in for a long wait.

Tuktoyaktuk in those days was still a large native village that had grown up round a Hudson's Bay Company post. It was a jumble of run-down houses, dusty streets, scruffy dog teams, fishing racks, and hundreds of small boats and canoes pulled up on shore. But the first winds of the oil boom, which ultimately would drastically change the town, were already blowing: Several ice-strengthened offshore oil field supply vessels were clustered in the harbor near Dome Petroleum's mazelike camp.

It was not until the fourth of July that two tugs in tandem, pushing several barges, hammered their way through the ice into the harbor. The next day the umiak arrived, followed shortly by the crew. First came Romayne, who would be in charge of the food supplies; then Kenny and Pat Hahn and Bib Tevuk from Nome and Ungsi Long from Point Hope—all old friends and traveling companions. The *National Geographic* sent a skilled photographer, Jonathan Wright, a quiet, lanky Coloradan who was also an expert mountain climber and cross-country skier. It didn't take long to realize that here was a man who could think on his feet and would be good in a crisis. Lastly came Billy Cockney, a young Eskimo hunter and trapper whom I had met in Inuvik only a few days before. Mark Fraker, an old friend of his, had introduced us, and we had liked each other immediately. He had a quiet dignity about him and a manifest aura of competence. As things were to turn out, he and Pat and Jonathan and I were to be together for the next three summers, working without any friction whatsoever, even under some pretty stressful times.

We finally left Tuktoyaktuk after lunch on July 16—under slate-gray skies, with wisps of fog blowing in and out of the harbor. The weather improved as the afternoon wore on, however, and we found ourselves sliding ahead in an almost perfect calm, along the grassy dunes of the Tuktoyaktuk Peninsula. Here and there we saw collapsed remains of trappers' cabins, and Romayne and I spotted the one at Tuft Point that had given us a little shelter in the storm of 1973.

Our luck did not hold. Midnight found us slicing through a mirror calm, but only minutes later a white line appeared on the horizon. Low and even, it indicated shore-fast ice extending far to the north. Soon we reached its edge and followed it in, toward the peninsula, finally landing at a tiny island, really a sandbar, called Refuge Islet, on which was perched a forty-foot radar-reflecting tower. It marked the western limit of a twenty-five-

Kenny and Pat Hahn (right) *work on the gunwhale in preparation for voyaging from Tuktoyaktuk in July 1978.* JONATHAN WRIGHT

Billy Cockney seated in front of the overturned umiak.

mile wide, very shallow bay, called Russell Inlet. Kenny and I climbed to the top of the tower, and through our binoculars, could see that the ice extended out to sea beyond the horizon, and we judged that in these shallow waters it was probably grounded and therefore might extend very far out indeed. There seemed to be no choice but to try to work inside it, along its melting edge in Russell Inlet.

The entire Tuktoyaktuk Peninsula consists of thousands of "oriented lakes" that have formed by the thawing of the mucky, frozen ground. Once the lakes have formed they expand at right angles to the direction of the prevailing wind, partly by thawing and partly by wind-induced currents and wave erosion. On the coast the ocean has quickly cut into these silty shores, and as it has invaded the lakes, it has produced a shoreline that is at once tortuously crenellated, constantly changing, and very shallow.

It was tiring work, running along the jagged edge of the ice in water that was only one and a half to three feet deep. There was a constant repetition of running aground, hauling on our hip boots and getting out, pulling the boats or poling, and sometimes using the sausage-shaped roller floats to get them over a small shallow spot. It took us four days to go sixty miles this way, right around to the other side of the peninsula, much of which we walked in calf-deep water in our hip boots. At times the tide would drop, leaving us stranded in inches of water on two to three hundred yards of mud flats. Then one of us, usually Kenny, would walk on ahead putting up sticks to mark the slightly deeper spots. We made camp a couple of times, and in the early morning found a thin skim of ice on the water. But the weather held beautifully, giving us absolutely clear skies, so that we had to wear sunglasses against the glare even at midnight—but our feet were always cold.

Once, when we were slogging along on foot, Jonathan Wright prepared to take a photograph of our travails, causing this rhetorical outburst from Pat: "Jonathan! What's wrong with this picture? I'll tell you—sunburn *and* trenchfoot!"

We learned to distinguish depths by slight variations in the color of the water and we learned to push the umiak along, heeled over at a twenty-degree angle to raise the false keel several inches. Twisting, turning, poling, rolling, pushing,

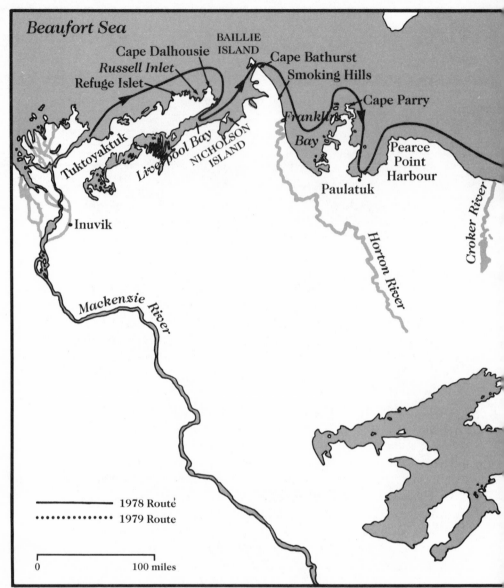

The Umiak's Route, 1978 & 1979

sometimes chopping through the ice or dragging the boats across it, we now measured our progress not in hundreds of miles, but in hundreds of yards.

At last, near Johnson Point, we broke free of the ice and worked our way across Liverpool Bay to the steep mud cliffs of Nicholson Island, camping there on a low sandspit in surprising heat, amid choking clouds of mosquitoes. As we were setting up the tents, suddenly Billy grabbed our only rifle, my old .22, and

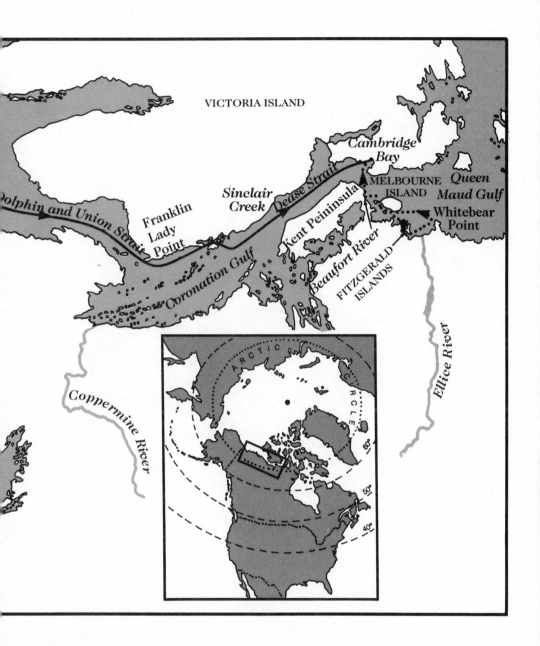

ran across the sandspit. We heard six shots, each spaced about a second apart and Billy returned with the news that he had bagged a caribou—very good shooting indeed. He quartered and boned it, then Bib and Ungsi cut the meat into strips and hung it to dry on a rack made from our oars and paddles. We woke the next day to find the mosquitoes replaced by a fog so thick that we could see only one hundred yards, so we stayed put and continued eating Romayne's delicious caribou stew.

Poling through the ice and shallows of Russell Inlet, July 1978. I pole in the stern while (left to right) *Bib Tevuk, Kenny Hahn, and Ungsi Long tend the bow.* NATIONAL GEOGRAPHIC SOCIETY, JONATHAN WRIGHT

Because the next place where we could buy fuel would be at Cape Parry, about two hundred fifty coastal miles ahead, I had put out a gasoline cache at Baillie Island, but finding the cache— or indeed even finding Baillie Island—in that cold, drenching fog proved impossible. I didn't want to run the risk of getting caught in a closing pack, so after weaving around amid the ice floes for several hours we gave up and made camp on some gentle sand dunes at Cy Peck Inlet, just as the wind came up strong from the northwest and the thermometer touched 32 degrees. Romayne had a hot meal for us fifteen minutes after landing, and we crawled into our sleeping bags at 4:00 A.M., depressed that we had only covered 175 miles in a week's traveling.

The next day was clear, making it easy to find the cache: The two drums of fuel stood out clearly against the sky on top of an eroding tundra bank.We stopped on Baillie Island only long enough to filter the one hundred gallons of gasoline into our jerry jugs. We always made it a practice to filter every drop of gasoline that we used, for in the North it is usually stored in metal drums and often contains water and rust. We simply saturated a piece of chamois skin in gasoline, then poured the contents of the drums through it in a funnel into the jugs. The skin filtered out all the water and impurities, allowing us the confidence to know that our engines would not quit at some crucial moment because of contaminated fuel.

It didn't take long to get underway again and right away we passed the little island that had marked our farthest advance in 1972, where we had spent a week pinned down in a gale. Neither Bib nor I had any desire to visit our former campsite. We were now in waters that were new to me and it was thrilling. Reaching the low bluff of Cape Bathurst, we turned south along the shore. The featureless mud bluffs gradually grew higher and higher, and after fifty miles they were steep mud cliffs, four hundred feet high.

Several hours later I began to notice a faint rotten-egg smell in the air. It puzzled me because I knew that the food in our grub box was fresh. Near midnight it grew stronger and quickly became fairly unpleasant. Soon in the twilight we saw a plume of thick white smoke billowing from the cliffside. It poured down upon the water amid the scattered ice and spread out like a heavy liquid. The smoke was acrid and sulphrous, and it sprang from seven or eight clusters of vents. As we passed through the vapors we thought we might be approaching the gates of Hades.

These were the famous Smoking Hills, one of the natural wonders of the Arctic. Only in 1826 did the first European see them. John Richardson, who was participating in John Franklin's Arctic expedition to meet Frederick William Beechey in western Alaska, passed along this coast leading an ancillary branch of the expedition. His voyage is one of the Arctic's great journeys of discovery, for he took two small boats, the *Dolphin* and the *Union*, eight hundred shore miles from the mouth of the Mackenzie to the Coppermine River—and then tramped back overland. One of the Arctic's finest naturalists, he was fascinated by the origin of these fires, which presumably have been burning for hundreds, if not thousands, of years. As we passed through that evil, sooty miasma, most of us began coughing (only the smokers in our party were immune), and we wondered what caused the fumes and how the fires had started burning.

Recently scientists have discovered that it is bituminous shale that is burning and that the shale is ignited by microscopic pyrite, which gives off an intense heat when exposed to oxygen. The smoke contains high concentrations of sulphur dioxide, as well as selenium, arsenic, antimony, and other unappealing elements. Because of these foul exudations botanists have begun studying the vegetation of the area to determine what sort of plants might grow in similarly polluted industrial environments.

At 2:00 A.M. we reached the small delta of the Horton River and paused for a rest at the foot of the mud cliffs. Nearby was a trading post built in 1905 by Fritz Wolki, a German harpooner from one of the American whaling ships. It was a small, tidy frame house, neatly covered with shingles. Unfortunately there was also a large round hole in the side, scored with deep claw marks all around the perimeter—evidence that a grizzly bear, searching for bacon grease no doubt, had had the bad manners not to use the door.

The post had been abandoned for many years, and lying around it were hundreds of old barrels, some of wood with iron hoops, some of heavy-gauge galvanized metal in the shape of

Jonathan Wright steers through the twilight of midnight at the beginning of the Smoking Hills.

wooden barrels, and some in the shape of a modern oil drum, but with two large rings around the middle for the ease of rolling—a virtual history of the changing morphology of the oil barrel. As we inspected these things a curious and frenetically energetic ermine ricochetted around them, chirping constantly and eyeing us with interest and caution.

It felt as if we had stepped back to the beginning of the century. In the twilight all around us was the litter of an earlier era—rotting leather dog harnesses, rusty fox traps and tin cans, empty cartridge cases, and pieces of dog sleds, and this scene was backed by the high cliffs which were a pale gray in the somewhat forbidding half-light.

After an hour or so we set off again, running south along the cliffs, which continued to rise—till they reached a thousand feet. I was hoping to get as far as the little harbor of Langton Bay, at the bottom of Franklin Bay, where we might pitch our tents, but at 6:30 A.M., twenty-five miles from there, we found the entire southern end of Franklin Bay still full of ice.

I didn't want to go back because we were getting low on

supplies and we had a box of food waiting for us across the bay at Cape Parry, which the DEW Line airlift had carried from Tuk for me. I should have made camp right there on shore and waited for the ice to move, but instead I decided to take the risk of standing offshore and running northeast along the ice edge, sixty miles to Cape Parry.

This was a mistake. After an hour or so the visibility began to get worse, and soon we could not see the cliffs behind us. Then it became foggy and a northwest wind sprang up, forcing a nasty swell on our beam. Nervously I navigated by dead reckoning, estimating the boat's speed and keeping a close eye on the compass, which unfortunately was getting a bit logey and unreliable. The needle moved as if set in molasses because of the weaker horizontal force as we drew nearer to the Magnetic North Pole. There the force is downward toward the center of the earth.

When the swell rose we found ourselves essentially trapped between it and the disintegrating edge of the ice. Had the ice been heavier, we could have landed on it and pulled the boats out and waited for the wind to die. But the ice had been melting for a long time, and the swells were rapidly turning it into a heaving mass of brash, through which we could not have forced the boats. We simply had to keep going, but I didn't know precisely where we were.

With growing anxiety, I marked our estimated position on the chart every fifteen minutes. After four hours, by my calculations, we should have been very close to the islands on the west side of Cape Parry. The ordeal ended when suddenly Kenny Hahn gave a whoop, and dimly in the fog was the outline of tiny Rabbit Island, less than a mile away.

Our spirits soared—but not for long, because drawing closer, we discovered that there was solid ice between the cape and its surrounding islands, and it looked as if Cape Parry was entirely surrounded by a wide fringe of shore-fast ice—ice which looked too rotten to walk on.

Very tired, we landed at Rabbit Island near noon. I called the Cape Parry DEW Line station on my portable radio, and the operator confirmed our fears that there was indeed ice all around the cape. Just as I began to think about having to camp on this barren scrap of limestone with only three days' food and little water, a voice broke in on the radio. It was Captain John Lennie of the Canadian Coast Guard icebreaker *Camsell*, who had overheard our conversation. He told me that there was indeed open water near the tip of the cape and that if we detoured far out around the islands we would find clear water.

We set off immediately and after an hour or so we spotted the icebreaker several miles ahead. I radioed that we had them in sight. Thinking that we were an ocean-going vessel, the radio operator replied that the men on the bridge could not pick us up on their radar scope. He asked, "What is your hull type?" "Walrus hide," I replied. The radio was silent for several minutes.

Rounding Police Point at the tip of the Parry Peninsula, we forced our way to the beach through a hundred yards of close-packed drift ice. We reached shore almost exactly twenty-four hours after having left Cy Peck Inlet. Captain Lennie, watching from the *Camsell*'s bridge, was impressed with our ice work and invited us to dinner on the strength of it. He sent his helicopter to ferry us over to a most welcome meal, while we, unwashed for ten days, felt quite embarrassed about our scruffy appearance. When I blurted an apology, Captain Lennie cut me off.

Oil drums of various ages lie strewn near the abandoned settlement at the Horton River delta.

"Nonsense!—Anyway we're repaying an old debt." He reminded me how, in 1972, off Wainwright, Alaska, we had given the ship a caribou when their fresh meat had run out.

Cape Parry is a foggy place. We were kept on shore for a week, while the north wind blew in ice and dank, heavy fogs. These were punctuated by strong southerlies that blew the ice out but kept us shorebound. In the meantime we explored the area, climbing over the eroding limestone cliffs and the three-hundred-foot hill, capped by the gleaming white dome of the DEW Line station. Here and there we found square depressions in the earth which were the collapsed remains of thousand-year-old Eskimo houses. But what struck me most was that these were the first rocks we had seen in more than a thousand miles of coast—the last were north of Bering Strait, near Cape Lisburne and everything between was sandy beaches or eroding mud bluffs.

As we camped on that chilly beach at Cape Parry I was amazed at the amount of food we were going through each day. Living out of doors in the cold, you have to eat mountains of food to stay warm, and we all found that fatty foods were particularly appealing because of their concentrated calories. I would guess that each one of us ate as many as six thousand calories a day during the summer when the temperature was in the thirties, and no one gained weight. Usually we would start the day with a meal of oatmeal and brown sugar and butter, as well as crackers and jam; lunch would consist of some sort of canned meat and crackers with mayonnaise; and dinner was heaping plates of rice or noodles with something like chili and whatever meat or fowl or fish was available. For snacks we added crackers and cheese, candy bars, or sardines (labeled by Kenny Hahn as "our Alaskan breath mints"). However, Jonathan Wright's taste ran to health foods, and one day, when he offered a plaintive bleat in their favor, one of the Alaskans cut him off gruffly with: "No food is worth eating unless it involves some risk."

A lot of time can be wasted on an expedition like this in a disorganized cooking effort. People want a hot meal fast when working outside, and if it is not there on time they can get grouchy very quickly. Romayne knew this and did her best to

make the cooking chores simple for us. During the winters she collected dry goods and staples for our trip and spent a lot of time drying fruits in our oven. She would seal the ingredients for a day's breakfast in a plastic bag, then do the same for the lunch and then the dinner. These three bags were put together in a larger plastic bag. For each week we had seven different basic menus; thus we never had to endure monotonous food, and this was a big factor in keeping our morale high—even in some fairly depressing times.

The umiak has been turned over and rests on its gunwhale to serve as a cook tent at the cold camp at Cape Parry. I am standing near the canoe.
NATIONAL GEOGRAPHIC SOCIETY, JONATHAN WRIGHT

When we landed on shore, after the usual flurry of unloading the boats, we would first haul the umiak up to a dry spot, then turn it over on its side (with the hull to windward) and prop it up on paddles. With its spray shield hanging down, the boat was almost a complete tent. Then, before doing anything else, we would set the Coleman stoves on boxes and arrange the kitchen so that the cook could get going on dinner. Meanwhile the rest of us set up and guyed the tents, arranged the caribou sleeping skins and distributed each person's duffle bag to the correct tent.

After that we secured the canoe and arranged the boat gear and gasoline jugs under tarps. This process took about half an hour, and by that time a hot meal was usually ready.

During the times when Romayne was not along on the expedition we usually divided ourselves into two groups: cooks and washers. Pat Hahn, being an able cook in his own right, organized a team of four cooks, each of whom would stand a three-day hitch before surrendering his duties to the next in line. When the meal was over, it was the washer's turn. I, being by far the worst cook in the group, was in charge of the washers. We also served three-day hitches, and it was our duty to make coffee after a meal, usually over a driftwood fire (to conserve our stores of pressure appliance fuel) and then to heat the wash water and clean the pots and pans and dishes. There was always a lot of grumbling when we found that one of the cooks had charred the macaroni to the bottom of the pan or had baked a fiberglasslike mixture of cream of wheat.

Our *Bishop's Ultimate* tents also made life much more pleasant. They had been designed for use in the high mountains, and as we learned in that storm at Tuft Point in 1973, they could take an incredible amount of punishment from the wind. With an integral, waterproof floor and sewn-in mosquito netting, each four-man tent weighed only fourteen pounds, including poles and a fly that completely covered the whole unit, and we could put one up in less than five minutes. I, however, decided to put only two people in each tent, thereby allowing everyone to have all his personal gear inside with him—with plenty of space to spare. The only one who demurred at this arrangement was Billy Cockney. He preferred to simply roll up in a tarp under the umiak. "I like the feel of the wind on my face" was his comment.

Paulatuk village is at the bottom of Darnley Bay. It consisted then of one hundred forty friendly people and a handful of brightly painted houses, a small church, but no post office, and one scheduled flight per week to Inuvik (which hadn't arrived for a month, however). When we reached there, nine hours from the fogs of Cape Parry, we reveled in its sunny warmth. Here Romayne had to leave us to return to her job, flying to Inuvik on

Romayne cooking under the umiak at Cape Parry. JONATHAN WRIGHT

a charter aircraft that happened to stop in Paulatuk. I was, of course, very sad to see her go, and so were the others, for she had kept everyone's spirits up in the slow progress. And, knowing that the quality of our cuisine would inevitably suffer, no one looked forward to the rotating cooking chores ahead.

The good weather was still holding when Romayne's plane took off, so we packed up and pushed on to the northeast in placid waters. We were heading for Cape Lyon at the northeast corner of Darnley Bay, but after only three hours' running we began to feel a greasy northwesterly swell coming out of Amundsen Gulf. Within twenty miles of the cape it had grown to five feet. Hobby-horsing badly in the steep seas, occasionally our propeller would come out of the water and race. The canoe was also laboring (at times in the troughs I could only see the top of Billy Cockney's hat) but the coast near Cape Lyon is a five-mile-long, forbidding wall of blue-gray slatey rock, fifty feet high, with no place to land. I decided to plug along to Pearce Point Harbour, a couple of hours ahead. Just then, however, a nasty-looking sky began to work its way up from the southwest. Soon a black line appeared on the horizon and the wind built to fifteen knots from that direction. Now, with the wind and the swells working at right angles to one another, we slogged along, pitching and rolling and taking on water.

We got into Pearce Point Harbour just in time and found it to be a gem: small and horseshoe-shaped with good protection and fresh water, and dominated in the middle by a large layer-cake block of limestone, through which there was a hole creating a natural stone bridge. There was a wild beauty about the place. It was surrounded by pinkish limestone escarpments which rose gently from the south and ended in steep cliffs at their north ends. In the low evening light the cliffs glowed red against the green backdrop of the tundra. The muted colors were a pleasant contrast to the monochromatic shores we had just traversed, and we were very happy to be secure and on shore there, while the wind roared above us.

The coast beyond Pearce Point Harbour runs southeast for more than two hundred miles of mostly even, gravel beaches backed by limestone cliffs. This coast has no harbors and is broken only by the mouths of a number of small rivers. In short, it is a vast lee shore, without shelter from the prevailing north-westerlies. For nine days, as we crawled along this exposed and dreary coast, we were repeatedly prey to the fast-traveling north-westerly gales that give Amundsen Gulf its cranky reputation in August. Our entire passage became a steady repetition of sudden gales, harrowing landings, abrupt departures, and sudden gales again.

Our landing at the mouth of the Croker River ended like so many of them. We had set off one afternoon in a flat sea, running along the featureless shore. We began to hope for a good long run, but, as usual, this was not to be. By 7:00 P.M. we were overtaken by drifting rain showers, which, though they thoroughly wet us down, had very little wind in them. Within half an hour, however, the sky began to look very black to the northwest, and soon we began to feel a heavy swell. At 8:00 the sky grew blacker and some gusts caught up to us, which should have been a warning, for within fifteen minutes the inky water was alive with whitecaps.

Kenny and I agreed that we had better get to shore fast because we could already see breakers on the beach, and we knew that we were going to have to unload the boats in a hurry—or risk having them battered to pieces in the surf. Because the umiak was sturdier than the canoe, I decided to take it in first so that we would have more hands to unload the canoe.

As we rolled down toward the beach I had the crew take down the spray shield on the starboard side only, as it would be the beach side during the unloading; the other, which would be on the weather side, we left up to protect us from the breakers. Bib Tevuk steered us in perfectly, and as soon as the boat scraped the bottom we lept over the side in a mad rush, heaving everything out onto the beach just above the water. The swells were battering the boat, and we worked furiously, driven by our adrenaline, throwing things up the beach and several times narrowly missing Jonathan Wright who was trying to get photos of the melee.

We were unloaded in about five minutes; then, with the motor still on the stern, we got it on the rollers and charged it up the slope. The swells were visibly rising when I signaled the canoe to come in. Billy brought her in beautifully, and we had it

out in half the time. We set up camp while the thirty-knot wind drove the breakers to five feet and sent in snow and sleet as well. This of course was the advantage of umiak travel: we were now safely on shore, with only a little sweat and some tense moments to show for it; whereas a larger boat might now have been in real danger of going ashore and breaking up, possibly with loss of life.

We race to unload the canoe at Croker River before the waves pound it to pieces. Left to right: *Billy Cockney, Ungsi Long, Kenny Hahn, Bib Tevuk, Pat Hahn, and I.* JONATHAN WRIGHT

It was not until August 14 that we reached Dolphin and Union Strait, the eighteen-mile-wide gut between the continental shore and Victoria Island. We felt we had now really achieved something, having reached the inner Northwest Passage waters which Europeans had first seen only in 1826 when John Richard's *Dolphin* and *Union* (boats as small as ours) had passed through here, searching for the mouth of the Coppermine River.

We were doubly glad to reach Victoria Island, for we now had the protection of its eighty-five thousand square miles against the northwesterlies that roar out of the Arctic Ocean with increasing frequency and violence as August wears on. In fact, almost as soon as we made camp at Lady Franklin Point on Victoria Island, we were hit by another thirty-knot gale from the northwest.

By that time we were so far behind schedule that we were running low on supplies again. There is a DEW Line station at Lady Franklin Point, and when the station chief, Keith English, heard of our problem, he sent us a huge load of food including fruit, cheese, pork and beans, a shoulder of beef, and fifteen dozen eggs. When I began to thank him profusely, he cut me off with, "Fuck, we'd only throw the goddam stuff away anyhow!" The attitude toward helping is different in the Arctic, where mutual support is often a matter of survival.

High winds kept us at Lady Franklin Point until August 19. We left in a thick fog and wormed our way along shore for nearly forty miles. After several more hours traveling along the monotonous coast we began to see bits of scattered ice, which grew thicker the farther we went. We had heard at Lady Franklin Point that Cambridge Bay, the town two hundred miles east of there, was still iced in, so we guessed that we were about to run out of open water. As we passed the mouth of a little river called Sinclair Creek I noticed a group of men on shore tending a fish net. Assuming they were Eskimos, I decided to stop to get information about the waters ahead. To our surprise, however, it turned out to be a group of genially tipsy Dew Line personnel on a Saturday spree from the station several miles away. They passed out gallons of beer, and, with a soppy bonhommie, told us that a few miles ahead Dease Strait was still completely blocked by ice.

We pushed on the next day but hadn't gone more than fifteen miles when, sure enough, we found the ice packed solidly from shore to shore right across Dease Strait—and to make matters worse, the pack was moving quickly toward us. Without other alternatives, we dropped back to Sinclair Creek to consider our position, and there an aircraft pilot told us that the ice was indeed packed solidly all the way to Cambridge Bay.

This was bad news. I knew that unless we got a strong wind directly from the north (an unlikely event) to open a shore lead for us, any other wind would merely keep the strait plugged up. We were all acutely aware that the nights had grown longer and colder and that there was now a skim of thin ice on the water in the mornings. There was no escaping the fact that this short summer was almost over and that we had to think about a place to cache our outfit for the winter.

Leaving the boats unattended on this exposed and lonely coast would be very awkward; on the other hand, Cambridge Bay, with its regular air service was by far the most sensible place to cache them—but the only way to get there was to hitch a ride

Billy Cockney (left) *and I, with the help of the crew, haul the umiak up on shore in a rising gale.* JONATHAN WRIGHT

on a large vessel that could force its way through the ice. I knew that the old tanker *Pinnebog* would be passing eastward soon to resupply the DEW Line sites, so I used the radio to call my friend Captain Douglas Thomas to ask if we could have a lift. He readily agreed.

We met the *Pinnebog* three miles off shore and managed to load our gear over the rail, hoisting the boats aboard with slings. Then, with the *Camsell* escorting, we pushed through about forty miles of close-packed ice and rain and fog. It was a chilling scene: The thermometer stood at 40 degrees, the skies were a uniform slate-gray, and the water was gray-black amid the dirty gray ice floes.

I watched Doug Thomas working his ship through the path that the *Camsell* was cutting. Copying the ice breaker's every turn and adding propeller revolutions or taking them off to keep the proper distance behind, we approached the entrance to Cambridge Bay, scrupulously following the range beacons into the harbor. Then, in a real tour de force, he eased his ship into the one-hundred-fifty-yard-wide West Arm of the harbor, gently putting the bow right on the beach—and holding it there in a fifteen-knot crosswind while the crew began discharging aviation gasoline for the DEW Line airport.

We camped on the beach, and the next day I walked up to the DEW Line site to ask permission to cache my outfit for the winter. While I was talking to Pat Murray, the station chief, a great bear of a man walked into the office. There suddenly didn't seem to be enough room for us all. When I was getting ready to leave the office, this big white man, Peter Semotiuk, an electronics technician for the DEW Line, offered to help us cache our gear and said that he would be glad to keep an eye on it during the winter. I quickly accepted his offer because it was easy to see that he was extremely competent—and rock solid. He and I were to become fast friends in the following years.

It took us several days to get our equipment stored, and during this time we had a chance to meet some of the Eskimos in the town of nine hundred. The summer had been so cold and icy, we heard, that many of them had been unable to reach their fish camps by boat and had worn their winter parkas all summer. While we worked, the weather became progressively more autumnal—cold, damp winds, and low, ugly clouds alternated with cool, crisp mornings. On the twenty-sixth we finished building the cover for the boats and gear and packed to fly south the next day. When we rose on the twenty-seventh, the first snow covered the hills. Thus ended our cold, thousand-mile trip of 1978.

Ice conditions in the Arctic are never the same in any two years, so I spent the winter hoping that our fortunes would improve, but in fact, the summer of 1979 was horrid. Shortly before my departure for the Arctic Bib Tevuk drowned in a boating accident at Bering Strait, and later I learned of Ungsi Long's death in an explosion at Point Hope. I reached Cambridge Bay on July 17 to find another cold and dreary season in progress. Dease Strait, which separates Victoria Island from the continental shore twenty miles to the south, was choked with ice, and Queen Maud Gulf, the island- and shoal-clogged basin east of there, was still frozen solid. The chances of reaching Resolute that year certainly didn't look good, and I realized that once again the fickle Arctic weather had got the better of us.

My crew trickled in over the next two weeks. Kenny Hahn was starting medical school that summer, so his younger brother Pat, who had now grown to be a strapping young man, took over as first mate. Billy Cockney and Jonathan Wright returned as well, and we were joined by three new men. As we painted the boats and got the gear ready, the ice melted with agonizing slowness, and it was not until August 10 that there was enough open water to allow us to get going.

At Cambridge Bay we were at the threshold of the most difficult part of the Northwest Passage: Behind us lay a thousand shore miles to the Mackenzie delta; ahead, a similar distance, was Barrow Strait, which, like Amundsen Gulf in the west, determines the eastern entrance of the inner Northwest Passage—but the difference was that ahead of us were infrequently traveled waters, occasionally poorly charted, and full of low islands, shoals and shifting currents.

We hadn't gotten far beyond the mouth of Cambridge Bay before drift ice in Dease Strait forced us to do some zigzagging to reach the continental shore at the Kent Peninsula. From there I had hoped to go east in a relatively straight line and to pass outside of the twenty-five mile, lozenge-shaped Melbourne Island, but even here the ice forced us south, between Melbourne Island and the mainland, where hundreds of shoals, rocks, and tiny, boulder-covered islets lay. Weaving in and out of these became very difficult as twilight approached, for the flat light merged them, to our eyes, into one solid black mass. To make matters worse, there were no large-scale nautical charts of the area, so we were forced to use small-scale topographical maps which omitted a number of islands.

Along this deeply indented, island-infested shore, we found the edge of the pack ice coming closer and closer to our line of travel. At the labyrinthine Fitzgerald Islands we found a massive pressure ridge twenty feet high, with impassable ice beyond. Fortunately the map showed a very narrow passage between the islands and the mainland, but finding the passage in the low light proved impossible; we missed the entrance and ended up in the darkness at a dead end in a shallow bay. The only choice was to camp for the night and push on when the light improved.

The next day we found the passage and saw that it was only about twenty yards wide, a tiny gut out of which the tide was running strongly and dropping a foot or two into a small basin a couple of miles across. Never having gone down a rapid in an umiak, I was worried that we might damage the boat, but we made it without a hitch. The low shoreline was so featureless that at first I couldn't see our way out, but eventually we spotted it and ran another small rapid into a larger basin, which we crossed in about half an hour. To get back into Queen Maud Gulf, we would have to run another gut—but here we would have to run *up* it against a five-knot current. Although we used poles to keep the umiak from swinging broadside to the flow, we grounded about halfway and had to jump out to keep the boat from being dashed on the rocks—and just then the outboard ran out of gas. After a few tense moments we were underway and into Campbell Bay, a bouldery and shallow embayment of Queen Maud Gulf.

After this day's exercise I decided to make camp at the mouth of the Ellice River about ten miles ahead. That turned out to be a fortunate choice, for when we neared the river's mouth the ice was hard on shore a few miles beyond. But to our surprise we couldn't even find the river mouth; the shoreline was so low, even, and featureless here that in the soft evening light everything simply blended together. We stopped on a small islet to get our bearings and realized that we had passed the mouth by about half a mile. Retracing our route, Pat sat dangling his legs over the bow, prodding the bottom with a harpoon shaft to test the depth until we found the meandering river channel amid the muddy shallows. We pitched our tents on a grassy slope across the river from a family of Eskimos who also had been unable to go farther east. Our little group then settled down to wait for a wind to shift the ice. It was to be a long wait.

The problem was Whitebear Point. A drumlin, covered with glacial till and marine sands, and totally devoid of vegetation, Whitebear Point juts up ten miles into Queen Maud Gulf like a giant thumb. A strong northwest wind had driven the pack ice down on it, grounding the ice many miles out to sea on its shoals. In the following days we and the Eskimos were repeatedly stopped as we tried to round the point, and each time we retreated to our river camp, hoping for a big south wind to move the ice. Instead we had nearly constant northerlies, with rain, fog, wet snow, and temperatures in the thirties and forties.

After waiting there for eleven days—and growing steadily more depressed—I finally concluded that the ice was unlikely to lift that summer (it never did, in fact) and that even if it did, it was already too late in the season for us to make any significant progress eastward. We all agreed that it would be best to return to Cambridge Bay and cache the gear for another try next summer. But even the return proved difficult.

On our way back, just as we were approaching Melbourne Island, the sea became mirror calm, and black clouds began to build ahead of us. Soon we felt a chilly wind, then a light rain, and suddenly we were hit by a strong northwesterly. Fortunately Melbourne Island and the Minto Islands gave us some protection as we pushed along in their lee, but there were big seas running out in Dease Strait, and only an idiot would have tried crossing the twenty miles to Victoria Island. So without other alternatives, we went into the rocky mouth of the Beaufort River to wait it out. We made camp on a nice sandy beach where the air was alive with the calls of loons, geese, ducks, and cranes.

It blew hard from the northwest without letting up for nine days. For much of the time the sea was a mass of wildly milling foam, all white above a dark, gray-green ocean, while billowing, majestic clouds thundered by, interspersed with patches of pale winter-blue sky and occasional snow flurries. Amid the boulders there were a few forlorn memories of summer: The daisies, buttercups, and cotton grasses were all withered, their brown, broken stems sticking up sadly through the light snow cover. Pervading all was the roar of the wind and the sound of the surf. It was a powerful and depressing scene.

Pinned down nearby was another group of Eskimos, one of whom turned out to be the grandson of the great Arctic explorer Vilhjalmur Stefansson. They had come across from Cambridge Bay for a day's caribou hunting and, not checking the weather, had foolishly arrived with very few supplies. We gave them what we could, although we were pretty low ourselves. Billy Cockney did not miss the irony of our position: We, the visitors—presumably the greenhorns—were bailing out the native hunters.

After nine days at the Beaufort River our spirits were as unrelievably gray as our surroundings and our supplies had run so low that we had very little food to spare—and the Eskimos had none at all. I knew that sooner or later the weather had to break and that we would make it back little the worse for wear—except a bit thinner perhaps. One of the hunters then asked me to radio Cambridge Bay with the news of their plight. I reached Peter Semotiuk in Cambridge and he passed the word on to the Royal Canadian Mounted Police. They in turn asked the captain of the Canadian Coast Guard tug *Nahidik*, which happened to be at the town dock, to run across Dease Strait to pick up the stranded Eskimo party. When I called the *Nahidik* on the radio I learned that her captain was my friend George Graham, and he offered to give us a ride as well, thus saving us a tiresome slog back.

Chapter 7

To Barrow Strait

It came out of the south the following summer, a warm wind carrying the promise of change. I flew to Cambridge Bay in July 1980 to find the season far advanced. While Peter Semotiuk and I painted the boats, the tundra sprang to life around us almost overnight, changing from a coarse gray into a soft green punctuated by bright clumps of wildflowers with song birds and terns nesting among them. Toward the end of the month the harbor was free of ice and the aircraft pilots reported open water east of us.

We delayed our departure until July 30 to wait for the arrival of Bill Graves, my editor at the *National Geographic*. By then Bill had been involved with the story for so long that he wanted to come along for the first leg of the trip to learn what umiak travel was all about. We arranged to have him temporarily replace Jonathan Wright, who would fly out by float plane a few days later, taking aerial shots on the way.

Full of hope we set off in the evening, and by five o'clock the next morning, we had covered one hundred ten miles. Nervously we approached our old bête noire, Whitebear Point, hoping things would be different this year, but no, we found the pack ice once again. It wasn't long before we saw that it was jammed down hard on the point, allowing absolutely no way of getting through. "Oh God, not another summer like last year," groaned Pat, who had forgone a lucrative job in construction to continue the voyage. Utterly depressed, I changed course for the mouth of the Ellice Rive to wait for better conditions. Suddenly all the frustrations of the past few years came washing over me. I remembered how, in the winters, I would sometimes toss and turn at night, realizing that I was locked in the embrace of an entirely personal challenge, a voyage which I seemingly couldn't finish, yet one which I certainly couldn't give up. And I would worry about the safety of my crew as I endlessly pondered all the things that might go wrong. At times I would wake to find myself drenched in sweat, wondering if the Arctic would ever let me through; then I would calm a bit and remember that the challenge lay before me and that there was no substitute for simply gritting it out and relentlessly making miles whenever the opportunity offered itself.

But when we reached the Ellice River, things again seemed better than in 1979. The place was warm and green and alive with birds, and a few musk-oxen and caribou.

A few days later the dull droning of a plane heralded the arrival of Jonathan Wright, who was being flown out by Willy Laserich. Arguably the finest aircraft pilot in the Arctic, Willy put the heavy, lumbering de Havilland single Otter down gently on the river, despite a moderate crosswind, and taxied to the bank in front of our tents.

There was a flurry of unloading and loading, as we replaced Jonathan's gear with Bill's. In the midst of the confusion Bill pushed through the flaps of our tent with a plastic laundry detergent jug in his hand. It was the large economy size. "I think you'll want this on the trip," he said. "Uh, Bill?" Pat replied, "we don't get a whole lot of opportunities to do our laundry up here." "Well, taste it then," was the answer. I unscrewed the cap and gingerly sniffed the neck. The jug was full of V.S.O.P. cognac.

We were all sad to see Bill Graves leave. It was frustrating to have produced so little progress for him in the last few years. "Don't worry, you guys. I know you'll make it this year," were his parting words, and amazingly enough, almost as soon as the aircraft flew out of sight, we began to feel a light wind springing up from the southeast. It was a hot, dry wind and it gained strength throughout the day and blew hard for the next forty-eight hours. Riffling our tent flaps, it rekindled our hopes with absolutely clear skies and temperatures in the seventies. We were delighted, for eventually it must set the pack ice in motion and lift it off Whitebear Point.

It was not until the evening of August 3 that we pushed off from the mouth of the Ellice River. I almost didn't dare to hope that the boats might finally get around that nasty point; for none of us wanted to repeat the emotional roller coaster of hope and disappointment.

As Whitebear Point approached it was clear that the ice had lifted a little, but still our route would have to go a long way outside it to cross the long shoal that extends off its tip. There was plenty of ice grounded on the shoal, so we kept on to seaward, trying to cross just before reaching the body of the dense pack. We could see the bottom shoaling up through the clear water, but we kept on pushing and made it across several hundred yards of boulders with only inches to spare under our keel. Then just when I thought the umiak must surely now hit the rocks, the bottom began to fall off a bit—and suddenly we were across and heading toward Perry Island. Immediately, Whitebear Point, with all its emotional baggage, seemed hundreds of miles behind us. I felt light-headed with relief.

Perry Island is a small year-round hunting and fishing camp near the mouth of the Perry River, one of the many rich streams that flow into southern Queen Maud Gulf. Before we left Cambridge Bay, Willy Laserich had flown me along the southern shore, searching for a good spot to put out a gasoline and food cache, which I knew we would need to get across the gulf. I could see that Perry Island was about the right distance from Cambridge Bay, and after Willy had made a perfect landing in the microscopic harbor, I decided to leave the cache there, at the little settlement of half a dozen plywood shacks, built amid great bare granite ledges. We then continued on along the south shore of the gulf, with Willy pointing out features and suggesting the best way to move along the coast.

I was stunned by what I saw. My topographical maps showed a profusion of tiny islands—perhaps three hundred of them in the hundred-mile stretch of coast—but in actuality there must have been five times that number. A few of the largest were as long as a mile, but the rest were much smaller, some only five or ten feet long. It was a vast flat wasteland, a field of Ice Age boulders and rubble left there by the retreating continental glacier only a few thousand years ago. In its retreat, the ice sheet had left its scrapings along this featureless plain that sloped gently to the north and eventually slipped beneath the waters of Queen Maud Gulf. Now, without the great weight of the ice sheet, the crust of the earth was slowly rebounding, raising these rocky islands out of the water a few millimeters per year.

I could see that it was going to be a nightmare working the boats through this rubble field. Willy screamed at me through the engine's roar, "Don't get caught in here. If the ice closes in, you could be trapped here all summer. Sometimes it just doesn't move." Remembering the summer of 1979, I wasn't about to argue with him.

Our boats reached Perry Island at 1:00 A.M. on August 4, only about five hours from Whitebear Point. We found the cache without difficulty and the crew got working right away filtering the gasoline while Jonathan cooked a meal of caribou meat. I busied myself on some chore or other, but my mind was still fixed on the treacherous waters ahead, which Thomas Simpson, the European discoverer of the area, had described thus:

> It would be an endless task to attempt to enumerate the bays, islands, and long, narrow, projecting points that followed. The coast . . . lost its bold character, and became low and stony. This lowness of the land increased the intricacies and perplexity of the route, rendering it necessary to ascend every elevation that presented itself to ascertain where to make for next. We had the disadvantage, too, of some bad foggy weather; but, as long as we could pick our way through

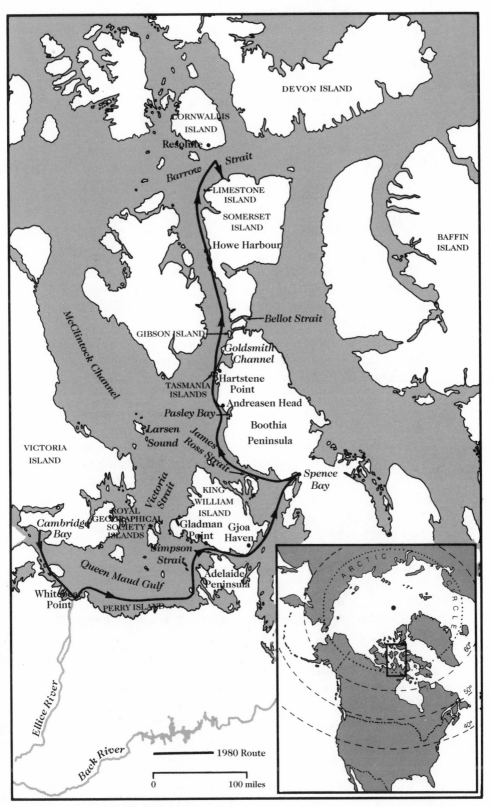

DEVON ISLAND

CORNWALLIS
ISLAND

Resolute

Barrow *Strait*

LIMESTONE
ISLAND

SOMERSET
ISLAND

Howe Harbour

**BAFFIN
ISLAND**

Bellot Strait

GIBSON ISLAND

McClintock Channel

*Goldsmith
Channel*

Hartstene
Point

TASMANIA
ISLANDS

Andreasen Head

Pasley Bay

*Larsen
Sound*

*James
Ross Strait*

**Boothia
Peninsula**

**VICTORIA
ISLAND**

*Victoria
Strait*

*Spence
Bay*

KING
WILLIAM
ISLAND

ROYAL
GEOGRAPHICAL
SOCIETY
ISLANDS

Gladman
Point

Gjoa
Haven

*Cambridge
Bay*

*Simpson
Strait*

Adelaide
Peninsula

Queen Maud Gulf

White
Point

PERRY ISLAND

Ellice River

Back River

————— 1980 Route

0   100 miles

ARCTIC CIRCLE

80°

50°

40°

The Umiak's Route, 1980

the open water among the bays and islands, we made
tolerable progress. Close without, the main body of ice
lay firm and heavy.

So confused were our people by the devious course
we were obliged to pursue as to lose all idea of the true
direction, few of them being able to indicate it within
eight points of the compass. I even overheard one
stoutly maintaining, in a cloudy day, that west was
east!

We were off from Perry Island in two hours. In the half-light
of predawn all the islands merged together into a low black mass
on the horizon, making it impossible to distinguish one from
another. As we threaded our way in and out of those red, bouldery reefs, it became so difficult to keep track of our position
that Pat and I both had to do the piloting, one directing the
helmsman, and the other keeping track of where we were. We
felt that if we should lose our position on the map, even for a
moment, it would be impossible to regain our bearings, so similar did all the islets look.

Of course, we might have gone farther offshore to avoid
those bits of rock, but the wind, which was still holding from the
south, had only pushed the ice off the coast a few miles, and the
pack still blocked us from reaching deeper water. In those shallows the job of the bowman was now particularly vital; for he had
to be constantly on the alert to warn us of the shoals, which were
everywhere. I was hoping that when the sun rose, the stronger
light would make our job easier, but it turned out to be quite the
opposite: We found ourselves heading right into a blinding sun
blazing out of a perfectly clear sky and reflecting off calm water.
Nevertheless, we were making good time, and no one was complaining about that glorious, warm weather.

After about eight hours the sun had swung well to the south
of our route, and the islands and the ice began to thin out somewhat. Soon, however, as we approached the southeastern corner
of Queen Maud Gulf, we encountered a dense stream of drift
ice—big, heavy, hummocked blueish floes, some of them thirty
feet thick.

This is famous ice. It begins its life many years before in the

Beaufort Sea. Throughout its first years sea ice gradually loses its salt content, becoming denser and harder until, after two years, it is as fresh as rain water. The floes are slowly carried along in the Beaufort Sea's great clockwise gyre and the powerful winter winds drive them against one another, creating massive pressure ridges that, through the succeeding summers, are melted down into gently rounded hummocks. It is this worn and rounded silhouette that distinguishes multiyear ice from the flatter and grayer first- and second-year ice. As the Beaufort gyre carries the ice along, some of it worms its way through the passages in the Arctic Islands and down McClintock Channel and Victoria Strait, which is essentially a cul-de-sac, blocked at the end by King William Island, the Royal Geographical Society Islands, and the shoals of Queen Maud Gulf.

In 1846, when Sir John Franklin was leading his third expedition in search of a northwest passage, he was on the threshold of linking his discoveries with previously charted coasts when he entered Victoria Strait. His ships were beset by the multiyear ice on the northwest coast of King William Island, and the ice held them there for more than two years. Eventually his scurvy-riddled crews—more than a hundred men—abandoned the ships in a futile attempt to walk overland to a Hudson's Bay Company post hundreds of miles away. As they walked along the shore they dropped off, one by one, and all died. The two ships have never been found, but judging from Eskimo accounts of the tragedy, it seems likely that one of them was crushed in Victoria Strait, while the other drifted south into the Gulf and rests there somewhere on the bottom. It was carried by the same stream of multiyear ice through which we were now moving.

As we neared the eastern end of the gulf the outline of the Adelaide Peninsula slowly came into view and we steered north toward Simpson Strait, the waterway between King William Island and the continental shore. Here we literally reached a turning point in our voyage: from Tuktoyaktuk our course had been always toward the east; now we swung to the north, toward the high Arctic and the water route to the Atlantic. Running along the coast of the Adelaide Peninsula we worked through dozens of larger islands, really drumlins, all of which were oriented toward the northwest, and finally, twenty-four hours after having left the Ellice River, we crossed Simpson Strait and pulled our boats ashore at Gladman Point on King William Island.

Sunburned and exhausted, we were exhilarated knowing that we had come through some of the most difficult waters in the entire Northwest Passage. We had been lucky with the weather—but had used our luck well, knowing all the while that with the next shift of wind the ice would come smashing back down onto the southern shore of the gulf. Pitching our tents on the bare rubble beach, the entire crew slept very well for the next twelve hours.

The little village of Gjoa Haven was slightly more than fifty miles beyond Gladman Point. As we entered the snug harbor it seemed as if all of the three hundred inhabitants turned out to meet us, surrounding us in great friendly waves of children and adults, who helped to pull our boats up the gentle beach. We were now in historic waters. Gjoa Haven was named by the great explorer Roald Amundsen, a Norwegian who completed the first water traverse of the Passage. He wintered here from 1903 to 1905 aboard his little herring sloop *Gjøa*.

The weather was still beautiful, but although I wanted to stay longer in this friendly town, I knew our stop here would have to be brief. As soon as I could, I introduced myself to the town's senior citizen, George Washington Porter. He was the son of Captain George Washington Porter, a Yankee whaleman, who, unlike most of his colleagues, actually married his Eskimo mistress and took responsibility for his offspring. After attending boarding school at Unalaska in the Aleutians, young George joined the American Expeditionary Force in the First World War. Later he returned north and eventually ran the Hudson's Bay Company store at Gjoa Haven, then the most remote outpost in the western Arctic. Still erect and fit at eighty-five years of age he sat in his comfortable house with his children, grandchildren, and great-grandchildren around him. "I have lived in Canada most of my life," he said, "but I still consider myself a Yank. Let's sing some of the songs." He chose some favorites from his years in the AEF, among them: "Over There" and "Yankee Doodle Dandy."

I desperately wanted to spend more time with this magnificent man, but not one hour of the good weather could be wasted,

The friendly people of Gjoa Haven help to haul the umiak up the beach in August 1980. JONATHAN WRIGHT

and after some rest we had to push on. The next day I walked over to say good-bye and found him sitting on his porch in the sunshine. He said to his many descendants nearby, "I want you to see a man who was brave enough to come here by skin boat all the way from Alaska." I took his hand and said I hoped I'd be seeing him again soon. There was a twinkle in his eyes as he said to me with a wink, "I doubt it, John. I'm pretty old, you know. But, no matter, I've had a good life, and I still feel good—I've got my appetite, I sleep good, and I can still pee."

On August 7 we pushed through Rae Strait enroute to the town of Spence Bay. By this time we had shaken down into an efficient routine. Pat and I and three others traveled in the umiak—this way Pat and I could discuss any navigation questions while we were moving. Jonathan usually chose the canoe as a vantage for photographing the umiak underway, and Billy, liking the freedom of the smaller boat, accompanied him. We carried hand-held radios for talking back and forth between the boats but rarely used them; for Billy, Pat, Jonathan, and I had by then covered nearly two thousand miles together and didn't

really need words to make mutual deicisions about boat move-
ments, camp sites, and other tactics—in fact hand signals were
seldom even necessary: For instance, once when a black cloud
suddenly loomed foretelling a blow, both boats, which were
nearly half a mile apart, simultaneously turned toward the same
landing spot, as if guided by remote control.

Spence lies at the end of the western Arctic shipping route;
it is the last town on the waterway that begins at "the end of
steel," the railroad terminus at Hay River on Great Slave Lake.
The water route descends the Mackenzie for a thousand miles
and traverses the Northwest Passage for another thousand before
reaching Spence. From the town it is only ten miles across the
rocky outcrops of the Isthmus of Boothia to the waters of the
eastern Arctic. For us, however, the water route to the eastern
Arctic demanded another three hundred miles of travel. But it
was clear that in one way, at least, we had already left the
western Arctic; for unlike the sandy and gravelly shores that
stretched behind us almost unbroken as far as Bering Strait, the
coast was now made up of great gray ledges of barren rock, part
of the Precambrian shield that had formed when the earth was
young, more than seven hundred fifty million years before. In
more recent geological time the great Pleistocene ice sheet
scraped the ledges free of overburden, and the town was built on
small scraps of earth between the granite outcrops.

Here I wanted to meet another Arctic elder of towering reputation. Ernie Lyall, who had founded the town about thirty
years before, was born in Labrador and had lived in the Arctic all
his life, working for the Hudson's Bay Company in a number of
outposts. In one of his postings he was stationed at Fort Ross,
located at the eastern end of Bellot Strait, a very tricky body of
water, one hundred fifty miles north of Spence Bay.

I was sitting under the umiak, talking on the radio with Peter
Semotiuk in Cambridge Bay, when an elderly gentleman, griz-
zled and wiry, appeared and quietly inspected our entire outfit,
especially the boat. When I had finished the transmission, he
opened our conversation by saying, "You're the first group of
travelers I've ever seen around here that look as if you know
what you're doing. I'm Ernie Lyall." Very flattered and very
pleased to meet this famous man, I immediately asked him

about the waters ahead, telling him that I hoped to reach the town of Resolute on Cornwallis Island. I explained to him that, once I reached Bellot Strait, I had charts that would allow me to go up either side of Somerset Island, depending on where the ice might be blocking the waters. "I'd only go up the west side of Somerset, if I were you," he replied. "There are cliffs on the east side and it is impossible to land for a hell of a long way. Anyway, Bellot Strait's currents run at more than eight knots, it can be a rugged piece of water, especially when you see it spitting out huge blocks of ice like bowling balls." Right then and there he saved me a lot of trouble, and I have always been grateful for his advice.

We were off again in a day and a half. Now we were heading into waters where only a handful of vessels had ever been and the land felt even more empty of human company than before. Going up James Ross Strait, we passed over and around the still-uncharted shoals where Roald Amundsen had nearly lost the *Gjøa*, grounding in a wild autumn storm in September 1903. We kept on along the beige limestone scree shores of the Boothia Peninsula, knowing that the pack ice would soon be lying in wait for us. It wasn't long before we spotted it: heavy multiyear ice like the stuff we had seen in Queen Maud Gulf. We twisted and turned through the floes as a thick fog descended. It was now desperately important that we stay near the shore, for our compass had ceased working—we were nearing the North Magnetic Pole, where the magnetic force was very weak, really more vertical than horizontal, and most of the time the sluggish compass needle pointed unerringly toward the outboard motor. All of us realized how easy it would be to lose our direction in that fog and inadvertently head offshore into Larsen Sound, where we could become trapped in a closing pack.

After fourteen hours' running in that cold, drenching fog, with visibility at times less than fifty yards, we wormed our way into Pasley Bay, a spacious and secure harbor. We were all shivering and tired from the tense run, and I was quite worried that the ice might be about to close in on us. Just as we began setting up camp, the wind did in fact come up strong from the northwest, forcing the pack hard on shore.

My memory of the next two weeks is a blur, for we were cold

and tired much of the time, and worried that we might get trapped in those remote and dangerous waters. We were held in Pasley Bay for four days, but on August 14, the wind swung into the northeast and began to push the pack ice offshore. We broke camp at once, but after only two hours of running, at the barren, glacial-till covered point called Andreasen Head, we ran out of open water once again.

Disgusted, we pulled the boats ashore to wait for a change in the wind. To pass the time and distract ourselves we began to build a cairn, but within four hours the wind swung into the southeast, and, accompanied by a soaking rain, started to move the ice off the land. We were underway at once, running for sixty miles up a narrow gantlet between the pack ice and the shore. Finally the fog set back in as thick as ever and we camped for a few hours at Hartstene Point, where it was mildly comforting to find a group of thousand-year-old Eskimo tent rings, evidence of other human beings. When the light improved we pushed off on a twenty-four-hour run, forcing our way through a dense patch of drift ice into clearer water at the Tasmania Islands.

What I remember most about those days is the sights and

The umiak moves at full speed through the fog and heavy ice floes of Larsen Sound. Pat Hahn is at the helm. NATIONAL GEOGRAPHIC SOCIETY, JONATHAN WRIGHT

sounds of moving through closely packed ice, of our wake sloshing against the floes and then exploding up in a dull *kerwhump* as it hit an overhanging lip of ice. Occasionally the wave would break off a ledge of overhanging, melting ice, destabilizing the whole floe, which would then roll over in a slow, seemingly agonized movement—all of this against the backdrop of the soft whiteness of the fog, the blue-white of the ice, and the light gray of the water—as floes first loomed indistinctly ahead, passed quickly, and finally vanished in the mists behind.

The land rose higher and higher on the west coast of the Boothia Peninsula, becoming bold, granite cliffs, and, to avoid more drift ice, we dodged behind Gibson Island and ran toward Bellot Strait up the steep, narrow gorge of Goldsmith Channel. As we approached the strait we were joined by schools of beluga whales, milky white against the dark water, flocks of ducks and fulmars, and we even saw a few polar bears swimming near shore. The sudden richness of the seas cheered us, for it was evidence of our approach to the fertile waters of Bellot Strait.

Shortly, we saw a white line on the horizon, and drawing nearer we could see big, bruised floes squirting out of the mouth of the Strait. Forced along the narrow channel by the eight-knot tidal current, the floes were all banged up on the edges and piled on top of one another in a confused jumble. I had only seen ice this tortured at Point Barrow, Alaska, where the full force of the Arctic Ocean's polar pack drives directly against the shore.

There was clearly plenty more ice in the strait, and remembering Ernie Lyall's warning about not going up the east side of Somerset Island, I kept on up Peel Sound, along Somerset Island's west shore. After another eighteen hours, we reached Howe Harbour, halfway to the north end of the island, just when the wind began to blow hard and cold from the northeast.

The crew wait for open water at Andreassen Head in Larsen Sound.

For a couple of chilly days the wind held us on shore, amid the harbor's dark Precambrian ledges. They were marbled with patches of snow, and it felt as if we had reentered winter. In fact, the temperature had been dropping since we left Gjoa Haven, and it now remained more or less constantly in the thirties. By then we were wearing almost all the clothes we could get on. I remember putting on two sets of long underwear, heavy wool trousers, two pairs of heavy socks, a hooded sweatshirt, insulated coveralls (the arms were cut off for ease of movement), muk-luks, a heavy parka, a wool cap, and two pairs of gloves. If it was raining I added foul-weather gear, and of course we always wore life jackets on top of everything, causing Jonathan Wright to remark, "We all look like a bunch of 'Michelin men' on a weird boating holiday."

When the wind finally died we pushed on for the final ninety-mile leg to Barrow Strait. Unfortunately, however, the calm and cold had allowed the formation of great mile-long patches of skim ice. This was only an eighth of an inch thick, and was very hard, being formed from a thin layer of fresh water, from rain or melt, floating on top of the salt.

Many years before, on Diomede Island, Dwight Milligrock had told me how this condition could be the most dangerous of all for an umiak: As the boat moves through this glassy skim ice, its edge acts like a razor blade on the walrus hide, slicing through it at the waterline in no time. At Dwight's suggestion I had always carried a large piece of old walrus hide for just such an emergency. We now drew the old hide over the bow and watched as the sharp ice systematically wore through it. We had only to raise or lower the hide an inch or so to expose an unworn bit.

At sunrise on August 20 we finally reached Barrow Strait, which separates Somerset Island from Cornwallis Island. The town of Resolute, population one hundred seventy, lay only thirty miles across the water. We were all restless and eager with anticipation. "Big city, here we come," said Pat with a grin— and then we saw the ice, a long, dense river of it flowing out of Viscount Melville Sound, through Barrow Strait, and into Lan-caster Sound. It was so closely packed that we had no choice but to turn back to the Somerset Island shore and to make camp, hoping for a change, as we had at Whitebear Point. But this

time, we had to break young ice to reach the shore, and we knew
that the summer was just about over.

We pitched camp at the northwest corner of Somerset Island
near Limestone Island. The land was appalling in its barrenness:
Not a blade of grass or even a piece of moss grew there, and, as
far as I remember, there were nothing but beige and reddish
limestone scree slopes. "It looks like we're on Mars," said Billy
Cockney, yearning for the lush willow and spruce thickets of his
home in the Mackenzie delta. Yet life was certainly sustainable
there, for at that very moment a mother polar bear and her cub
came into view high on the great sloping side of Limestone
Island.

Once we had the tents up and had cooked a meal we all
crawled into our sleeping bags. None of us realized how tired we
were, having been running on the thrill of reaching Barrow Strait
which leads to Lancaster Sound, a short two hundred miles from
Baffin Bay—but two hours later, when a helicopter landed within
ten feet of one of our tents, four of the crew never even woke in
that racket. It was not until I showed them the skids' marks in
the mud that they would believe that I had just gone up several
thousand feet to check on the ice in Barrow Strait.

What I saw up there was not cheering: The north side of the
strait was choked with ice, with no apparent way of clearing.
Several days later Pat, Billy, Jonathan, and I climbed to the top
of Limestone Island, eight hundred feet high, and from there we
could see that things had not improved—a vast band of drift ice
stretched from horizon to horizon in the strait.

As I stood at the top of the island with my three friends I
began thinking about the future of our trip. We all wanted to
complete the Northwest Passage, but it had grown increasingly
clear that this would not be possible. The umiak's walrus skins
now had three years' hard wear on them, and I remembered how
Dwight Milligrock had told me, point blank, not to use them for
four because they would lose some of their strength and resil-
iency. I knew that I could not take this chance, because the rest
of the trip to Davis Strait would be in very deep water, past long
reaches of bold cliffs and glaciers; if the skins started to give out
and leak, there might be absolutely no place to land, and we
certainly wouldn't last more than a few minutes in that cold
water.

The umiak and canoe cruise through Goldsmith Channel. JONATHAN WRIGHT

The umiak next to the Canadian Coast Guard icebreaker Pierre Radisson *in Barrow Strait.* JONATHAN WRIGHT

As we walked back down the steep slope of the island, the four of us, who had come so far together, sensed that our voyage was over, and each grew quiet, thinking sadly, I suspect, that we would probably never have a chance again to experience our unique teamwork and camaraderie.

As it happened, five Canadian icebreakers were standing by in Resolute, waiting to escort the summer's shipping into and out of the Arctic. When I called Resolute on the radio, one of the breakers, under the command of my friend Captain Patrick Toomey, offered us a lift to Resolute. I gladly accepted, and the *Pierre Radisson* crunched through the ice to rendezvous with us off Limestone Island. We hauled our boats and gear aboard with a cargo boom, and on the afternoon of August 24, 1980, we went ashore for the last time.

A day before, when I stood on the top of Limestone Island, I recalled the previous ten years and the adventures that had led me to that spot. I remembered something that George Porter, the oldest resident of Gjoa Haven, had said to me only a few weeks earlier. A man of bravery and resourcefulness, he had traveled over most of the same route that had brought me from Alaska, and he had asked why I had wanted to make such a long and difficult trip. I found, to my surprise, that I did not have a convenient answer. It had all seemed very clear ten years before, simply to traverse the Northwest Passage, but now I found that although I had a dozen reasons, I could not explain even one of them. I was simply overwhelmed by the experience of the whole thing. So, I mumbled, "I don't really know." I suspect he knew exactly why I was so tongue-tied. "It doesn't matter," he replied. "It was worth it."

He was right. It *was* worth it. I had learned a vast amount; I had had a wonderful adventure; I had gained respect for and understanding of the North; and I was now confident in my ability to travel carefully and safely in the Arctic. *But,* I had not yet traversed the Northwest Passage, and this, the greatest challenge of my life, remained before me.

Chapter 8

North Pacific

"What are you going to do now, John?" said Peter Semotiuk as we swatted mosquitoes and sweated, loading the umiak's gear into a shipping container. It was late July 1981 in Cambridge Bay, and it was a good question.

I had returned to Resolute earlier in the month to pack my equipment. It was a cheerless task, for I had no clear plans about what to do next in the North—and all that well-worn equipment now lay silent and evoked only memories of my friends who only a year before had been lugging it around and laughing and cursing. Worst of all was finding Jonathan Wright's coffee cup—for within only two months of leaving Resolute in 1980 he had been killed in an avalanche near Mount Everest in Tibet.

Resolute had also become a far different place from when I first visited it sixteen years before. It was now the logistical support hub for all the Canadian Arctic islands, servicing the frantic search for oil and gas going on in the Sverdrup Basin, as well as the lead-zinc mining both on Little Cornwallis Island and on the north end of Baffin Island. With so many people scurrying around in high-tech machinery and aircraft, shipping in those icy waters had also become relatively commonplace: The M/V *Arctic*, an ice-strengthened bulk carrier, was around frequently, hauling lead-zinc concentrate to Europe; and a couple of cargo ships, one or two tankers, and four or five ice breakers were roaming about, while above them roared Canada's ice-patrol planes, guiding them through the floes. As I hammered together a wooden pallet on which to ship my umiak south by sea—she was heading for Mystic Seaport Museum in Connecticut—there was a constant buzz of helicopters, Hercules cargo planes, light aircraft, and the roars of daily jets carrying passengers and freight from Edmonton and Montreal. Tourists were now reaching this remote spot in only a few hours. I remembered how it had once taken me nearly twenty-four in a DC-3—and we had all been rather pleased with our speedy progress.

One advantage to all this traffic was that I was able to return my canoe and gear to Tuktoyaktuk. Most of the jets going south had empty cargo bays, so it wasn't difficult or expensive to pack the outfit in an airfreight "igloo" (the canoe went by itself) and accompany it south to the plane's next stop, Cambridge Bay. There Peter Semotiuk and I put it all on a barge for the haul to Tuktoyaktuk, where I stored the stuff in my rusty, banged-up shipping container—the same one that carried my boats north from Seattle in 1977.

I could not have known it then, of course, but the changes I was witnessing as I completed those last chores of my umiak expedition would precisely foreshadow my Arctic voyages of the rest of the eighties—that wrenching change, both historically and in the present, would be the central theme in my research work as well as in my quest to complete a traverse of the Northwest Passage; in fact my travels from now on would seem simultaneously to be through time and across large distances.

As I padlocked the container's door in Tuk, Peter's question was very much on my mind. I knew that although the umiak voyages had allowed me to travel safely along huge stretches of Arctic coastline, I had been unable to cross big bodies of water—but to complete my field research on the history of the Arctic whaling industry and fur trade, I still needed to reach the islands far offshore. Of course I still wanted to complete a recognized

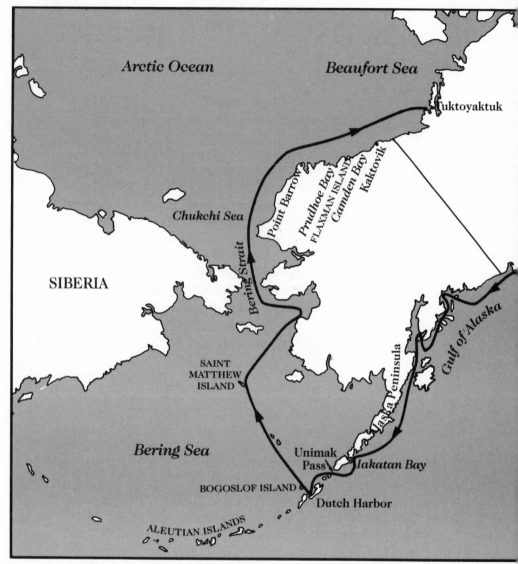

Belvedere's *Route, 1983 Voyage*

traverse of the Northwest Passage too, and I remembered something that Captain Tom Pullen had said to me. Now retired, he was a famous Canadian icebreaker captain, and is the arbiter of the history of the Northwest Passage traverses. "John," he said, "to make a recorded transit you have got to start at one end and come out at the other. You've got to go all the way in one voyage, whether you have to winter over or not. It can take any number of years, but it's got to be one discrete voyage, beginning at Bering Strait and ending at Davis Strait, or vice versa."

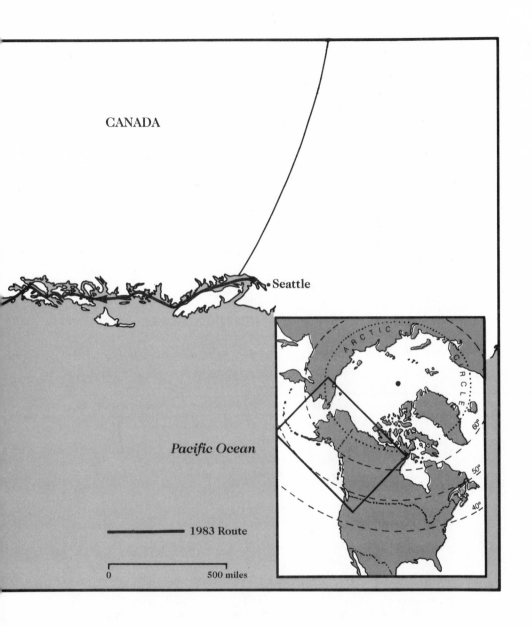

CANADA

•Seattle

Pacific Ocean

1983 Route

0   500 miles

Soon it dawned on me that what I needed was a sailboat. During
the winter I began looking for one. I knew that it would have to
be rugged and capable of long ocean passages, but beyond that
I hadn't thought very far.

The solution came in April 1982 when a marine broker sent
me a prospectus for a sixty-foot cutter-rigged motor sailer that
was berthed in San Diego. I learned that she had been both
designed and built by George Sutton, who was well known as a
skilled naval architect specializing in sea-kindly and very livable

long-range cruising boats. Better yet, she was heavily built of steel with big water and fuel tanks, and she carried a 6-71 marine diesel engine—the DC-3 of marine propulsion, steady and very reliable. She looked perfect for my needs, in fact, so perfect that I wanted to see her at once. The only problem was that I had to leave the next day for a lecture and research trip in England, so I phoned my friend Sven Johansson, who had moved to the West Coast from the Arctic, and asked him to have a look at her.

"She's a really fine craft, John," I heard over the crackle of the phone lines in London. "She's in good shape, and with a few conversions she'll make a really good Arctic boat." I flew to San Diego as soon as I could and bought her.

Beginnings are important and the first thing I did was to rename and register her as *Belvedere* of New Bedford, Massachusetts. Her namesake was one of the greatest New Bedford whaleships, a steam auxiliary bark that spent her working life in the Arctic fishery, a long-lived, sturdy, and lucky ship that was one of the first commercial vessels to enter the eastern Beaufort Sea. I hoped some of her good fortune would encompass my boat, and as far as I can tell, it has.

In June 1982 Peter Semotiuk and I and Bruce Courson, my old friend and colleague from Massachusetts, joined Sven Johansson and a few others in San Diego and set off for Puget Sound, where I had arranged to have *Belvedere* refitted for the Arctic. It was a good trip, full of head scratching and profanity as we all tried to cope with an unfamiliar boat. Peter worked on the creaky radio and radar equipment: "John, do you want to donate this crap to the Smithsonian, or should I just chuck it overboard right here?" Our only tense moment was when we were right under the Golden Gate Bridge in San Francisco and the engine went dead (dirty fuel), just as a huge Japanese container ship came roaring in. "My epitaph isn't going to read, 'Run down by a load of microwave ovens'!" said Bruce as he set the jib in a flash. Sven got the filters changed just in time, however, and the engine came back to life.

During that winter I had *Belvedere* refitted for the Arctic, adding extra ballast, heavier anchors, radars, a satellite navigator, a long-range radio, and an enclosed pilot house to protect the crew on watch. While work was underway, I often thought fondly of how simple the umiak had been—all she needed was a compass—but of course in the umiak we were always near shore and could haul the boat out at a moment's notice. Now I would be in a heavy boat, sometimes far from shore, and I had to plan for occasionally violent weather. And thinking about these things gave me an even greater respect for the skills of the nineteenth-century whalemen who sailed in the Arctic year after year without the benefits of any of our modern electronics.

Operating a boat like *Belvedere* is a complicated job: The mechanical, electrical, and hydraulic systems all require more or less constant attention. I knew that if I was to get on with the archaeological and historical research that I needed to do for my next books, then someone else would have to keep an eye on the boat for me, and fortunately my friend Sven Johansson offered to lend a hand. He had finished his own underwater geological survey work in the western Arctic and had sailed his boat *North Star* to the Pacific Northwest, but he was itching to get back up there. So, when we cast off *Belvedere* from the dock in Seattle on May 1, 1983, aboard were Romayne, our six-year-old son Johnny, Sven and I, as well as a few other friends.

Belvedere performed wonderfully. With her mainsail and jib drawing she had the feel of an ocean rover, moving effortlessly over the big, long swells of the North Pacific, and during calms or periods of headwinds the diesel engine, "our iron mainsail," as Sven put it, drove her easily ahead at a steady seven knots.

When we reached the eastern Aleutian Islands we passed the treeline, and now, with only tundra-covered shores ahead of us, it seemed as if we had returned to the Arctic and to my quest for the Northwest Passage. Anchoring *Belvedere* on a sparklingly lovely day in Iakatan Bay, between the western tip of the Alaska Peninsula and the eastern end of Unimak Island, Romayne and Johnny and I rowed across the bay to the island shore. We traversed a wide sand beach and immediately entered a dense thicket of wild flowers and grasses. The Aleutians are treeless; the brutal winter winds and summer temperatures that rarely exceed 50 degrees Fahrenheit prevent their growth. However, the marine climate also prevents the temperature from ever falling far below the freezing point, and the result is the densest green cover of vegetation I have ever seen in the North.

"I think I'm in heaven," said Romayne, an avid gardener, as she stopped to examine a wild iris. Only her head and shoulders were visible above the grass, and I couldn't see Johnny at all. All around us were purple lupines and violets, yellow buttercups, red fireweed, and tundra roses. We climbed higher up the steep hillside of Mount Dora (an extinct volcano) until, reaching the top of the spine, we looked straight south to the Pacific. Johnny crept to the edge on all fours and a hundred feet below discovered a six-foot eagles' nest alive with eaglets, while above us their parents flew nervously back and forth. Along the bay shore were the rotting remains of pilings and a few buildings from a long-abandoned prewar salmon cannery; while farther out, a

Belvedere *in Iakatan Bay in the eastern Aleutian Islands in June 1983.*

great school of herring rippled the calm surface of the water. Above wheeled hundreds of gulls, feeding on the school, and high above the gulls a dozen bald eagles glided in lazy circles.

The Aleutians are one of the few places in North America where bald eagles are common. Here, away from egg-destroying pesticides, they have huge fish resources to feed upon—as well as plenty of isolation. It was exciting to have so many eagles about. For a short time at least, we were thrilled when these birds discovered that the radio antenna crosstree at the top of *Belvedere*'s mast was a made-to-order perch. From there they could rest while simultaneously keeping a sharp lookout for any fish that were unlucky enough to swim close by. One flap of their wings and they were airborne, then it was just a short swoop before their talons flashed out and snatched a fish from the water.

Unfortunately we found that these birds were so well fed that *Belvedere*'s decks soon looked like the bottom of a gigantic bird cage. If you know what one comparatively scruffy herring gull can do to the decks of a boat, imagine the capacity of a robust young Aleutian eagle, four or five times its size. . . .

In a few days we reached Dutch Harbor, the best anchorage in the Aleutians and its fishing capital. Amid the steep, rocky hills lay a very secure harbor which was crammed with fishing vessels and processing ships. Dutch Harbor was the midpoint of our voyage of 1983. We paused there to take on supplies, to carry out a few repairs, and to change one or two of the crew. Johnny and Romayne would leave us there—for a long-standing visit to her family in England, but Bonnie Hahn, my good friend from Nome, had come aboard and would take over the cooking chores. Eyeing the stout industrial-strength diesel stove, which not only did its job, but also provided some welcome warmth as well, Bonnie let out, "The last time I saw something that sturdy was in a mining camp on the Seward Peninsula." It proved to be a good friend and a reliable one that never let us down—except at the times when a particularly stiff head wind would stuff smoke right back down the stack and fill the galley with soot.

Bogoslof Island was our next destination. After rounding Makushin volcano on Unalaska Island, we spent the night in Makushin Bay before heading northwest for Bogoslof, the youngest of the Aleutians. Bogoslof is an island with a cranky reputation. Born from a submarine volcanic eruption, it was first reported in 1768. In 1796 a second peak sprang from the sea with such ferocity that Russians of Umnak Island reported "Large flames of such brilliancy that on our island . . . night was converted into day and an earthquake occurred with thundering noises, while rocks were occasionally thrown on the island from the new crater." Eight years had to pass before the island had cooled enough to allow people to examine it.

Bogoslof continued erupting over the succeeding years, always changing shape, with one to four peaks, one hundred fifty to five hundred feet high. In 1883 only one peak was visible—

Johnny Bockstoce lies at cliff edge on Unimak Island in the eastern Aleutians.

until a second one rose in an eruption, "throwing out large masses of heated rocks and great volcanoes of smoke, steam and ashes." But it did not take long for life to establish itself there, for when the volcanologist Thomas Jagger reached the island in 1907, he found "the rocky cliffs were covered with thousands of murres, their chicks and eggs; and the birds darkened the sky in flight." He added, "The stench from offal and rotten eggs was intense. . . . The sea was full of fish, the beaches were full of sea lions, the hot lava and air were full of birds. Thus life and deadly volcanism lived together."

Belvedere crept toward Bogoslof in near-calm seas, under low clouds and fog. It was so murky, in fact, that we were using our radar for the approach. Suddenly the clouds parted a bit, and out of the fog about a mile ahead appeared the island, jet-black, with a huge sugar-loaf-shaped cone jutting up from it. We could hear the cries of thousands of gulls and murres, and as we inched closer at dead slow, I saw that the beach was covered by hundreds and hundreds of sea lions. This was catnip to me. The place looked so forbidding and eerie that I decided that I had to go ashore. We launched one of the small eight-foot aluminum dinghies, and I began to row in—but I hadn't counted on the kelp beds.

This kelp was impressive: Dense forests of brown streamers twenty to thirty feet long surround all the islands of the Aleutians, growing wherever they can get a foothold in shallow water. The great fronds in turn provide grazing and refuge for many forms of sea life, including the sea otters. As I rowed toward shore I could see a wide band of it encircling the island a few hundred yards off the beach, blocking my way to the black sand. On the beach the sea lions had clearly spotted me and were getting very nervous indeed, grunting and milling and eyeing me anxiously.

I assumed that I could row right through the kelp and keep right on to shore, so I forged ahead—and within a few yards was stopped dead. The great fronds entangled my oars and, scraping against the hull, brought it to an abrupt halt. Try as I might I just couldn't make much progress, so I decided to row back out and look for a better route to shore. But now even getting out proved difficult, and I began to worry that I might have to wait here until the crew saw my predicament and brought *Belvedere* near enough to throw me a line.

But just then the entire herd of four or five hundred sea lions panicked and raced down the beach to the water and directly toward me. This herd was a lot of animal on the run—the females are as much as six hundred pounds and the males can reach a thousand pounds—and their sheer mass, coming off the beach, scared the hell out of me.

I must not have been as badly mired in that kelp as I thought, for I spun the dinghy in its own length and flew out of there, nearly skipping the boat across the water. When I reached *Belvedere* Sven Johansson leaned over the rail chuckling: "I'll bet you never rowed that fast for Yale or Oxford!"

My ardour to land on Bogoslof had suddenly cooled appreciably, so we kept on north into the Bering Sea toward Bering Strait.

The Bering is the world's third largest sea, and is smaller only than the Mediterranean and South China seas, but it supports one of the world's richest marine ecosystems in which one hundred seventy plant species and three hundred faunal species flourish. The birds, seals, whales, and fish are near the top of a pyramid of life that begins with microscopic algae (phytoplankton), which is in turn nourished by the great ocean current that sweeps north, out of the Pacific at abyssal depths, then rises over the continental shelf carrying a wealth of nitrates, phosphates, silicates, and other nutrients. These mix with the oxygen-rich upper waters to produce a fertile broth that has been calculated to produce 274,000,000 metric tons of phytoplankton per year, and this great mass of phytoplankton allows a concentration of zooplankton (tiny marine animals that feed on phytoplankton) of as many as ten thousand individuals per cubic meter of water. From this base the food chain rises.

Three days and five hundred miles from Bogoslof, we approached Saint Matthew Island in the Northern Bering Sea. Saint Matthew lies two hundred fifty miles from both Alaska and Siberia, and lacking even a rudimentary harbor or airstrip, it is one of the most remote places in the northern hemisphere. The island is only about two hundred fifty miles south of Bering Strait, so its climate varies between the Pacific-moderated, like the Aleutians, and the Arctic-dominated, with winds that howl out of Siberia.

It had turned foggy on the approach, so we motored toward it cautiously, using our radar and keeping a close eye on the depth sounder. Soon we began to get a solid "paint" on the radar's twenty-four-mile scale—it was Cape Upright's fifteen-hundred-foot basalt face at the southeastern corner of the island. Again amid the cries of seabirds we crept toward the island, and I thought that it may have been just like this in 1764, when a Russian explorer, Ivan Sindt, found the island. Presumably the cliff-dwelling auklets and murres would have indicated the presence of land as he groped through the fog, but the bottom soundings certainly wouldn't have helped: The northern Bering Sea and entire Chukchi Sea is remarkably shallow and even. Sindt, I thought, would have broken out of the fog, just as we did, into a clear patch of air on the leeward side of the island, and the bold rock cliffs, topped by the green tundra would have been right before him. Of course I have no way of knowing whether Sindt discovered the island this way, but on the spot the scenario seemed vivid and plausible.

I grabbed a pair of binoculars and began scouring the beach a few hundred yards away. In the mid-nineteenth century, Yankee whalemen had frequently reported summering polar bears peering down at them from the cliffs, but it all looked empty this time. Sven volunteered to keep an eye on *Belvedere* while the rest of us took the dinghy to shore. Bonnie and I were the first to land, and as soon as we had crossed the narrow beach we were confronted by vast piles of driftwood that had been flushed out to sea by the Kuskokwim and Yukon rivers which debouch less than four hundred miles to the east. Some of the logs were thrown high on the side of the bluff, fifty or more feet above sea level, testimony to the appalling force of the autumn storms— and tangled amid the wood was an amazing mass of flotsam from the fishing fleets that operate in the Bering Sea: big shreds of green plastic nets, tangled skeins of cordage, bits of life rings, and everywhere net floats and buoys. There were big Day-Glo plastic floats from the American boats, and the somewhat smaller Japanese and Soviet glass floats of every size, shape, and color.

Bonnie, an inveterate beachcomber, was ecstatic and seeking treasures, immediately disappeared into the mounds of wood. Occasionally I would hear a whoop as she discovered another gem, all of which would end up decorating the walls of her house at Cape Nome. Later, as she fought her way out of the driftwood, her pockets bulging with glass floats, I reminded her about the beachcomber on Montague Island in the Gulf of Alaska who had discovered a rusty World War II sea mine, but she easily trumped my story: "Back in the early sixties I found a Russian satellite on the beach in front of my house at Cape Nome. It was spherical and heat-scorched, and we didn't know what on earth it was, but as soon as the story got out the Army came down there and confiscated it."

Then Bonnie trumped her own story. "One day at Cape Nome I saw something floating in the water right near the beach. I thought it might be a dead walrus that I could take the tusks from, but when I waded out to it, I saw it was a human corpse, facedown. I was pretty shaken up, so I drove into town right away to tell the police. I ran into the station and blurted out the story, but the cop on duty didn't even look up from his desk. He just asked, "Did he have a glass eye?"

While Bonnie went back to the dinghy to deposit her gleanings, I climbed a hundred feet up the steep bluff to the rolling tundra meadow on top. Here were not the dense growths of grasses and flowers that we had seen in the Aleutians. They were gone, replaced by a low, even, but nevertheless luxurious, tundra cover of reindeer moss and occasional grass tussocks. It was a scene of surpassing beauty—immensely silent and seemingly timeless as I walked across the soft moss while the mist swirled about me, moving gently over the green carpet. Occasionally a bird would cry, and somewhere beyond my soft perimeter I heard the grumbling cackle of a crane. Once or twice I picked up the hiss of surf far below me but all else was quiet. I surprised a molting arctic fox; dirty gray-brown in its summer coat, it scampered off toward the cliffs, no doubt to raid some murre or puffin eggs, and once, when the fog lifted a little, I caught sight of a pair of swans on a small freshwater lake.

I found myself wondering what this island would have been like in the Pleistocene, eighteen thousand years ago, when the sea level was three hundred feet lower and when this twenty-two-mile spine of rock was, in effect, a great mesa overlooking the broad and rolling tundra plain of Beringea. It would have been part of a cold subcontinent a thousand miles wide where musk-oxen and moose and wooly mammoths and lions and bison and bears roamed. Slightly more recently man wandered into this region and must have used high ground such as this to spot his game.

After the great continental glaciers melted and the seas rose, surrounding the island, it is unlikely that any human beings visited Saint Matthew until the eighteenth century, when several Russian and English explorers passed by. Except for an ill-fated polar bear hunting expedition of 1810–1811, when a party of Russians and Aleuts mostly perished from scurvy, it is unlikely that there were any overwinterings until the 1920s, when the price of Arctic fox pelts rose above fifty dollars apiece and prompted a few trappers to try their luck—but the grim winter weather, with wind speeds averaging over thirty miles per hour and temperatures hovering just above zero, must have made them feel that they had earned their money dearly.

All across those lovely meadows I saw old trampled-down

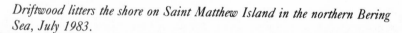

Driftwood litters the shore on Saint Matthew Island in the northern Bering Sea, July 1983.

trails leading here and there, and once in a while a bleached antler poked up through the green cover, testimony that the island had formerly been teeming with reindeer. This was not a remnant population left over from the Ice Age, but rather, during the Second World War, an Army weather station and a Coast Guard loran station were hastily established on the island—and in case their supplies might have run low, the Coast Guard introduced twenty-nine reindeer to the island as an emergency food source. Soon Saint Matthew was abandoned by the military, leaving the reindeer behind in what was for them an ecological paradise: no predators, plenty of food, and no competitors.

The herd exploded. By 1963 visiting biologists estimated that it had reached six thousand animals and reported that they had overgrazed the range to an alarming extent—the precursor for disaster. The following winter was extremely severe, with record snowfalls, and the reindeer starved by the thousands. In 1966 scientists again reached the island and they could find only forty-two animals—although the ground was littered with piles of bleaching bones, among which were clumps of stomach remains containing mostly woody crowberry stems, nutritionless plant material that the starving reindeer had been forced to resort to before they died. In 1982 only one lame old female was seen, and in 1983, when *Belvedere* reached the island, we did not see her during our short visit.

A few weeks later we joined my old umiak route of 1972 and soon were at Barrow. As we glided along shore amid the lightly scattered ice floes, it was clear from the skyline and noise that the place had changed dramatically since my last visit. Working through the ice and rounding Point Barrow, *Belvedere* entered Elson Lagoon. We could see the heavy pack ice only half a mile to the north of the point, and with a rising westerly, it was clear that we were going to be bottled up for a few days until the wind changed. I thought how easy it had been to pull the umiak up on the beach and simply camp under it: Now we had to man anchor watches in case a rising wind might cause our ground tackle to drag.

This enforced idleness did not bother me at all. I wanted to take the time to visit with my old friend Tom Brower. Tom's father was Charles Brower, who, in 1884, was the first white man to settle permanently in northern Alaska. He became a mainstay of the local whaling industry and fur trade by founding the Cape Smythe Whaling and Trading Company near the site of the present town of Barrow. We were anchored about eleven miles north of the town, so I decided to take one of the dinghies through the lagoon to Pirginik, the duck hunting camp at the head of the lagoon, and then to walk the five or six miles into town. I hoped that if I was lucky I could hitch a ride from there on the back of a motorized three-wheeler, as I had in the seventies. It turned out to be a lot easier than that.

As I hauled the dinghy up on shore a city bus pulled up to the encampment a couple of hundred yards away. "You'd better hurry," someone shouted, "it only comes here every hour." Dressed in mukluks and an old hunting parka I hopped the bus. As I rode in I saw a couple of multistory buildings and masses of expensive single-family houses with pickup trucks and trailered aluminum boats parked outside. The old scruffy town I remembered had been transformed. Gone were most of the rundown houses and general hodgepodge. In its place were an ultramodern high school, a large supermarket, a hospital, a fire station, several restaurants, and a huge atriumlike building housing the offices of the North Slope Borough, a county-type government whose jurisdiction stretched six hundred miles from Point Hope to the Canadian border.

"Yup, our ship really came in when they struck oil at Prudhoe," said a paunchy and blow-dried native civil servant as he flicked a speck of dirt off his fake-alligator cowboy boots. He was right in a way. The North Slope Borough, having incorporated Prudhoe in its boundaries, was able to tax the real property there, and these funds, plus the state's wellhead oil revenues and inflated wages, had created a boom in the area and allowed the borough to assume the highest per capita municipal indebtedness in the nation. The income from the bond issues had fueled the construction I saw.

Now in his seventies, Tom Brower was in the paradoxical position of being at once a venerated elder of the community (hence a guardian of the area's traditional lifeways) and the president of Cape Smythe Aviation, which owned, among other aircraft, an executive jet—and the antinomy was not lost on him. "John, it used to be that a man here was proud to be a good hunter and to own a good team of dogs and a big umiak. Some of the guys around here now wouldn't even know how to use either one. Their big thrill in life is a set of car keys and a briefcase."

I returned to *Belvedere* with Craig George, an old friend and fellow student of shore whaling, who is a wildlife biologist for the North Slope Borough. A dedicated naturalist, Craig wanted to cruise along the north coast of Alaska to search for bowhead whales that might be returning early from their summer feeding grounds in the eastern Beaufort Sea, and I immediately offered him a lift because he was, and is, a boon companion and a skilled boatman.

We set off the next day and almost at once found loose, drifting pack ice as we worked our way eastward. I pulled on my parka and climbed to the spreaders with a hand radio to talk to Sven, who was on the helm as we picked our way through it. One thing I definitely did not want to do was to take an ill-advised turn and run off down a lead—only to find that it was a cul-de-sac. The old whalemen knew that the waters off the north coast of Alaska can be dangerous; for offshore leads usually close up, and when they do, any ship caught in the ice is carried away in the great clockwise gyre that slowly grinds round the Beaufort Sea.

Standing at the spreaders I remembered how, ten years before, I had met one of the last of the old Arctic whalemen who, as a sixteen-year-old, had been the engineer of the schooner *Polar Bear*, going after bowheads in these waters. Ben Kilian was eighty years old then, but his mind was sharp and his eyes flashed as he told me how his captain, Louis Lane, had avoided being caught in the pack in 1913. Others were not so skilled. That same summer, 1913, the old whaleship *Karluk* was carrying the main party of the Canadian Arctic Expedition eastward in the Beaufort, when her captain, unused to the ways of the western Arctic, took the chance of making progress by running down one of these offshore leads. The *Karluk* was caught in the pack and swept away to the western Chukchi Sea, where the ship was crushed, far from shore, and many of the crew and passengers perished on the ice floes.

Louis Lane had been tempted to follow the *Karluk* offshore, and for a while he did head down one of these leads, but when he found it a dead end—and planned to wait there in the assumption that it would open further—an ancient retired whaleman, Captain William Mogg, who happened to be taking passage aboard the *Polar Bear*, stepped forward and advised returning to shore and staying as close to it as possible. Ben Kilian recalled his words: "Captain, don't tie up here. I always like to sleep with the mud on one side of me." Lane turned the *Polar Bear* back to shore and safety.

This is the sort of advice that isn't found in the modern sailing directions, and I have always been grateful for Ben Kilian taking the time to pass on his wisdom.

Eventually a dense fog blew in toward *Belvedere* from the main body of the pack, and our only choice was to work along close to shore, using our radar to guide us. With no visibility I was now useless at the spreaders, so I went below for some much-needed sleep.

Sometime later the crunching hiss of ice grinding along the hull snapped me awake, and just then Craig George's face appeared in the cabin door.

"John, I think you'd better come topside. There's something really odd out there."

"What is it? Pack ice?" I asked anxiously, assuming we were getting into a tricky spot.

"No," Craig replied in a slightly confused voice. "It's something weird on the radar scope—something really big, and it's dead ahead."

I was out of my berth in a flash, groggily pulling on my clothes as I raced up the ladder into the pilot house. I saw Sven hunched over the radar, his face washed in the sickly green light emanating from the scope.

"John, whatever it is, it's really big," he said.

"A huge piece of drift ice?"

"I don't think so. The water's too shallow here. A piece of ice that big would have grounded farther off shore in deep water, and so would a ship of any size."

I thought back to 1972 and 1974, when I had passed right over this spot in my umiak, and I couldn't remember anything being here then, so I went over to the navigation table to have a look at the chart. It showed only empty water. Very puzzled, I stuck my face in the scope. Whatever it was, it was huge and now only a mile away—and squarely in our path. It seemed the size of an aircraft carrier.

Pulling on our parkas Craig and I made our way along the deck to the bow to peer through the gray murk, while Sven throttled the engine way back. In the Arctic silence we could hear the light ripple of water on the ice floes, the occasional cry of a gull—and somewhere to the north of us the great whooshing blast of a bowhead whale lazily blowing.

Then I heard something else—a faint clank-clank-clank of machinery—and suddenly Craig let out a cry: "What's that?" he said, pointing above the fog bank. I whirled and saw the top of an oil drilling rig projecting above the mist. "A drill ship?" I thought out loud. "Can't be. The water's too shallow here."

Then the fog wisps parted and we could see that it was not a ship at all, but an artificial island, built for oil drilling—and it must have been built recently, for it was not on our up-to-date chart. As *Belvedere* edged closer through the floes, the chug of generators and the banging of machinery grew louder. We saw it was a large circular island built of gravel dredged from the sea floor and rimmed round with thousands of black plastic "berm bags" filled with sand to keep the island from washing away in the summer storms. Atop all was a huge accumulation of modular buildings, tanks, drill pipe, odd machinery and, of course, the oil rig itself. It was all bathed in an eerie yellow light shed from the sodium vapor lamps and punctuated here and there by the searing blue flashes of arc welders.

I thought how odd it was to be here in a sailing vessel, in waters where few ships had ever been; here, in the Northwest Passage, we were on a mission to study the first search for oil (whale oil) in the western Arctic and we had nearly collided with the second (petroleum oil).

We pushed on and found the edge of the pack ice encroaching closer and closer to shore—and when we reached the Midway Islands (so named by the whalemen because they were halfway between Point Barrow and their outpost at Herschel Island), we went into the lagoon behind them. With the barrier islands holding the pack ice off, we proceeded east in nearly ice-free water.

Finally, at 4:00 A.M. on August 13, everyone needed some rest, so we dropped the anchor behind Belvedere Island. This island had been named by Ernest deKoven Leffingwell who had almost singlehandedly mapped the northern coast of Alaska in the early years of the century. Working mostly alone—and without subsidy—he spent eleven years patiently setting up triangulation marks throughout the coast and interior. He had come north in 1906 on an expedition to discover new land in the Arctic Ocean north of Alaska. He and his partner sailed the little schooner *Duchess of Bedford* up from the West Coast and allowed her to freeze in behind Flaxman Island—where the ice promptly pulled the caulking from her unsheathed seams and she settled to the deck line. Unfazed, Leffingwell switched his focus to surveying, moved ashore, and tore off the *Duchess*'s superstructure to build himself a little house on the island. From there he carried out his surveys year round, by dog team in the winter and by umiak and pack dog in the summer.

The sand barrier islands on the north coast of Alaska proved to be so numerous that Leffingwell needed a lot of new names to differentiate them. In some cases he simply used the names of the whaling captains who had helped him through the years (Cottle, Bodfish, Leavitt, and Bertoncini) and in others he used their ships' names (*Belvedere, Narwhal,* and *Karluk*).

I wanted to visit Leffingwell's cabin on Flaxman Island, so the next day, in a dense fog, we raised anchor and motored over there. After several hours we reached the bight behind the island, and although the fog remained extremely thick, Craig and I donned parkas and hip boots and took the dinghy in to shore.

Immediately *Belvedere* vanished behind us in the swirling mist, but we soon reached the bouldery beach that was backed by an eroding tundra bank. The entire coastline of northern Alaska and western Arctic Canada is gradually washing away in the summer storms. The waves melt the permafrost that holds the silt, and even boulders, in suspension—in some places the erosion is more than thirty feet per year, thereby making the

Belvedere *is hauled out at Tuktoyaktuk, August 1983.*

charts of this coast more of an approximation than a reality. It was difficult making our way from the dinghy, for the soft muck sucked at our boots, forcing us to hold onto the tops as we staggered along. But once we had clambered to the top of the bank, walking over the tundra was easy, and soon the outline of Leffingwell's cabin appeared in the mist ahead.

Its plank sides and driftwood uprights were windburned and weatherbeaten to a silver-gray, and the rectangular pieces of tundra sod that had been placed on the roof for insulation were sprouting their own green growth. Inside, the soft foggy light spilled through the empty skylights and gently illuminated the tongue-and-groove woodwork and brass fittings that were obviously the remains of the *Duchess of Bedford*.

Standing in his simple cabin, it was easy to feel that Leffingwell was certainly a man with a mission. From 1906 to 1914 he spent nine summers and six winters working out of this tiny building, making thirty-one major trips by sled and boat and covering forty-five hundred miles. He later wrote: "In addition to the astronomical observations . . . I triangulated about 150 miles of the coast and mapped the details on a scale of 1/250,000, and entered the positions of about 1500 soundings. I made a sketch map of the entire coastline between Point Barrow and the Canadian boundary . . . mapped the main geographic features of an area of about 50 by 80 miles of the mainland [,] drew the known and probable distribution of 15 geological deposits. . . ." He added, "My report of petroleum seepages near Point Barrow attracted more attention than all the rest of my work."

Through the fog Craig and I could hear another oil rig clanking away, this one right on Flaxman Island itself.

Less than a week later we were at Tuktoyaktuk, where, with the help of the Northern Transportation Company Limited (NTCL) shore crew, we built a skid for *Belvedere* and pulled her out of the water with bulldozers. Thus ended the four-thousand-mile season of 1983. We had completed the first leg of my return to the Northwest Passage, and had seen some dramatic changes. It was clear to me that my Arctic voyages aboard *Belvedere* were going to be very different from my travels in the umiak—and this would have nothing to do with my choice of boats.

Chapter 9

Change in the Eastern Beaufort

The change in Tuktoyaktuk was astonishing. In August 1983, as we were crossing the Mackenzie delta, it was not the houses there that we saw first, but rather, three or four large cranes, projecting above the horizon. When I few in from Inuvik in 1984, the oil companies' camps were the most obvious feature from miles away. The noise washed over me as soon as I opened the aircraft's door—the roar of earth-moving equipment, the *beep-beep-beep* of reversing alarms, and the juddering of helicopters.

The place was milling with activity because of the frantic search for oil in the eastern Beaufort. This in turn was based on the Trudeau government's quixotic program that mandated "energy independence for Canada" and paid eighty cents out of every dollar expended by Canadian-owned oil companies exploring in frontier areas. By the time the Mulroney administration canceled the program, the government had paid out five billion dollars, which amounted to the largest single tax-payer handout to Canadian industry.

At Tuk this had resulted in a mass of new projects. Dome Petroleum's old, bolted-together modular camp maze was now dwarfed by a new fifty-acre storage yard bristling with stacks of drill-pipe and well casings, cement mixers, and machine shops—and by its new two-story camp building which was capable of housing 344 people, complete with a gymnasium, racketball court, sauna, Jacuzzi, sick bay, laundry, mud room, and a huge dining hall serving four meals a day.

Nearby Gulf Canada had put up an equally impressive structure, and, as if to trump Dome's card, had included a swimming pool as well. To support all the oil activity, the Northern Transportation Company had built a new camp for its expanded shipping work, which entailed hauling freight down the Mackenzie and out to the offshore drill sites; a new company, Arctic Transportation Limited (ATL), had also built a camp to service its offshore supply fleet; and Imperial Oil's facility had grown as well.

The harbor was full of ships. From the air I saw three or four tugs and more than a dozen barges, a dredge ship, a couple of floating dry docks, two oil exploration vessels, five or six ice-strengthened offshore supply ships, two high-speed crew boats, and several others—all this where, until the early seventies, there had been only a sleepy town that had grown up round the Hudson's Bay Company post.

As it happened, my friend Billy Cockney, who had been with me on the umiak voyage from 1978 to 1980, was aboard the same flight into Tuk. He was returning from several months' work in Alberta, and after we landed on the newly lengthened airstrip (which now had one 737 flight a day from Calgary), we decided to walk to his parents' house to borrow a pickup truck for our bags.

We started along the edge of the dirt road into town, but we hadn't gotten very far before we had to jump for the ditch as a Kenwood eighteen-wheeler crashed past us, showering us with dust and flying gravel. As we climbed back up on the road, I saw Billy first glance at the little hamlet of seven or eight hundred people on the tip of the sandspit, then turn his head to gaze at the airstrip, beyond which we could see the oil camps. At that moment a Sikorsky Sea King twenty-two passenger helicopter rose in a violent chatter and headed out over the water toward one of the drill sites.

"Jesus," he said, "I've only been gone for three months, but half this shit wasn't here when I left."

The winter of 1983–1984 had been a cold one in the Canadian Arctic, causing the government's ice-forecasting bureau to predict a later than usual breakup in the Northwest Passage, with lots of heavy ice all summer. It was unlikely that *Belvedere* would make it through the Passage that summer, a fact which didn't bother me a lot. I still had plenty of field research (site surveys and personal interviews) left to do to complete the work for my book on the history of whaling in the western Arctic—and I also wanted to get started on collecting information for its sequel, a book on the history of the maritime fur trade in the same area. Furthermore, it seemed as if I could tackle both of these tasks at once, for in the early years of this century, while the whaling industry was declining, the price of furs was rising, and many of the people made an effortless transition from one livelihood to the other. Not only were a few of them still alive, scattered among the villages of the western Arctic, but their children were also a great source of information on their activities—and *Belvedere* was perfectly suited to take me to all those remote settlements. For the next few years as I researched this cultural transition in the Passage's past, I continually ran up against the wrenching change underway in the present.

So, in July 1984, when *Belvedere* sailed from Tuktoyaktuk, we headed west for Herschel Island. Aboard were Romayne and Johnny and I, as well as Sven Johansson and Bonnie Hahn. Both Sven and Bonnie had been eager to return, Bonnie especially so, for as an inveterate traveler she couldn't resist the lure of those seldom-visited shores.

As it turned out, the forecast proved accurate: The ice had not melted much, and we were forced to work along inside the ice edge in very shallow water, within only a mile or two of the delta islands. Normally this wouldn't have been a problem, because the silty bottom is very flat and uniform there. But as the search for oil intensified, the oil companies moved from onshore

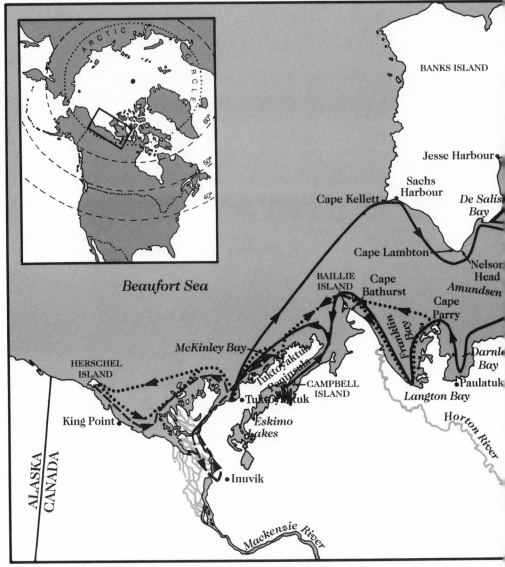

Belvedere's *Route, 1984–1986 Voyages*

exploration in the delta to offshore drilling—and the simplest
way to do that was to build an artificial island. They built these
islands by using dredges to suck up sediments from the sea floor
and to deposit them, either by pumping them through floating
pipes or by using a hopper dredge, which is like an ocean-going,
self-loading dump truck that, when full, goes to a spot and deposits its load through a set of bottom doors. This island building
is economical in water up to ninety feet, though at the outer

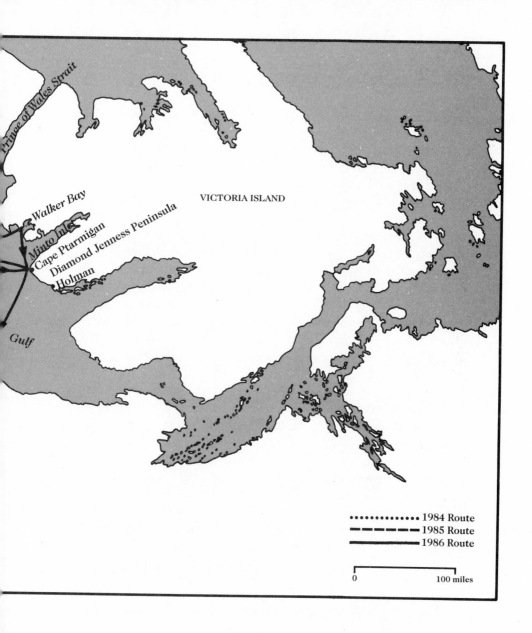

Prince of Wales Strait

VICTORIA ISLAND

Walker Bay

Minto Inlet

Cape Ptarmigan

Diamond Jenness Peninsula

Holman

Gulf

·············· 1984 Route
− − − − − − − 1985 Route
━━━━━━━ 1986 Route

0   100 miles

range the sediments are pumped into a retaining metal caisson rather than being merely heaped into a pile and protected from wave erosion by plastic "berm bags" full of sediment.

The theory goes that, once the drilling is completed, the caisson or berm bags can be removed and then the island will simply wash away. But if in fact this is true in the long run, it was clear to all aboard *Belvedere* that it certainly was not so in the short—for we occasionally saw these abandoned islands awash and unmarked. Between 1973 and 1985 twenty artificial islands were built in the delta, and the presence of these unbuoyed hazards certainly kept us on our toes as we threaded our way through those shallow waters.

I was glad when we finally reached deeper water west of the delta because I was anxious to get to Herschel Island to continue my survey work on the turn-of-the-century whalers' village there, and I eagerly anticipated visiting this ghost town of empty houses, rusting machinery, and lonely graves interspersed among fields of wild flowers. But long before we reached the island, *Belvedere's* VHF radio was alive with chatter and static crashes— for it turned out that Gulf Canada was using the island, as whale- men had a century before, as an Arctic advance base for their offshore exploration, and the place was full of barges and dredges and supply vessels and launches and helicopters charging around twenty-four hours a day.

In fact most of Gulf's fleet—a ninety-thousand-ton tanker; two icebreakers; two supply boats; the construction barge; the *Munaksee*, a converted railroad ferry now serving as a floating command post; a huge mobile arctic drilling caisson called the *Molikpaq;* and the *Kulluk*, a deepwater floating conical drilling platform—spent the winters frozen in Thetis Bay at Herschel. Once the ice was thick enough, they were serviced by a hundred- thirty-mile ice road, built over the ocean and through the delta to Inuvik, where it joined the Dempster highway, linking it with southern Canada. This way two million pounds of freight were hauled out to Herschel in one winter. The company also built a seven-thousand-foot ice runway at the island, allowing 737 jets to land right near the fleet for personnel changes.

A week later, when I had finished my survey work on the remains of a whaleship in Herschel's Harbor, we headed south to the mainland. For the first time in my life I was glad to leave the island. Romayne, noting my slightly glum look said sensibly, "Never mind. The place probably wasn't any quieter when those nineteenth-century whaling ships were jostling around the har- bor." She was right. The place had been seething with activity in those days, and it probably was very little different then, as now—save for the aircraft and the size of the ships.

At Pauline Cove, Herschel Island I inspect a plank from the whaleship
Triton.

I hadn't visited King Point since 1973, when I had stopped briefly on my umiak trip as we were fleeing the heat and mosquitoes of the delta. Now I had a more compelling reason: It was here that Roald Amundsen had been stopped by ice and forced to spend the winter of 1905–1906 as he was heading toward the completion of the first water traverse of the Northwest Passage. Just after he had worked past the Mackenzie delta, he was forced right in to shore, only about forty miles short of the shelter of Herschel Island. He had no choice but to allow the *Gjøa* to be frozen in on the exposed coast.

As we were sailing out of Tuktoyaktuk harbor in July 1984, I had told Bonnie Hahn about Amundsen's difficult summer of 1905, and Bonnie, looking at the floes that were going to force us right down to the delta's outer islands, said cheerfully, "Well, at least we'll get a real feeling for what slowed up Amundsen. The conditions are exactly the same!" I had agreed with her as I silently wondered how much work the ice might allow us to do that year.

It took us only a few hours to reach King Point, which is really not a point at all, only a slight seaward protrusion marking a small lagoon. Nevertheless, for someone traveling along the coast in a small boat—as Sir John Franklin did in 1826, when he named the point—its small river-worn cut sticks out just far enough from the procession of hundred-foot-high mud banks to merit the title.

Johnny and I took the dinghy ashore. He hopped out of the boat and immediately spotted a long trail of very fresh grizzly tracks in the sand. Exchanging my camera for my old shotgun I then set out for the mud bluffs, following Johnny. Once we had clambered through the mass of driftwood logs we worked our way to the low willows on the top of the bluff. I was worried that we might meet the grizzly, so when John let out a *whoop* I almost jumped out of my skin. But he was merely holding up a weathered old board with the name GUSTAV WIIK deeply inscribed on it.

All at once I felt very close to history and very sad, for this was all that remained of the grave of one of Amundsen's men who had died aboard the *Gjøa* in the winter of 1905–1906. The waves have been cutting into this coast at the rate of about two feet a year, and the grave had long since washed away—and now the marker was about to tumble down too, so Johnny and I dragged it thirty yards inland to a safer position.

A few days later we returned to Tuktoyaktuk and changed part of the crew. Romayne and Johnny flew south for the rest of the summer, while Craig George, my whale biologist friend, flew in from Barrow, Alaska, and another old friend, Steve Lirakis, a highly skilled ocean sailor and a manufacturer of marine-safety harnesses, flew up from Newport, Rhode Island. We were out of Tuk again at the end of the month, heading east this time, first, to help Craig out with some whale reconnaissance. A number of biologists were concerned by the possibility that the noise from oil exploration activities might spook the whales; hence everyone was anxious to learn more about their whereabouts. Craig also wanted to see them in relatively undisturbed surroundings and observe their behavior in open water; so we headed toward Baillie Island, where they were historically known to congregate.

"What the hell are those things?" said Steve as soon as we had cleared the harbor and begun to run parallel to the coast. He was not pointing out to sea, but rather inland, at the circular hills that thrust up everywhere from the monotonous plain. We had grown familiar with these things called Pingos, but to a stranger they certainly look odd. There are hundreds of these mounds on the Tuktoyaktuk Peninsula. Ranging in height from a few feet to more than two hundred, they appeared to one explorer to be "mud volcanoes"—and that is a fair description. Scientists now know that they are a cold-region phenomenon that occurs when a lake is drained (by erosion, for instance), thus removing the insulation layer of water from above the underlying unfrozen and moisture-laden sediments. These sediments then freeze and the ice in the lake's center is thrust upward, rather like the dome on an ice cube in a freezer tray. Some are also fairly short-lived, with cycles of growth and decay measured in hundreds of years. Pingos twenty feet high are known to have formed since 1950, for instance, and some have been measured to grow at a rate faster than a foot-and-a-half per year. Each pingo has a distinctive profile, and the Eskimos have always used them as navigational aids in this otherwise featureless region. In fact, we often relied on them too: When approaching Tuktoyaktuk, it is well known that by lining up two of the biggest, "Ibiuk" and "Split Pingo," a course can be followed safely through the shoals off the harbor.

As we worked our way along the coast, we spied a hydrographic research ship farther out, making a detailed chart of the waters off the delta—for it turned out that pingos had been discovered underwater as well. Prior to 1969 everyone assumed that pingos were restricted to dry land, but in that year, the 1,004-foot, 155,000-ton tanker *Manhattan* headed through the Northwest Passage on an experimental voyage to determine the feasibility of tankering the oil out from Prudhoe Bay. She was being escorted by the Canadian Coast Guard icebreaker *John A. MacDonald* when the Canadians made a frightening discovery. As the two were traveling in shallow water off the Tuk Peninsula, over a supposedly flat and regular bottom, suddenly the recording depth sounder showed an abrupt rise from more than one hundred fifty feet to less than seventy, and just as quickly, an equally steep descent. Aboard the icebreaker the shocked crew were staring at this terrifying spike on the printout—and contemplating the consequences if the *Manhattan* had torn her bottom open on such a thing—when the admiral appeared on the bridge. The story goes that he walked by the depth graph, then did a "double take" as he realized that the water depth had shoaled by half and shreiked "What's that!" poking his finger at the anomaly—right through the paper. Henceforth this underwater pingo has appeared on the hydrographic charts as "The Admiral's Finger."

As we continued on east, the wind suddenly rose to more than twenty knots, right on the nose, and quickly built a steep, short sea, making *Belvedere* hobby-horse violently. Rather than beat our brains out all day in this seaway, I decided to go into the only harbor nearby and wait out the blow. When I had traveled along this coast in my umiak in 1972 and 1973, McKinley Bay had been, as it always was, a large, very shallow, and generally useless bay that had the added detraction of being exposed to the northwest, where the big storms come from. But Dome Petroleum, which in 1976 became the first company to work far offshore in the eastern Beaufort Sea oil play, quickly found that Tuktoyaktuk's harbor was too shallow to hold its marine fleet that eventually consisted of an icebreaker, four drillships, and eight suppliers, as well as many other vessels. So in 1979 the company dredged a channel straight into McKinley Bay, excavated a large ship basin for its flotilla, and used the dredge spoil to build a low barrier island to protect the ships from moving ice.

The wind died the next day, and we were off toward Baillie Island and on the lookout for whales. A century ago this area near Cape Bathurst was the last whaling ground discovered in the Arctic. By then the bowheads had been extirpated from almost every other area of their former range and the population had been driven close to extinction. These waters, seven hundred miles east of Point Barrow, were so difficult to reach that the whales were not molested there—until their scarcity elsewhere had driven up the price of baleen, making it worth the risk to take a ship into such remote waters.

The whaleships mostly had to rely on steam auxiliary power, and because the trip from San Francisco was so long, about four thousand miles, they began to winter in the only good harbor nearby, Pauline Cove at Herschel Island. Each spring for a few years it was "Cape Bathurst or bust the boiler," as one whaleman put it, while the fleet hammered its way three hundred miles through the ice toward the Baillie Island grounds near Cape Bathurst.

Even before the island came into sight we began to see whales blowing all around us. "Now I understand why they hang around here," said Craig. "I noticed a few miles ago that we passed out of that muddy delta water into much clearer stuff. All those nutrients that are flushed down the river finally reach some waters where the sunlight can penetrate enough to trigger a plankton bloom. The whales are feeding at the edge of these two water masses. There weren't any whales farther back because the water's too turbid there, and the plankton bloom just doesn't take off without light."

Absolutely flat, and only about fifteen feet above sea level, Baillie Island is a five-mile, triangular plane of eroding mucky silt. We anchored for the night in the whalers' harbor behind the sandbar at the southwest corner of the island. The wintering whaling fleet moved here at the turn of the century to give themselves a better chance in the spring at the few bowheads that by then were left after the assaults from Herschel. Baillie Island was "a nasty place to winter," according to one of the whaling captains. The only protection was the sandbar, which was barely above sea level, and at most a handful of ships could be wedged in there, with their bows almost on the beach and spaced only about a hundred feet apart—far too close in the event of fire. They had no protection from the southwest, and there was no water on the island; the whalemen had to get their drinking water from drift ice. Exposed, dangerous, and isolated, it made Herschel Island look cosmopolitan and luxurious by contrast.

The Parry Peninsula juts northward a little more than fifty miles into Amundsen Gulf. In contrast to the greenery and high mud hills behind us, the peninsula was low and tan-colored—a glacial-drift-strewn isthmus that rose slightly as we traveled along the coast, until outcrops of crumbling limestone cliffs appeared. They had been deeply eroded by the sea into a myriad of islets, inlets, and reefs, making the going quite complicated. I knew that the steam whaling bark *Alexander* had been wrecked here, and I wondered what, if anything, was left of her.

On August 13, 1906, she was charging along in a dense fog under both sail and steam. At 7:00 A.M., just as the officers were sitting down to breakfast, the ship struck so hard on Cape Parry that her bow was driven into only nine feet of water. Immediately the crew was thrown into a panic because it knew that the entire whaling fleet was going to leave the Arctic early that year, and the men realized that for any hope of rescue they would have to race in their whaleboats nearly five hundred miles to Herschel Island to catch the ships before they sailed. In an hour the entire crew was in the boats in a mad rush for safety, and amazingly enough, they all made it, the first boats reaching Herschel on August 26, just an hour before the last ship was scheduled to sail.

The derelict was, of course, a godsend for the resident trappers, both white and Eskimo, who found it to be a wonderful source for all manner of supplies, and the 158-foot ship, which had been built in New York in 1855 as the S.S. *Astoria* and then served in the Russian American Company's fleet, was gradually picked apart—while the autumn storms pounded her to pieces.

Craig George kneels on top of the boiler from the whaleship Alexander *at Cape Parry.*

Rounding one of the low limestone outcroppings, I spotted a massive rusty iron boiler lying against the crumbling foot of the cliff. This was all that remained at the site of the *Alexander*'s wreck, but farther up in the bay the beach was littered with bits of the *Alexander:* large pieces of her decking and hatches, timbers of all sorts, a piece of the mizzen mast, and barrel heads and staves everywhere. We all found it spooky to be at the site of a shipwreck, even though it had occurred nearly eighty years before. It reminded us how fragile all vessels are in the Arctic.

Above the wreckage, on a barren hillside, stood two grave markers. These were not from the *Alexander* disaster, but rather ten years earlier, when the whaleships *Balaena* and *Grampus* had cruised too late in Amundsen Gulf and found their way back to Herschel Island blocked by a large field of ice. With no other options available they were forced to stay here in Balaena Bay for the long winter of 1895–1896. They were short on rations and, thus weakened, eight men died.

Bonnie and I walked to the graves. Both were made of heavy boards that were now gray and deeply weatherbeaten. One had a low and rounded top like a seventeenth-century New England gravestone. Carved into the wood were the names E. ELOPSON and A. LARSON, and at the base, STR. GRAMPUS. I could just make out a few bits of white paint at the base that had been protected by the gravel heaped around it.

The other was seven and a half feet tall and was pointed like a New England church spire. Below the peak in bas-relief was a rosette on one side and a flower on the other. Names were carved into both sides: A. LAROUE, O. CLURE, EUG. COTE. EPH. COTE, JOHN A NATIVE, BEN A NATIVE and the ship, STR. BALAENA. At the base I could again make out a few traces of white paint. Along the edges, there were also a number of puncture marks, with fresh wood showing, evidence that grizzlies had recently been gnawing on the boards. A few bits of fluffy hair were stuck on the splinters as well, testifying that the bears had been using the marker as a scratching post.

Perched atop the apex of the head marker was a lovely carved dove of peace. Gray and weathered, it looked serene and sad; indeed the whole scene was lonely and melancholy. I imagined how in the summer of 1896, as the ships were preparing to sail away forever, the carpenters would have prepared these handsome monuments resembling the grave stones in their hometowns in the United States. The crews would have dug the shallow graves, chipping away the frozen ground with their whaling spades and pickaxes; the head markers would have been set up; and then after a brief service, read by the captains, they would have slowly walked back down to the shore and their whaleboats. I wondered if the men had embellished the graves a bit more, perhaps transplanted some tundra flowers in that brief spring, for on each grave little clumps of yellow Arctic poppies were blooming.

The following summer, 1985, started badly for us. A month of northwesterlies had pushed the pack ice nearly to shore; nevertheless I needed to visit Herschel Island one last time to complete my work there, but it was only through a lot of wriggling and doubling back that we were able to get there at all, and then a couple of stiff northwesterly gales shoved the ice right down onto the delta's islands, so that returning to Tuk proved difficult. It was clear that we weren't going to get much work done that summer, so I decided to do some exploring up the Mackenzie River—but the heat, dust, and mosquitoes quickly drove us back out for the cool of the pack ice and the Beaufort Sea. We made a stab at getting eastward, by running close along the shore of the Tuktoyaktuk Peninsula, but even that modest goal proved impossible, and we were only able to get as far as McKinley Bay, sixty miles from Tuk.

After visiting for a couple of hours with some friends at Dome Petroleum's camp, we started back, westbound, and found that even this was tricky. When we reached Beluga Shoals, where we had been only eight hours before, we discovered that the ice had closed back in, forcing us to zigzag with some difficulty in the shallows.

In the evening, just after we broke into clearer water, the wind dropped to a mirror calm. The sky was perfectly clear, and it was 50 degrees on deck, but when I climbed twenty feet up to the lower spreaders, I was surprised to find that it was 60 degrees up there and that the wind was blowing twenty knots from the

southwest. We had encountered one of the delta's famous atmospheric inversions, and the light, refracting through the different densities of air, put up a fierce mirage, making the scattered floes seem as if we were constantly approaching a solid wall of ice forty feet high, but one which, of course, we never reached.

It would have been nice to stop on that beautiful evening and go ashore for a walk on the dunes, but we had a hunch that the southwesterly might push some ice onto the shoals at Toker Point, blocking our way back to Tuk. Thus we wanted to keep going and get past there as quickly as possible. It turned out to be a well-founded hunch.

At 2:00 A.M. we reached Toker Point, only about fifteen

The whalers' graves stand out against the barren coast at Cape Parry.

miles from Tuk, and, sure enough, found our way blocked by a solid wall of compacted drift ice. First we tried to get inside it by going into very shallow water near shore, but we were never quite sure whether or not we might make it because the mirage made everything look impenetrable. Finally, with the keel scraping the bottom, it was clear that we couldn't make any progress by this route, so we swallowed hard and headed out to sea, running along the ice edge, searching for an opening to get through—and hoping we would find one before this drift ice joined up with the main pack which was not far off shore. But the mirage made it almost impossible to tell whether we were heading for open water or not.

We had to motor fifteen miles off shore, past Toker Point

shoals, past the shipping channel between them and James Shoal, and past James Shoal, until we began to fear that the drift ice had indeed come into contact with the pack and that therefore we were trapped east of Tuk. At last, near 4:00 A.M., we managed to work into a bit of looser ice and began twisting and turning toward the southwest and ultimately broke out by simply pushing our way through into clearer water.

In retrospect, one of the few interesting things to happen in the 1985 season was the arrival at Tuk of the forty-four-foot, ice-strengthened research sloop *Vagabond Deux*, from France via the Panama Canal. She was crewed by a friendly group of Polish émigrés, and we were to see her occasionally in the next few years.

My book on the history of whaling in the western Arctic, *Whales, Ice and Men*, was published in the summer of 1986, and I turned my attention to the successor industry in the western Arctic, the maritime fur trade. Now I needed *Belvedere* to take me farther afield—to the trapping camps and trading posts on the shores of Amundsen Gulf, the great eastern embayment of the Beaufort Sea.

My crew for the season consisted of the usual group of friends—Sven Johansson, Bonnie Hahn, and Craig George— plus a few new faces, and principally among them was Rich Perkins, a friend from home who had had extensive experience sailing in Greenland and now wanted to see the western Arctic. We were off for Banks Island in the latter part of July and almost at once found ourselves working under a low overcast with a light-gray sky and cold, dark-gray sea. For a while we dodged in and out of patches of densely concentrated ice, but at 8:00 P.M., when we were twenty or thirty miles northwest of Baillie Island, we broke into open water, and almost at once we picked up an ugly sea coming at us from smack on our bow. I saw no point in bucking this, so we dodged back into the ice, to wait until a forecast high-pressure system arrived and allowed the seas to settle somewhat.

We found an old piece of hummocked ice fifty yards in diameter and rigged a long "running line" like a bridle: out from one of the bow hawse holes, around a natural ice bollard, and back through the other hawse hole. We could now comfortably

Belvedere has been secured to an ice floe during a gale in Amundsen Gulf.

lie in the lee of the ice and yet be ready to cast off quickly if need be. It seemed odd to be there in calm water, miles at sea, with thirty knots of wind blowing.

That done, we all decided to get some exercise on our floating island. Rich broke out his frisbee and Craig nearly broke his leg chasing it over the undulating hummocks; then Craig dug into his duffle bag and found a bottle of beer that a friend had brought him from somewhere in Micronesia, which he shared. Thus fortified, Craig set up his hydrophone and began to listen for bowhead whale calls but succeeded only in hearing someone peeing from the rail.

Almost as soon as *Belvedere* was under way again we spotted a long, thin, hazy line of white on the horizon, under the gray and murky drizzle. What we were seeing was "ice blink," the reflection of the ice on the undersides of low clouds, and it is a convenient way of telling where the ice is—and isn't. All we had to do was steer toward the "water sky" (the black line on the horizon) to get around this large ice field.

Shortly thereafter "feed slicks" began to appear on the water. These long, slightly greasy-looking strips were in fact dense concentrations of plankton. We knew that bowhead whales graze through these slicks, and within a few minutes we spotted one, and behind him we could see a wide swath he had cut through this marine garden.

Just before midnight Rich Perkins let out a yell of "Land ho!" It was Banks Island which even by Arctic standards is remote. A hundred miles north of the continental coast, its twenty-four-thousand square miles of rolling tundra were first glimpsed by Europeans in 1820 when Lieutenant Frederick William Beechey gazed south from Melville Island and saw the loom of land. His commander, Captain William Edward Parry, named it in honor of Sir Joseph Banks, the great eighteenth-century naturalist and fellow voyager with Captain James Cook. The island was not visited by foreigners for another thirty years until Commander Robert McClure, sailing H.M.S. *Investigator* in the search for Sir John Franklin, landed on the south coast and took possession of "Baring's Island" for the crown, not knowing, of course, that it was one with Beechey's discovery. After spending one winter in Prince of Wales Strait on the east side of the island,

McClure sailed the *Investigator* up the west side and half way along the north side before putting into Mercy Bay for the winter. Unfortunately the bay never unfroze in the following summer, and the ship was forced to remain there for another winter. The weakened and scorbutic crew was extremely lucky to be found by a scouting party from another of the searching ships, which had entered the Arctic from the east, via Greenland. They abandoned the ship and walked over the ice, eastward, to safety. In 1909, when a party from the Canadian ship *Arctic* visited Mercy Bay, they found no trace of the *Investigator*—and to this day no one has. It is assumed that she drifted out into Viscount Melville Sound and eventually was crushed in the ice.

In the early hours of July 30, 1986, we closed with the southwest corner of the island. I saw masses of heavily pressured drift ice that had floated down the west side of the island from the Arctic Ocean, telling something of the dangers that waited up there. In the early morning twilight the white ice line, jagged and menacing, floated above a slate-gray sea and below a peach-colored sky on the northern horizon.

When we were within a mile of the fishhook-shaped gravel spit called Cape Kellett, we turned east and ran along the high, eroding mud banks of Duck Hawk Bluff toward the village of Sachs Harbour, and shortly after lunchtime we crossed the shallow bar into the comfortable embayment in front of the village. Craig and Rich immediately got the dinghy over the side, and we all went ashore.

Sachs Harbour turned out to be one of the cleanest, neatest, and most "pulled together" northern villages I had ever seen. I had grown accustomed to the litter and general sloth of the more southerly towns, but this one was quite the opposite. I would guess that two hundred people lived there, most of whom were active trappers and hunters. A group of Eskimos from Tuktoyaktuk had colonized the island in 1925, when the price of white fox pelts was soaring. They built their own houses, trapped all winter, then sailed back to the mainland in their boats on a fifteen-hundred-mile round-trip voyage to trade at Herschel Island or Aklavik. Each time they left Banks Island on one of these trading expeditions they took all their possessions, including their dogs, with them—because they could never be sure in any year whether the sea ice might block their return. In that case they would simply make camp wherever the trapping seemed good, repeat the annual cycle, and then try again for Banks Island the following autumn.

Bonnie and I walked to the top of the hill behind the village. From there we counted seventy or eighty buildings: There was a one-teacher school for grades one to eight (the high-school students boarded in Inuvik); a co-op store stocked with everything from vegetables to traps to baby clothes and mukluks; a nursing station; a Royal Canadian Mounted Police post; and quite a few red, metal-sided municipal buildings interspersed among the houses. Near the beach, up on blocks, was the little motorized "schooner" *Fox*. A beamy cargo sloop, like all the fur trade "schooners," and only about forty feet long, it had been one of the vessels making the annual voyage between Banks Island and the mainland trading centers (the *North Star*, now owned by Sven, was another). It had now become an artifact symbolizing the community's pride in their self-reliance and competence.

We were off again late the next day, heading southeast, toward the southern tip of the island. The mud bluffs that we had followed all the way from Cape Kellett gradually changed to dunelike sand hills, and then suddenly raw basalt broke through these soft features and stood out in powerful, rough, abrupt cliffs. Here and there, they became palisades rising to more than five hundred feet and farther on, to nearly twenty-five hundred feet. With talus slopes at the bottom, and on top, fields of rolling green tundra ascending into the gray clouds, they were immensely dramatic, looking like a great fortress's walls. Meanwhile, at the base of the cliffs we saw bowhead whales, mothers and calves, proceeding along unconcernedly. As we sailed on, the long line of cliffs seemed to rise out of the water ahead of us, reach into the sky, and then sink back into the sea behind us.

But all of this was a mild preamble to the majestic sight of the southern tip of the island. It was near 4:00 A.M. when we rounded Cape Lambton and saw Nelson Head about eight miles away. The sun was on the horizon and slightly to the northeast, putting the great cliffs west of Nelson Head into a penumbra. The wind fell to a calm, the sky was clear, and the sea was nearly flat.

We saw that the twelve-hundred-foot vertical face of the

headland comprised bands of delicate pastel colors: pink, white, and buff quartzites, interbedded with dark basalt—then suddenly we passed out of the shadow into blinding horizontal sunlight, and these colors became more vivid in the reddish sunlight. For once I was speechless.

The coast of Banks Island runs northeast from Nelson Head and slowly recedes into more gentle hills. At 10:00 A.M., in perfect weather, we dropped anchor in the quiet and beautiful harbor, De Salis Bay. On the sandspit Craig and I found the remains of four or five trapping camps, which we judged had been abandoned forty or fifty years ago. There were hundreds of blocks of sod that had been cut from the nearby tundra, apparently to provide insulation for, amazingly enough, wall tents in which those hardy people spent the winter. Everywhere were rusty pieces of fox traps and other deteriorating debris: polar bear skulls, seal bones, musk-ox horns, rusty cans, bottles, broken guns, cartridge cases, reloading tools, enamel cups and pans, bits of coal, dog chains, and old batteries. We wondered what it would have been like to spend the winter in that lonely place.

The ice charts that we received on our weatherfax indicated open water on the Victoria Island shore between two great fields of ice that virtually covered all of eastern Amundsen Gulf; nevertheless it looked like we might be able to get between them and possibly reach the village of Holman on the Diamond Jenness Peninsula. As we motored across in the near calm, we saw ice blink on either side of us and thought we might make it, but the open water ran out at Cape Ptarmigan, about twenty-five miles from Holman. I went ashore with Craig and climbed to the top of a two-hundred-foot hill to get a better view of the ice ahead of us. First we had to cross a lowland full of seaweed flotsam, then beyond, a small grassy meadow, but when we reached the top, most of what we saw was a vast barren expanse of glacial boulders and reddish raised beaches. This was the legacy of the land's rebound from the ocean after the great weight of the Pleistocene ice sheet was removed. The only things moving were a few logey mosquitoes that floated around us in the 45-degree air. "There's so little growing here that it seems as if this place only rose from the sea last March," said Craig.

We hauled up the anchor and headed back for the more open

seas near Banks Island, then steered north, up Prince of Wales Strait. The coast we ran along was a dark umber color, bare glacial till and uplifted mud, dotted with large erratic boulders on the hillsides. In the shallow valleys the faintest indication of pastel green revealed a tundra growth and in each we saw small groups of grazing musk-oxen.

At 2:00 A.M. on August 5 we anchored in Jesse Harbour at 72 degrees 14 minutes N. It was similar in proportion to De Salis Bay, but smaller and more beautiful. There were rafts of eider ducks in the bay, and one hundred yards away, on the boggy sandspit fluttering with lapland longspurs, eight musk-oxen foraged contentedly, digging in the wet turf with their hooves to expose willow roots. As soon as we headed toward our berths, they too sank down, quietly chewing their cuds.

The next morning we headed up Prince of Wales Strait, but it wasn't long before we were stopped cold—ice stretched from shore to shore, twenty-five miles across the strait. It was in one solid piece and clearly had been there since freeze-up. This did not surprise me; and I certainly hadn't held much hope of getting through the Passage by this route, for it was not far north of here that the super tanker *Manhattan*, 1,004 feet long, was brought to a halt with its two escorting icebreakers. In 1969 she was trying to pioneer a new route through the Passage while simultaneously testing the feasibility of tankering Prudhoe Bay's oil out to markets on the Atlantic coast. The trio tried to break out into the Beaufort Sea via the deep and wide McClure Strait on the north coast of Banks Island—but there met the great river of old polar ice that flows into the Passage from the Arctic Ocean.

"You can't imagine the strength of that ice," Captain Donald Graham, one of the *Manhattan*'s skippers, told me. "There we were with a hundred and fifty-five thousand tons of ship, with her turbines putting out forty-three thousand horsepower, and the ice stopped us cold. There wasn't a thing we could do. The pack was from six to fourteen feet thick and jammed solid under heavy pressure between Banks and Melville islands. As it was, it took us three days to retreat the few miles to Prince of Wales Strait."

For *Belvedere* there was no choice but to turn back. Going back down the strait, we found lots of ice drifting from the east into formerly clear water. At first I was worried that it might have trapped us, but after Sven and I talked it over we realized that it probably had opened the eastern shore at Walker Bay, where I very much wanted to go.

Walker Bay is a name graved deep in the history of the western Arctic. The few people who have visited the area have been struck by the raw beauty of the eroded limestone cliffs. For sailors, however, the compelling attraction has been shelter the harbor provides from moving sea ice. From 1851 to 1852 Captain Richard Collinson and the crew of H.M.S. *Enterprise* became the first Europeans to winter there, while they were searching for the lost Franklin expedition. More than half a century later Captain William Mogg brought the whaling schooner *Olga* there. With the whaling industry dying and the price of furs on the rise, he thought that it would be an excellent place to trade with the Copper Eskimos who had had almost no contact with white men. The motor schooner *Polar Bear* was in the bay from 1915 to 1916 supporting Vilhjalmur Stefansson's Canadian Arctic Expedition, and in the 1930s both the Hudson's Bay Company and their American competitor, Captain C. T. Pedersen's Canalaska Company, maintained trading posts there. For me, however, the most important reason to visit the bay was its association with the history of the Northwest Passage: I knew that Sergeant Henry Larsen of the Royal Canadian Mounted Police had put the schooner *St. Roch* into winter quarters there from 1940 to 1941—while he was on his way to completing the second traverse of the Northwest Passage.

There was not a cloud in the sky as Rich, Craig, Bonnie, and I climbed the low hill above the bay to the *St. Roch*'s great beehive-shaped cairn. Below us *Belvedere* floated peacefully on still blue water marbled by brillant white ice floes—and beyond, the dun limestone cliffs were highlighted by lime-green valleys.

We made another unsuccessful try at reaching Holman, and judging from the weatherfax ice charts and Peter Semotiuk's radio reports from Cambridge Bay, it looked as if there wasn't much point in making a third attempt, so I decided on yet another return to Tuktoyaktuk. Nevertheless, I estimated there was still enough good weather left in the summer to let me squeeze in a little more work on the way back. I made my mind up to head directly south to the continental shore to continue my survey of Amundsen Gulf.

I hadn't visited the village of Paulatuk since 1978. It is at the bottom of Darnley Bay and almost 125 miles due south of Nelson Head on Banks Island, and the difference was dramatic. Here, warmed by the continental winds, the vegetation was lush; the hills as well as the valleys were a rich green and the tundra around the town felt mossy and springy under our feet. The town was much as I remembered it: small (less than two

Rich Perkins sits near St. Roch's *cairn at Walker Bay, Victoria Island, August 1986.*

hundred people), with a few houses painted in a variety of garish purples, oranges, and yellows—"Like some paint salesman arrived here with a hangover," said Rich—and a small co-op store with nothing much in it. The only new structures seemed to be government housing, a school, and a few other buildings.

Right in the middle of the village stood a small, neat Roman Catholic church shaped somewhat like a quonset hut with a low peaked roof. Next to it was a very small two-story vicarage that, like the church, appeared to be about fifty years old. Craig and I knocked on the door and introduced ourselves to the Oblate priest, Father Leonce d'Hurtevent, an immensely likeable man of great dignity, about seventy-five years old. He told us that he had arrived in the Arctic from France in 1937, and that he had traveled throughout the region by boat, resupplying all the missions. In those years the village of Paulatuk did not even exist; there were only mission buildings. The local people were dispersed in trapping camps, and the priest traveled to them by dog team. The only congregation took place at Christmastime, when everyone in the area came to Paulatuk. I imagined how the small, spare room in which we sat—lined with benches and a coal-oil stove in the middle—must have looked then: the people quietly shoulder to shoulder, steam rising from their parkas, children running around. . . .

Father d'Hurtevent said that the local population had remained in camps until 1955, when many of them moved to Cape Parry to work as laborers on the construction of the DEW Line station. It was only in 1964 or 1965, after the government had decided that the Paulatuk area had plenty of game and other resources, that it offered subsidized housing and other services there, firmly rooting the settlement.

After rounding Cape Bathurst, a week later *Belvedere* anchored at the bottom of Liverpool Bay. We were near Campbell Island at the mouth of the Eskimo Lakes, and Craig and Rich and I wanted to inspect the countryside. It was very green and pond-covered, full of grass tussocks and berry bushes and, here and there, willows six feet high. On arrival I said, "Looks like good cover for bears." Then, after a stroll, I returned to *Belvedere* while Craig and Rich kept on walking.

About an hour later there was a yelp on the VHF radio and I

heard Craig's breathless voice: "We've just met a grizzly!" I jumped into the dinghy and raced to shore. A couple of shaken men met me at the water's edge, and luckily neither was hurt. Here is Craig's report in *Belvedere*'s logbook.

> . . . went ashore after dinner to try our luck fishing some tundra lakes about ½ mile inland. JB and I both commented that the country looked to be good grizzly habitat, with good ground cover, berries and abundant ground squirrel signs. . . . JB turned back at the first lake, Rich and [I] unwisely soldiered ahead over a ridge to a second lake. We descended the ridge on the north side quietly chatting and I stopped to glass the hillsides for wildlife. Suddenly I heard very loud grunts. I looked to my right and saw a grizzly charging. I then noticed two cubs standing together but remaining still. Richard was about five yards uphill and we both tried to escape. The bear had instantly closed within 30 feet of me and I turned to face her. She stopped. I yelled with all I had and took up my pack to defend myself. Her lips were curled back showing her teeth in a terrifying display. She turned away and then charged a second time closing to within about 20 feet. Surely I thought she'd attack this time. In one fluid motion she stopped, reeled around and ran back to her cubs. The threesome ran away nearly touching each other, across the drainage and far into the distance. . . .

On our way back to Tuk things went nicely until we were within fifteen miles of the harbor. We were motoring along in a very light southwesterly, with 50 degree weather, when suddenly a black wall appeared to the west and northwest, and then the line squall hit us. The wind came out of the northwest in gusts up to forty-five knots, the temperature fell to 38 degrees, and it began to rain hard. In no time the wind put up an ugly steep chop in the shallow water, and we began to roll like a bucket. We had no choice but to keep going through the rain and scud, and we were mighty glad when we picked up the outer fairway buoy on the harbor approaches. We dropped anchor in Tuk harbor having covered nearly two thousand miles for the summer.

The next day I went ashore to arrange our flights to the south, and just as I passed a TV set in the Northern Transportation Company's camp, word was coming out in a newscast that Gulf Canada was going to shut down its Beaufort Sea operations, laying off seven hundred fifty people. Dome Petroleum had apparently done the same thing. It turned out that OPEC had been unable to maintain its price discipline, and the result was a tumbling price of oil—far below the twenty-four dollars per barrel that was needed to make eastern Beaufort oil profitable.

Once I was back on board *Belvedere* the gale hit again with a vengeance, gusting this time to fifty-five knots. Our anchor line was tight as a piano wire, and although we were only a hundred yards from the windward beach, the waves were already two and a half feet high by the time they reached the boat. We kept anchor watches all night, as the wind sang in the rigging.

I woke to find the gale down to twenty to twenty-five knots and the land all white with snow, contrasting eerily with the blackness of the water—while overhead the dark clouds thundered by, occasionally interspersed with snow flurries or small patches of pale-blue sky. The temperature was 36 degrees and it seemed a fitting end for the summer.

Chapter 10

The Northwest Passage

I spotted Tuktoyaktuk's familiar skyline of cranes and big buildings long before we lined up for the final approach to the runway, but what was remarkable was the new stillness to the place once we landed. There was no frantic scurrying up and down the dirt roads and gone were the whines of jet aircraft and twenty-four-hour-a-day helicopter racket. It was July 1987 but in fact Tuk sounded as it had in the early seventies.

The reason of course was the low price of oil. The only game in town was now Gulf Canada, which planned at best a modest drilling operation for the 1987 season. Consequently Arctic Transportation Limited was sending much of its equipment back to Vancouver and Dome was trying to sell or lease the ships in its fleet. Imperial Oil's camp was completely shut and Dome's housed two caretakers: As I walked past it the only noise was the creaky flapping of some metal strips that the wind had partially torn off the side of one of the modular buildings. Several for-lornly mothballed ships swung on their anchors in the harbor, and the only movement seemed to come from a couple of North-ern Transportation Company tugs and from our old friend, the

Coast Guard ship *Nahidik*. We were witnessing the same boom-and-bust cycle in the oil industry that had happened in the fur trade, and before that, in the whaling industry.

It now seemed a good time to try to move on from Tuk: I had finished almost all my work in Amundsen Gulf, and now I wanted to turn my attention to the waters east of there—and to complete the traverse of the Northwest Passage if possible.

Of the possible routes through the Canadian Arctic islands from the Beaufort Sea to Davis Strait, only one, the southern-most, is usable by boats the size of mine. Because of greater exposure to heavy, moving ice, all of the other routes can only be traversed by larger, ice-strengthened ships. My plan this time was to go first into Coronation Gulf between Victoria Island and the continental shore; then into Queen Maud Gulf's myriad of shoals; then south of King William Island; and later, north along the coast of the Boothia Peninsula, through an exposed section, Larsen Sound, before breaking out into deeper and more open waters.

Even in April, however, I knew that getting through the Canadian Arctic islands to the Atlantic in 1987 would be a tall order. I could see from the U.S. Navy's ice charts that lots of heavy old polar ice had blown into the important straits, and this, plus the fact that the winter of 1986–1987 had been very cold, meant that the breakup would probably take place later than usual (and in some places, perhaps not at all); yet it was defi-nitely worth trying to go into the inner Passage, and possibly beyond, for I still had plenty of field research and interviews to do on the history of the fur trade.

At first it looked as if even getting to the inner Passage was going to be a problem because heavy ice still covered the whole area. Nevertheless I could see from the ice charts that a month of strong northeasterly winds had opened a V-shaped lead of water up the west coast of Banks Island, and I very much wanted to see this rarely visited place.

Craig George and Rich Perkins were involved in other projects that summer and in their place was Rich's aunt Judy Perkins, a veteran of a number of voyages to Newfoundland, Labrador, and Greenland, who joined me, Sven, and Bonnie and one or two others. Judy immediately proved her worth. We

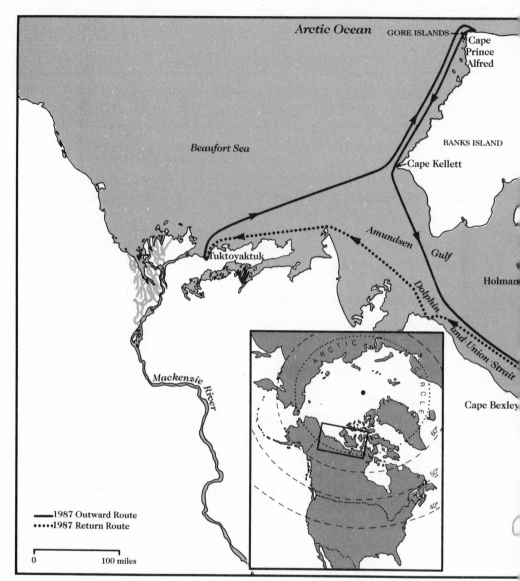

Belvedere's *Route, 1987*

were motoring along the Tuk Peninsula in a flat calm when she spotted some small breakers on the port bow. It was very disquieting to see such a thing in otherwise empty, placid seas, but a glance at the chart showed a small black square marked "abandoned 1980." Barely awash, utterly unmarked, and obviously hazardous, it was one of the artificial islands that the oil companies had built.

Keeping our course directly for Cape Kellett at the southwest

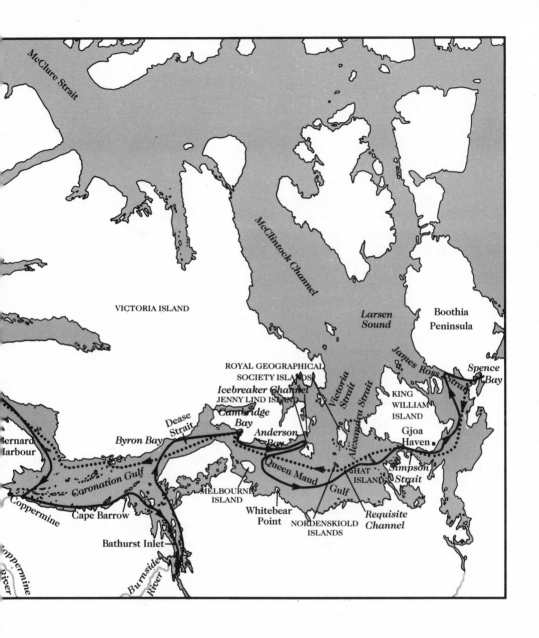

corner of Banks Island, we gradually drew away from the peninsula and reached the cape in the early morning. We were fairly tired, so we dropped the anchor with relief, looking forward to a good sleep. But about 6:00 A.M. we were all awakened by a deep, reverberating *GUC-GUC-GUC-GUC-GUC-GUC-GUC-BOOM-BOOM*—a large ice floe rumbling up our anchor chain, then banging into the hull. On deck, I found that the current had carried a fifty-foot-by-fifty-foot piece of old pressure ridge around the point and down onto us. It was alternately striped with blue of old ice and dirty brown from dust blown off the land. I got to work with a pike pole while Sven started the engine, and with the anchor still down we steered around it and went back to our berths—but the episode repeated itself at 8:00 A.M. and then at ten, by which time the current had begun to run hard from the west, putting us broadside to the wind and bringing more of these unwanted intruders down on us. By then I was fully awake and decided to keep my own anchor watch.

As I stood on deck, occasionally fending off drifting ice, I gazed at the gravel spit a hundred yards away. I could see where a couple of small houses had stood long ago, and I remembered a story that Roy Vincent, one of the elders of Point Hope, Alaska, had told me many years before. The son of a Yankee whaling captain and an Eskimo mother, Roy was raised by his mother and Eskimo stepfather, Peter Koonoonoruk, and went with them in 1916 when Captain C. T. Pedersen landed them at Cape Kellett with a year's outfit to spend the winter trapping foxes and bears. Unfortunately the summers of 1917 and 1918 were so icy that despite his best efforts, Pedersen, the consummate ice pilot, was unable even to get close to the island. "By then we were so low on bullets that we would only take a shot at a caribou when it was in line with another farther away. That way the bullet would hang up in the second one, and we could dig it out and use it again," I remember Roy saying. "We weren't starving. There was plenty of game, but boy were we glad to see Pedersen's ship when he picked us up in 1919!" he added with a chuckle.

By noon the weather forecast was for stable conditions for a few days, so I decided to start up the west side of Banks Island. Almost as soon as we were underway the fog descended, making us a little tense as we worked through the scattered ice floes, but in the evening it cleared, leaving us with a glassy calm and a low overcast. All was an even, flat grayness as we motored ahead, and the only thing to break the monochrome was the occasional blowing of a bowhead whale, its back and head standing out deep black against the uniform light gray.

We stayed a couple of miles offshore because the coast is very low on the west shore, with sandspits and lagoons that hold the shorefast ice, which now was slowly disintegrating and drifting out, making near-shore travel quite difficult.

In fact, we only closed with the coast as we approached the Gore Islands at the northwest corner of Banks Island. They were low and a deep-burnt-umber hue, reminding me very much of the land near Cape Ptarmigan on Victoria Island. Girdling them was a belt of heavy rubble ice shoved high up the shores by the immense force of the Arctic Ocean's winter winds. As we rounded the Gore Islands, heading toward Cape Prince Alfred, we passed more heavy old floes with big, crushed edges. It was a frighteningly beautiful scene, the deep azure blue of the old sea ice against the even gray of the sea and the sky.

We passed the latitude of 74°20′ N and from there could see ten or fifteen miles along the north coast of Banks Island. The pack ice was hard on shore, and it was clear that we weren't going to get much farther in that narrowing shore lead. In fact, we were in the waters now where as far as I know only four other surface vessels had ever been—an ice-strengthened whaleship, an ice breaker, a canoe, and Robert McClure's H.M.S. *Investigator*, which, as I mentioned earlier, never returned.

Moving east into McClure Strait, I noticed the air had a deep, fishy smell, suggesting a dense plankton bloom—and almost simultaneously a bowhead rose close to the boat. We were now less than five hundred miles from the known summer range of the eastern Arctic bowhead population, the one that winters south of Davis Strait, and I wondered if there might be any contact between the two. Scientists today assume the populations are discrete, but during my logbook research I found records of British whaling irons from the eastern Arctic fishery taken from whales that were captured in Alaska; and now being in the presence of a "western" whale, and so close to the eastern range, the thought was tantalizing.

With no open water anywhere but around the corner behind us, we began our return toward Cape Kellett. Holman Island, where I had been iced-out in 1986, was again enclosed, so I decided to head southeast to inspect the continental shore of Coronation Gulf. But because of the lobe of ice off Holman, it would be necessary to aim for the mainland near Pearce Point Harbour and work east along that coast.

After we passed the southern end of Banks Island, it was fog, fog, and more fog. We could see only a couple of boat's lengths ahead, and at about one-thirty in the morning we came upon some low, disintegrating strips of ice. The ice cover was denser than the ice chart we received on the weatherfax had indicated, and we quickly became enmeshed.

I was at the helm, backing and filling and trying to work through it, and when that proved futile, simply trying to get out of it. It was dead slow, neutral, reverse—over and over—as we maneuvered our way in and out of the tightly packed floes. After an hour of this we began to notice a slight swell in the water, indicating that we were getting close to the windward edge of the ice field. Farther on, the swell grew to about two feet, heaving the floes around a bit, a situation that could easily become dangerous if a piece got under the stern and tore off our rudder or bent a propeller blade. The whole time, we were more or less constantly pushing ice, with the dull rumble of the floes scraping past the hull—waking the entire crew and making them extremely nervous. We all knew, and I most of all, that *Belvedere* was not built to be an icebreaker and that the steel of most of her hull was only one quarter of an inch thick. We finally broke out into clear water near the end of my watch. I was exhausted from heaving on the wheel and gearshift lever. For the rest of the day it was just dank, dense fog which eventually settled into rain.

Near midnight a day later the skies cleared and we saw the sun set, only to rise fourteen minutes later, giving us a beautiful morning. But as the sun continued its progression across the eastern horizon, it was soon right in our eyes, making the waters dance and sparkle and visibility extremely difficult. In order to see and avoid the scattered ice we began to "tack" across the path of the sunlight. Even so, I hit a low, waterlogged piece of ice that gave a hiss and rumble as it passed under the hull breaking in two without any damage to the boat.

Cape Bexley marks the beginning of the constricted part of Dolphin and Union Strait, where it is less than twenty miles from the mainland to the southwest corner of Victoria Island. There was a large plug of ice blocking the strait, but we worked in to within one hundred yards of the low, rubbly drumlin-like cape, and with only twelve feet of water under the keel, made it across the Cape Bexley shoal inside the ice. There was so much ice around that I had no idea how much farther we might get, but I wanted to push on a bit in the hope of reaching Bernard Harbour about thirty miles ahead. The capes there are all long, narrow, glacially sculpted limestone fingers reaching northwest, so we kept on, working from promontory to promontory through the scattered ice. West of each small cape we found a little open water and were able to squeak across the shoal off the headland— and so on, hopping right to Bernard Harbour.

It is very difficult to spot the harbor's entrance because the off-lying islands all seem to meld together into one undifferentiated mass when viewed from seaward. This kept us confused for a bit, but eventually we picked out a couple of very old oil drums, one stacked on top of the other, and ran toward them. They turned out to be a rough-and-ready navigational beacon of the fur trade era, but an effective one, for eventually we saw the opening between two of the islands—and suddenly arrived in a nice little harbor with nothing but one dilapidated cabin and an abandoned DEW Line site on a far hill.

Soon the wind piped up to thirty knots, gusting to forty-five, from the northwest and began shoving the ice down Dolphin and Union Strait, making us very glad that we had pushed ahead from Cape Bexley to our safe anchorage. Judy and I went ashore and found that the cabin was an abandoned Royal Canadian Mounted Police post. Inside was a name board from the *Fort Hearne*, a Hudson's Bay Company supply schooner that had been holed by the ice in the strait and had sunk in the harbor. Judging from the speed that the ice was now shooting down the strait, driven before the gale, we could well imagine how the *Fort Hearne* might have been damaged.

We left Bernard Harbour July 29, with the wind down to fifteen to twenty knots from the northwest and the temperature at 35 degrees Fahrenheit. As I mentioned, the gale had blown lots of ice into the strait, and some of it had even been forced into the mouth of the harbor. Leaving was going to be tricky, so I went to the masthead with a VHF radio while Sven took the helm—and for the next four or five hours we twisted and turned our way down Lambert Channel into the clearer water of Coronation Gulf. In the evening the wind fell to a calm, and the flat-topped, narrow islands ahead seemed to swim on the surface of a mirror sea, while behind us was a crimson sky.

The next morning was cloudless and still, and I went ashore at Coppermine and walked into town to mail some letters. The place was absolutely quiet. It was a national holiday, and many of the nine hundred people were out in their summer fishing camps, while the rest seemed to be operating in the normal Arctic summer mode of staying up until four in the morning, then sleeping till noon.

In the quiet I passed one of the old "schooners" from the fur trade days. This one was up on blocks and had a doorway cut through its hull, apparently because some entrepreneurial soul had taken advantage of it to open a coffee shop—but the venture had collapsed and now the boat looked very shabby.

From the top of the hill behind town I could see out across Coronation Gulf and the green delta of the four-hundred-mile Coppermine River. For thousands of years this place had been a seasonal campsite of the Eskimos as they harvested the rich runs of Arctic char. The river got its name from a garbled eighteenth-century Indian tale that it ran past some copper mines, debouching into northern Hudson Bay, and creating a waterway to "ye western ocean"—a northwest passage. The Hudson's Bay Company sent Samuel Hearne to investigate, and in 1771 he found the river and descended it to the ocean. It was a disappointing discovery: There was little fur; the river was not navigable; and there were no copper mines, save for some small surface finds where the "Copper" Eskimos collected ore to cold hammer.

We were off the next day on a sparkling morning, heading east along the mainland shore of Coronation Gulf. On our port side were the Couper, Berens, and Lawford islands, a hundred or so narrow strips of rubbly black-brown basalt columns, each rising from west to east and ending with abrupt fifty-to-one-hundred-foot cliffs. Halfway between Coppermine and Port Epworth, on our starboard side, the gentle rolling tundra and basalt dikes suddenly changed to a wild bubbly upwelling of gray granite with very little tundra in between. We kept on east along the coast, which in the low overcast and drizzle, presented a dismal scene: a low brooding shore, full of scarps and ledges and glacially smoothed rocks.

Soon the skies cleared, and we began our run south, picking our way through a multitude of islands down the one-hundred-fifty-mile gash that is Bathurst Inlet. To the south, perhaps a hundred miles away, were massive cumulus clouds, testifying to the stultifying heat of the interior, away from the cooling effect of the sea water—while to port and behind us a thin line of white stretched along the horizon, confirming the presence of ice that, temporarily at least, blocked our further progress eastward.

We continued on down the inlet all night and well into the next morning, often traveling through waters where no charting had been done. The bottom here was very irregular, occasionally rising from nearly 400 feet to thirty feet or less in a quarter of a mile. At such times, not wanting to slam into an uncharted reef, we would throttle back and inch ahead with our eyes glued to the depth sounder. Because we were now heading so far south—Bathurst Inlet actually ends twelve miles south of the Arctic Circle—the night was very dark, so we kept going by radar, barely being able to see the headlands in the deep twilight.

Belvedere reached the mouth of the Burnside River at four-thirty on the morning of August 5. We were the farthest south *Belvedere* had been since 1983 and more than five hundred miles south of the latitude of Cape Prince Alfred on northern Banks Island.

Two days later we went back up the inlet in a perfect flat calm, heading for Ekalulia Island for water. This small island has a circular lake, two or three miles across, in the middle, and it empties into the inlet via a narrow river only three hundred yards long. We carefully eased into the tiny, rock-bound bay and watched as the bottom rose from two hundred feet to nothing in less than a hundred yards. We put the bow right into the river mouth, almost resting on the beach while we still had ten feet of water under the stern. It was a simple matter to take the fire pump ashore and with the aid of a couple of garden hoses, to pump directly into our tanks.

After wrestling with the ice for a bit, we crossed Dease Strait to the Victoria Island shore, where I had last been nine years before in my umiak. A gale was forecast from the northwest, and we were running for the shelter of Byron Bay. The blast caught up with us on the way, and although we were less than half a mile from the windward shore, where we had good protection from the seas, it blew so hard that in one gust the anemometer needle went right off the gauge at sixty knots (nearly 70 miles per hour), blowing out the stove, and filling the boat with a noxious diesel smell and flying soot. There was so much spray in the air that the windshield wipers could not keep up with it; hence we were very glad to put the hook down in Byron Bay a couple of hours later.

When we arrived in Cambridge Bay, Peter Semotiuk was waiting for us on the town dock. Not only were we glad to see him, but he also had our mail and an offer of showers. Cambridge was much as I had remembered it: dusty and dirty, full of scruffy children on the dock throwing rocks, the occasional stumbling, muttering drunk, and otherwise full of very nice people, many of whom remembered me from my years there in the umiak.

But Cambridge, as a town, was only a few decades old. Dease and Simpson were the first Europeans to pass here, mapping the bay in 1839. Dr. John Rae traveled along this shore in 1851, searching for the lost Franklin expedition, and then Captain Richard Collinson, in the same search, wintered H.M.S. *Enterprise* in the bay from 1852 to 1853. During the winter the local Eskimos visited the ship and Collinson noted that they passed through the area regularly for sealing, fishing, and wildfowling. Foreigners did not reach the bay again until Roald Amundsen anchored the *Gjøa* briefly in 1905 during the first water traverse of the Northwest Passage. Using Collinson's chart of "this narrow and foul channel," he gratefully wrote:

> Sir Richard Collinson appears to me to have been one of the most capable and enterprising sailors the world has ever produced. He guided his great, heavy vessel into waters that hardly afforded sufficient room for the tiny *Gjøa*. But, better still, he brought her safely home. His second in command, Sir Robert McClure, who had to abandon his vessel, the *Investigator* . . . on the northeast coast of Banks Island, and who was then helped home by others, received all the honour. . . . Both of these expeditions were of the greatest importance as a

guide to the navigation of the passage. McClure had proved that it was impracticable to make the passage by the route he tried. To Collinson belonged the still greater merit of pointing out a really practicable way for vessels—as far as he reached. In other words, McClure found a North West Passage which was not navigatable; Collinson found one which was practicable, although not suitable for ordinary navigation. . .

Permanent settlement did not begin at Cambridge Bay until 1923, when the Hudson's Bay Company opened a post here. A few years later it was joined by Captain C. T. Pedersen's Canalaska Company and an RCMP detachment, and in time both the Anglican and Roman Catholic churches opened missions. In 1955 construction began on the DEW Line, and Cambridge became a major transportation and supply center, which at its peak of activity employed as many as two hundred Eskimo laborers, virtually all the region's able-bodied men between the ages of sixteen and sixty-five. Today there are about a thousand persons in the town, whereas forty years before there were a hundred.

One visible link with the past is the submerged hulk of Roald Amundsen's three-masted schooner *Maud,* the remains of which lie awash in the east arm of the harbor. Long after he had completed the traverse of the Northwest Passage and become the first man to reach the South Pole, Amundsen built the *Maud* and sailed her through the North*east* Passage, from Norway to Bering Strait in the years 1918–1920. The Hudson's Bay Company then bought her—it is said, to keep such a sturdy and ice-capable vessel out of the hands of its competitors. Rechristened *Baymaud*, she was used briefly at Cambridge as a floating depot and radio station—until a leak along her shaft put her on the bottom.

One morning, as I was working on *Belvedere's* deck, I noticed an intelligent-looking and fit white-haired gentleman inspecting the boat from the dock. He introduced himself as Carl Emil Petersen, a Norwegian who had just canoed down the Horton River and was now touring some of Amundsen's route by aircraft. I later learned that, in addition to his virtually annual sailing expeditions to the east coast of Greenland, he had skied alone across the Greenland ice cap and had twice sailed round the world. He obviously enjoyed the Arctic as much as I did, and on the strength of that, no less than his manifestly pleasant character, I offered him a berth on our voyage eastward. He accepted at once, and I asked him to come on board that afternoon. "Good!" was his reply. "That will give me just enough time to go snorkeling on the *Maud*." He turned out to be a great addition to the crew, and a hardy one, for every morning he would dive overboard naked, "just to get my blood flowing," he said.

We were all glad to be underway out of Cambridge's dust. Working east into Queen Maud Gulf, along Victoria Island's monotonous fawn-colored shore, we almost made it to Jenny Lind Island before being stopped by a river of ice advancing down from Victoria Strait through Icebreaker Channel—and for the next six days it kept advancing, chasing us back more than forty miles to Anderson Bay, which is only a few miles as the crow flies from Cambridge.

Finally, the ice charts started to show some possibility of navigable water to the south of Queen Maud Gulf, so we swung down by Melbourne Island, and at 7:45 P.M. on August 21 White-bear Point, my old nemesis of 1979 and 1980, was abeam. The going was reasonably good amid scattered floes, but as the light began to get weaker it became harder and harder to pick an intelligent route among them, so at about 2:00 A.M. we shut the engine down and drifted for a while in a small bit of open water.

By 4:00 A.M. the light had improved enough for another try, and try we did. I was off watch, but through the hull I could hear the crunch and hiss of ice scraping by and the deep boom of the bow hitting piece after piece—contrapuntal with the accelerating engine, the sudden pops into neutral, and the heavy reverses, again and again.

Queen Maud Gulf can be fairly described as a navigational nightmare. Although it is well charted in some places, there are thousands of tiny islets, shoals, and boulders in the gulf, all drumlins and glacial erratics. To make matters worse, the compass is virtually useless there, and during the navigation season there is plenty of fog and a constant stream of ice trickling south between the islands. This ice disgorges from a river of multiyear

Carl Emil Petersen and Bonnie Hahn sit aboard Belvedere *in Queen Maud Gulf, August 1987.*

ice that has been forced from the Arctic Ocean, through Mc-Clure Strait and Viscount Melville Sound, then down Mc-Clintock Channel, where it is blocked in a cul-de-sac formed by the Boothia Peninsula, King William Island, and the many islands between there and Victoria Island. Here the ice has nowhere to go, and can only melt slowly or dribble into Queen Maud Gulf.

We knew from our weatherfax ice charts that there was nearly solid ice on the south shore of the gulf, but it looked as if we might squeeze through between that and a flow of ice coming down out of Alexandra Strait along the King William Island shore. This meant using Requisite Channel, the main shipping route, between two clusters of reefs—one around the Nordenskiold Islands to the northwest, and the other around Hat Island on the southeast. For a while it looked as if we might make it, but soon we were halted by a big plug of multiyear ice blocking the strait, and we spent a tormented week groping through the fog, shallows, and never-ending streams of ice feeding down from the north.

Finally, getting tired of this game, I decided to drop back a few miles to Hat Island for some shore leave. We wove through first, the ice, and then the multitude of shoals and low islets off the east side of the island until we reached a beach near an abandoned DEW line station. The island is only about five miles

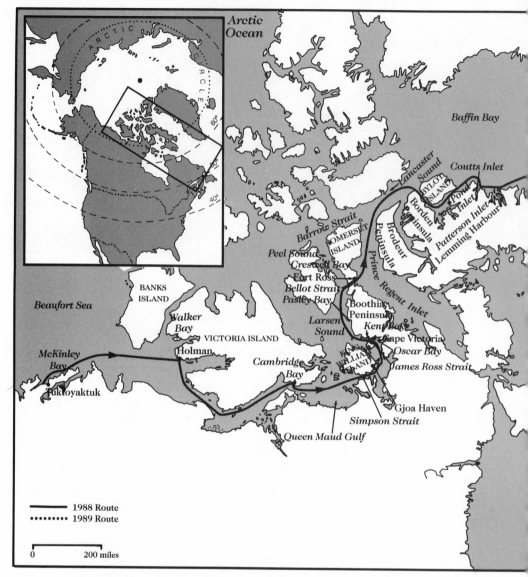

Belvedere's *Route, 1988 & 1989*

long and a little less wide, and it looks remarkably like a flat-brimmed hat: It is mostly low and level, but right in the middle is an abrupt limestone mesa seventy-five feet high. As such it is virtually the only good natural navigational landmark in the 175-mile-wide gulf.

Most of us went ashore and wandered across the mossy tundra, past a long-abandoned trapping camp, to the top of the bluff. It was a stunningly beautiful, if depressing, vista: The sky

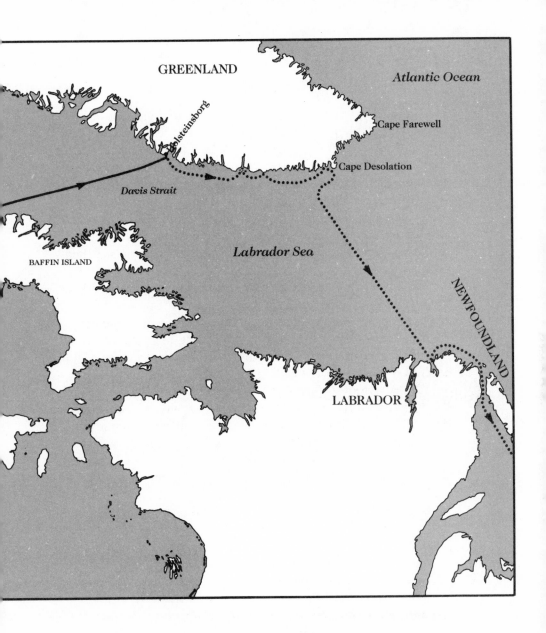

was clear, and the sea all around us was a deep blue, contrasting with the sheer white of two streams of ice, flowing from the north, past either side of the island, which itself presented the third dominant color in the land and seascape—the limestone's even ocher hue. From what I saw it was fairly difficult to imagine how we might make any progress to the east, or indeed even make it back to the west.

When I returned on board I kept my regular radio schedule

with Peter Semotiuk in Cambridge, and he told me that my old friend Willy Laserich, the pilot, was going to fly over to us and help with some ice reconnaissance. Willy put the King Air down gently on the DEW Line airstrip, and Carl Petersen and I went with him on a thousand-mile loop, heading directly to Spence Bay for fuel, then up the coast of the Boothia Peninsula. Amazingly enough it looked just possible that we might make it to the eastern Arctic that summer, and more important, I thought I could see a way out of Hat Island by heading first southeast, then turning northeast.

We hoisted the anchor at 4:00 A.M. the next morning. I had the first watch, but because there was so much ice around I gave the helm to Sven and pulling on several layers against the damp 31-degree air, climbed to the icy spreaders to guide the boat from there. In two hours we had broken out of the ice stream and entered Storis Passage, heading for Simpson Strait.

We had a brief, happy reunion in Gjoa Haven with my friends the Porters, and I was sorry to learn that my friend George Porter, Sr., had died. Carl had a chance to inspect Amundsen's wintering site, and after waiting out a brief gale, we were off again. With *Belvedere*'s bow now pointing north, rather than east, all of us hoped desperately that this might be the year that we made it through the passage.

But it was not to be. Here is my journal entry for August 30, 1987:

> At about 18:00 yesterday we found thick, closely-packed ice extending across James Ross Strait from shore to shore. We were brought to a halt—very depressing. This morning at 06:00, when the light had improved, we started off again and were stopped in just about the same place—wall to wall 9/10's of ice. Damn! So near and yet so far from Resolute.

Although we had covered twenty-seven hundred miles since leaving Tuk, it was clear that we weren't going any farther that summer: The weather forecast was gloomy for the near future—strong northwesterlies, that would really pack the ice in hard in Larsen Sound and James Ross Strait.

Belvedere *takes on water from an ice floe in Queen Maud Gulf.*

The autumn in the Arctic is no place to be wasting time, for the gales increase in frequency and ferocity, and up there autumn begins in mid-August. So, thoroughly depressed at having been stopped once again, I reluctantly gave the order to head back. After dropping Carl Petersen in Spence Bay, on September 1 *Belvedere* turned west to begin the thousand-mile return to her winter quarters in Tuk.

All that autumn I watched the weekly ice charts that were sent to me by the Canadian "Ice Central." Throughout September and October 1987 the heavy multiyear ice remained fast in James Ross Strait and Larsen Sound. This was bad news, for ice like that would take a long time to melt the following summer. But then in November there was a big change. Suddenly the ice charts reported first-year ice in a wide strip along the west coast of the Boothia Peninsula. A strong easterly gale must have shoved the heavy ice over to the west side of Larsen Sound, and I could see that the young ice that replaced it was already thick enough that it would be impossible for the old stuff to blow back in. This meant, of course, that the summer's melt in 1988 would go a lot faster on that relatively thin, salty ice than it would have on the heavy old floes. I spent the winter biting my nails.

As the spring wore on in 1988 the Passage was blessed by relatively warm winds, and the melt began several weeks ahead of normal. It suddenly looked as if we might have a fighting chance to make it through, and I began phoning my friends to put the crew together. Sven, Bonnie, and I formed the core of the crew. Judy Perkins was at work on some whale counting projects that summer, and replacing her were my son Johnny, now twelve years old, and Peter Semotiuk from Cambridge Bay. Peter had been our shore-based radio contact every year since 1979 but this year he had passed his duties on to his wife Alma and had decided to take a crack at running the marine end of the radio link instead.

We sailed out of Tuk on a hot sultry day and immediately were hit by the only really bad weather of the summer. Within a couple of hours it was gusting to forty knots and the seas built to eight feet, making everyone more or less queasy. We were in only seventeen feet of water, so we bucked and rolled pretty badly in steep, muddy seas until we got into McKinley Bay to ride it out. We tied up to the rusty pilings at the artificial island, and then it really began to blow, gusting to fifty-seven knots and sending great billowing clouds of silt over us, coating the entire boat in a sticky layer of salt and mud.

It was a still, dreary scene; for the price of oil had remained low and Dome Petroleum's operations had almost ceased. "This place is the way we expected Herschel Island to look!" exclaimed Bonnie, recalling how in 1984, instead of a ghost town, we had found the entire Gulf Canada fleet there. She was right; now the ghost town was here. It was eerie. Ashore there were only empty buildings, and rusty machinery stuck out of the drifted sand at odd angles. In the bay only one of three drill ships was lighted; the floating dry dock was filled with two mothballed boats; and several work barges, a fuel barge, and the supply boats were all silent and dark. I realized that in 1978 in Tuk I had seen the beginning of the boom; in the early eighties I had been there at its zenith; and at the end of the decade I had witnessed its temporary collapse.

I was glad to leave McKinley and begin washing its mud off *Belvedere*'s hull and sails. We reached Cambridge a week later and paused there to take on fuel, water, and provisions, as well as to await the arrival of Craig George and Richard Olsenius, a photographer from the *National Geographic*. As soon as we had tied up at the town dock, Willy Laserich came aboard and offered to take me on a quick ice-recon flight up to Creswell Bay, north of Bellot Strait, while he collected a load of *muktuk* (whale skin and blubber) from some Eskimo beluga whale hunters camped there. "You'll be back in the evening, or at the latest the next morning, so all you'll need is a sleeping bag and a light jacket," he said. Knowing well that Willy's "one day trips" can easily expand to encompass an entire week, I brought along the necessities for four or five days.

We flew nearly five hundred miles to Creswell Bay on the east shore of Somerset Island, and Willy put the twin Otter down perfectly on the minute seven-hundred-fifty-foot gravel strip. Unfortunately the Eskimo with us, who was the buyer for the local co-op stores, pronounced the *muktuk* (stored on the beach in cardboard boxes under tarpaulins) to be rancid: "No good, no good," I heard him mutter darkly as he kicked at the fetid load—so the hunters were dispatched to go knock off a new batch of whales, which we had seen from the air. After eighteen hours of waiting nothing had happened, so Willy, the copilot, and I slept on the floor of the plane (the Eskimo stayed with his relatives in one of the tents on shore), eating tins of sardines and bits of second-rate sausage from my knapsack. What with one thing or another it took a couple of days to get back to Cambridge, but the time spent was well worth it: To my joy I saw only fifty miles of ice blocking the route north of James Ross Strait—and it was in a fairly advanced state of melt.

Amazingly enough, we had almost no ice, fog, or wind in Queen Maud Gulf as we picked our way through the islands to Simpson Strait. I had a hunch that I might not pass this way again, so we dropped anchor in the strait and took the dinghy to the featureless shore to inspect a group of cairns that explorers have left to honor Sir John Franklin's men; for it was in 1848 on the west and south coasts of King William Island that most of his men died in their futile attempt to walk from the frozen ships in Victoria Strait to the safety of a trading post on Hudson Bay. Franklin had made the mistake of trying to sail down the west coast of King William Island, rather than the east coast—because the charts of the day showed "King William Land" connected to the Boothia Peninsula by an isthmus. The river of multiyear ice from McClintock Channel closed in around Franklin's ships in the autumn of 1846, and a year and a half later it still had not released its grip, when the weak and scorbutic crews abandoned the vessels in an heroic but utterly futile attempt to walk to safety. When we sailed from that sad and dreary spot, we flew our ensign, as Amundsen had in 1905, to honor those brave, doomed men.

Then it was on to Gjoa Haven where we were given the usual friendly welcome, with crowds of kids and adults coming down to the shore to wave at us. George Porter Jr. and his wife Effie immediately came on board, and Johnny was swept right up by all the Porter children and grandchildren. The ice charts showed that James Ross Strait was still not passable, so for once I didn't have to rush leaving Gjoa Haven.

The next day George Porter returned with a couple of fat Arctic char that he had just taken from his net on shore. He and I began to talk about the old days. In the 1930s, when his father was running the Canalaska Company store in Gjoa Haven, he sent young George to the nearest school—which happened to be a thousand miles to the west, at Aklavik in the Mackenzie delta. George and his little sister spent a couple of years there, and then one summer, when he was about fifteen years old, the teachers simply told him he had finished and that it was time to go home. Unfazed by the task, George took his sister by the hand and walked to the trading "schooners" at the water's edge and got a job washing dishes on one that was going as far as Cambridge Bay, then hitched a ride on another for the last two hundred miles to Gjoa Haven.

He told me that his father had guided for Sergeant Henry Larsen when the *St. Roch* was wintering in Walker Bay, and he reminded me that the *St. Roch* had passed by here in 1941 on its way to becoming the second vessel to traverse the Northwest Passage—and the first to go through eastward. I knew that the next two transits had been by large ships via the deep-water route, Prince of Wales Strait: the *St. Roch* in 1944, and the Canadian icebreaker *Labrador* in 1954, both westbound. George recalled that during the DEW Line construction in 1957 a convoy of three U.S. ships, an icebreaker, the U.S.S. *Storis*, and two buoy tenders, the *Bramble* and *Spar*, had gone through eastward, past Gjoa Haven. After that I knew that the eighth and ninth traverses were by U.S. submarines in the early sixties, both using McClure Strait, and that the tenth was by the Canadian Coast Guard icebreaker *John A. MacDonald* in 1967. But all these were essentially preamble to 1969 with the historic voyage of the 155,000-ton tanker *Manhattan* and her Canadian and U.S. icebreaker escorts. These three did not complete a traverse of the Passage, for they stopped short of Bering Strait. But by reaching Prudhoe Bay and then returning to the east, they had finally proved the commercial feasibility of the transit, and thus essentially had ushered in the modern era to the waterway.

Although the words were never spoken, I think that George and I preferred the earlier, and to us, heroic, era in the Passage, before the advent of massively powered and reinforced vessels. The later achievements somehow seemed jejune in comparison to the transits of the *Gjøa* and *St. Roch* and the voyages of H.M.S. *Enterprise* and the whaleships and the fur-trading fleet. I saw a nostalgic look cross George's face as he gazed off into the distance and our conversation returned to the years before the war. "It was real nice then. Sleep when you want. Get up when you want. No welfare. No one to tell you what to do." Then George looked straight at me and said, "John, we really enjoy your visits. You are helping to preserve our history and no one else cares about it." I quote Amundsen to express my feelings on my departure the next day. "I left Gjøahavn with nothing but happy memories."

On the afternoon of August 21, 1988, once again we found our old bane, the pack ice, blocking James Ross Strait, just as it had the year before. This time, however, it was broken up and moving, and I felt sure that it wouldn't be long before we made some headway, so we dropped back a few miles to wait in an unnamed cove just west of Oscar Bay. Here we were joined by our friends aboard the research sloop *Vagabond Deux*.

The next day began foggy, and in our enforced idleness, after having been frustrated by the ice for so many years, we could barely contain our impatience. Seeing that we were all twitchy and that none of us could relax, Peter Semotiuk suggested that we should go ashore and build a cairn to commemorate our voyage. It seemed like a good idea for burning off some energy, so I appointed Peter as "cairnmeister," a job he was well suited for, being six feet four inches and stronger than any two of us put together. Our model was the *St. Roch*'s cairn at Walker Bay on the far side of Victoria Island, now nearly a thousand miles by water to the west of us. After three hours of lugging rocks and placing them at Peter's direction, we had a pretty good monument, seven feet high. "I hope no one mistakes this for one of Sir John Franklin's undiscovered cairns and tears it down, only to find a Tupperware box with our business cards in it," said Peter.

In a sunny calm the following morning we found that the ice edge had moved a few miles north to Cape Victoria. With nothing else to take up our time, Craig and Johnny and a few others decided to go swimming. I believe it will remain one of the shortest swims of their lives—the water temperature was 35 degrees Fahrenheit. Only Johnny went for a second plunge. After going ashore at Cape Victoria we dropped back to "Belvedere Harbour" again for the night.

The time passed with agonizing slowness, but the next day the ice had started to move a bit, and we pushed on in a narrow shore lead past Cape Victoria into Kent Bay. Suddenly Craig and Richard Olsenius let out a whoop from the spreaders. "I can see another sailboat coming toward us!" Richard shouted. It was the small yawl *North Hanger* of England, and I believe it was the first time eastbound and westbound vessels have met in the Passage. An hour later we met another, the motor lifeboat *Mabel E. Holland*, also of England, with my friend David Cowper aboard. He had wintered the boat for two years at Fort Ross at the east end of Bellot Strait, waiting, like us, for an opening. He was underway to circumnavigate the world, alone, under power. It was a

In "Belvedere Harbour" on the Boothia Peninsula at James Ross Strait, Johnny Bockstoce poles his way in the shallow water on a small ice floe in August 1988.

series of ecstatic greetings, frantic toasts, and hurried good-byes—for none of us wanted to waste time with that menacing pack ice lurking out there to the west of us in Larsen Sound. (Both *North Hanger* and *Mabel E. Holland* were stopped by heavy ice just west of Herschel Island and wintered at Inuvik, completing their traverses to Bering Strait in 1989.)

That afternoon we passed Pasley Bay, where the *St. Roch* had wintered in 1941–1942, and where I had camped in 1980 on my umiak trip. Less than twenty-four hours later we reached Bellot Strait, which is the fulcrum point of the Northwest Passage. This is where the waters of the western Arctic meet those of the east, and it is the first meeting of the tides of the Atlantic and

Pacific north of Tierra del Fuego. The strait is narrow and deep: twenty miles long and less than half a mile wide at its narrowest, where it separates Somerset Island from the Boothia Peninsula, which is the northernmost point of the continent of North America. Tidal currents race through its fiordlike, rocky walls at more than nine miles per hour, which is about as fast as *Belvedere* can go under full power.

I was worried that the current might be holding a nasty surprise for us in the form of drift ice. As I mentioned earlier, in 1980 I had stopped at the village of Spence Bay, about one hundred fifty miles south of Bellot Strait, and there had met the late Ernie Lyall, who told me that the current could shoot the ice floes through "like bowling balls. And the conditions can change fast," he added, reminding me that in 1977 the Canadian hydrographic survey ship *Baffin* had entered the strait in relatively clear water one August morning, but three hours later the current had sucked in so many floes that the strait was covered from shore to shore with heavy old ice under very strong pressure. The *Baffin*'s crew found itself trapped right at the midpoint, and was only able to hold the ship's position by running the engines at full power. When the tide turned the ice slacked off and the ship moved on safely, but it was a close call—and one that I certainly did not want to replay in *Belvedere*.

In 1980 I had heeded Ernie's advice and didn't go into Bellot Strait in my umiak, but kept on directly north, up Peel Sound; nevertheless, in 1988 our destination was Greenland, and this route would save at least a hundred miles. I had prepared a detailed set of tide tables for the strait, showing the brief periods of slack water and the directions the currents would run at each change, and when *Belvedere* approached the western end of the strait on the morning of August 25, 1988, I discovered that we had luckily coincided with one of the slack periods.

Craig and Richard and I got into the dinghy to photograph *Belvedere* coming through the strait. Gazing right down the slot, Craig let out: "It looks like a chainsaw cut through a mountain range here." It was impressive, forbidding scenery: steep thousand-foot reddish basalt cliffs rising from the water, interspersed with dun-colored limestone, and punctuated here and there by colonies of nesting sea birds which showed as bright orange swaths of lichen above a green base.

Gray fulmars, gull-size birds, soared and swooped around *Belvedere*, skimming low over the waves, then rising with rapid wing beats. The birds were here because Bellot Strait is one of the Arctic's great polynias, a place where there is open water year-round. Here the tides do the job of preventing an ice cover forming, and the mixing of the water masses creates a rich plankton bloom; in fact we could see it in the water, and the presence of four or five bearded seals sleeping on separate floes testified that there were plenty of fish to live on. It reminded me that in 1980 I had seen beluga whales and polar bears at the west end of the strait, whereas the waters south of there had seemed almost devoid of life.

Once Richard had gotten his photographs we sped on down the strait in the dinghy to Fort Ross, an abandoned Hudson's Bay Company post. We saw two weatherbeaten and lonely-looking buildings standing near the shore at the foot of a big ledge. They had been built in 1937, when the company decided that it would be an ideal location, and one which could be supplied from either west or east. Scotty Gall, then a young post factor at Cambridge Bay, had told me how he had taken the

Craig George works on the Belvedere *cairn near Oscar Bay on the Boothia Peninsula.* Belvedere *is in the distance.*

sixty-foot schooner *Aklavik* east with supplies to meet the freighter *Nascopie*, which had arrived from the Atlantic with construction materials. But it turned out that the company had overreached: The summers of 1942 and 1943 were so icy that the *Nascopie* could not reach Fort Ross, and Ernie Lyall was forced to undertake a five-hundred-mile sled expedition across the moving ice of Prince Regent Inlet to collect supplies from the post at Arctic Bay on Baffin Island. In 1948 the company closed the post and set up a new one at Spence Bay.

Two hours later, the current had begun to run hard again, and I could see evil tide rips eddying over Magpie Rock, a formidable hazard to large ships. I remembered how my friend Captain Tom Pullen had described the discovery to me. He was in command of the Canadian icebreaker *Labrador*. "We were doing exploratory work in 1957 and entered the strait with the tide flooding strong behind us. Suddenly the depth sounder started to rise almost vertically, and I threw the engines into full astern. We just missed scoring a bull's-eye on that rock. The name was my navigator's: a hit is a bull's-eye; a miss is a magpie."

We rejoined *Belvedere* at the eastern end of the strait, and almost as soon as we were underway, we were welcomed into Prince Regent Inlet by a school of bowhead whales that were lazing along in the flat calm on the surface, blowing and occasionally showing flukes.

At the north end of Prince Regent Inlet our course closed with the thousand-foot limestone cliffs on the Brodeur Peninsula of Baffin Island. All day we worked along with huge icebergs (visible ten miles away) on our port side and the bleak, buff-colored cliffs to starboard. They seemed lifeless: no animals, no vegetation, and only the occasional fulmars, dovekies, or black guillemots. Moving on into Lancaster Sound, we began to feel a westerly swell, which increased substantially by the time we rounded the northern tip of Baffin Island (73°52′ N), but now it was more on the stern. We rolled along all night and finally turned south, into Navy Board Inlet with a twenty-five-knot wind following us. Soon the skies cleared; the sea became deep blue; and in the sunlight, the cliffs tan and red. Ahead four or five glaciers poured down the steep cliffs of the Borden Peninsula and all around us were large, pure-white icebergs—while off to port, between the five-thousand-foot peaks on Bylot Island, I saw the ghostly white glow of its ice cap.

We reached the village of Pond Inlet and paused to take on fuel and see a few friends, principally Father Guy-Marie Rousseliere, a widely respected Arctic archaeologist and thirty-year resident of the settlement. By 6:00 P.M. on August 29 we had run far enough out of the mouth of the inlet to find a big residual swell setting in from the northeast, the legacy of an earlier gale. This, plus a twenty-five-knot wind, made the going pretty unpleasant, giving *Belvedere* a corkscrew motion in the cross seas. None of us wanted to be thrown around all night, so I decided to put into the first place that offered shelter, the forty-mile-long, Y-shaped fiord system called Coutts Inlet. It was now quite dark, with a heavy overcast and snow flurries. I found it difficult to pick out anything but the biggest features in that murk, but fortunately the cliff walls showed up clearly on the radar. The bottom was deeper than a thousand feet, so we decided to try anchoring in the alluvial gravel at the mouth of a stream. We found that it sloped down so steeply that our anchor couldn't get a bite, and furthermore, that the creek valley funneled the wind to about forty knots. The best we could do was to run a little farther up the fiord and simply drift all night with "anchor" watches.

In the morning we woke to a stunning scene. The fiord was narrow and very long, with bold cliffs, three thousand feet high, topped by an ice cap. Here and there they were broken by steep grayish-white glaciers that descended almost to the water's edge plowing beige moraines ahead of them. The pinkish granite cliffs were streaked with black and had been smoothed by the great grinding pressure of the glacier that had been in the fiord, but the peaks were ragged. A snow line began halfway up the cliffs and ended under a cold gray sky.

Emerging from the inlet we found the old heavy swell still running, so we only made about sixty miles before we ducked out of it into Patterson Inlet. At the southern end of Bergesen Island we found a gem of an anchorage in Lemming Harbour, which is only two hundred yards long, by fifty wide, a small low cleft in the pinkish granite. Around the edges of the harbor was

a dense, mossy tundra cover that had gone into its autumn colors: deep greens, tans, and reds. Across from the harbor's mouth,
only a mile or so away, was the eighteen-hundred-foot vertical
cliff face of Adams Island, topped by its own glacier.

As soon as we dropped anchor Bonnie spotted a large polar
bear lying on the tundra about a hundred yards from the boat. It
got up, stretched, then slowly made its way over a ridge. Near
the creek in the harbor we found five or six lichen-covered remains of prehistoric Eskimo houses. They were semicircular and
built into the scree slope below a great ledge. It was easy to see
how the stone slabs had been used for the walls of the entryway,
for the sleeping platform, and for the lamp stands. I saw one
large bowhead whale rib that must have served as a roof beam,
and here and there were scattered moss-covered seal bones. The
structure reminded me very much of the houses I had seen on
Diomede Island in Bering Strait, but the place looked so bleak
that it hardly seemed possible that life could be sustained there;
yet the house, and the seal bones, and the polar bear, and some
caribou dung all pointed to the contrary.

That evening the forecast was light winds for a couple of
days, so at 4:00 A.M. on August 31 we left Lemming Harbour and
shaped a course directly for Holsteinsborg, Greenland, at Davis
Strait, nearly six hundred miles ahead. On our starboard side
thirty miles away were the great black cliffs of Baffin Island, with
wisps of snow blowing off their peaks in the purplish haze—
while all around us were hundreds of icebergs of vastly different
shapes and sizes, reminding us of things as diverse as birds,
powerboats, houses, and cathedrals. Johnny spotted one that he
claimed was a dead ringer for a gigantic Big Mac.

Icebergs were a new phenomenon to us, making us feel like
the strangers from the western Arctic that we were, where there
are none—because there are no glaciers there. A few of these
bergs may have calved from Canadian glaciers, and some may
have originated in east Greenland and then been carried by
ocean currents around the southern tip of the island, then around
the entire perimeter of Baffin Bay, but the vast majority of bergs
are produced on the west coast of Greenland, where twenty
thousand to forty thousand are calved annually. Those that reach
the sea are carried first to northern Baffin Bay, then down the

coasts of Baffin Island and Labrador. Completing a two- to three-year cycle, an average of about seventeen hundred bergs pass south through Davis Strait each year and about three hundred reach the waters east of Newfoundland, where the *Titantic* had her fatal encounter in 1912. Some bergs, in fact, have gone farther: One was sighted off Bermuda in 1907 and one south of the Azores in 1909.

Bergs calve in any number of sizes, from large tabular-shaped bergs with flat tops that are from one to thirty miles long (although bergs more than twice that length have been reported),

Peter Semotiuk watches the coasts of Coutts Inlet, Baffin Island, August 1988.

Sunlight reflects off of a small iceberg on the southwest coast of Greenland as Johnny Bockstoce looks on, June 1989.

down to bergy bits, the size of a house, and growlers, less than about twenty yards square.

Being glacier ice, hence compressed snow, they have a luminous appearance from the large amount of air trapped within them. "Up close, you can hear them hissing as the air is released while they melt," Vice Admiral George Steele told me. He made the first submerged transit of the Passage, in 1960, in U.S.S. *Seadragon*. "When we entered Baffin Bay we never had a problem identifying icebergs. Sea ice, of course, doesn't make that noise."

And being fresh water ice, it is very hard, as the crew of the ice-strengthened super tanker *Manhattan* found in 1969 on their return from Prudhoe Bay in sea water ballast. "We hit a bergy bit in Bafflin Bay that rolled under the hull and punched through some unreinforced plates. You could have driven a truck through the hole," Captain Donald Graham told me recently.

On the evening of August 31 we were crossing diagonally through the stream of bergs, and as the light got weaker, it became more difficult to steer through all the bits of ice. The bergs were easy enough to spot, but as they melt, many pieces of ice slough off them and drift away downwind. The combination of an overcast, some mist, and poor light made the helmsman's work really tricky. The simultaneous jobs of staying on course, peering into the radar scope full of targets, then squinting through the windshield to dodge the ice that we knew was coming at us, kept us on our toes all night.

By daylight on September 1 we were through the worst, and things continued to improve as we kept on southeast across Baffin Bay, drawing ever closer to Greenland. On the second we crossed onto Store Hellefiske Banke ("Big Halibut Bank") and saw one or two Greenlandic trawlers at work. I couldn't sleep at all that night I was so excited, but when I came on watch at 4:00 A.M. on the third, I was dismayed to find that our clear skies had been replaced by thick fog. This was definitely a problem, because our approach charts and harbor charts for Greenland had never caught up with us; so we were forced to close with that rocky, reef-strewn coast on our radar and depth sounder alone. I can say without fear of contradiction that we were a happy crowd when the massive granite headlands of Holsteinsborg Harbor showed above the fog. We had reached Davis Strait, the eastern entrance to the Northwest Passage, and *Belvedere* had become the first yacht to traverse the Passage from west to east.

We were underway again in June 1989 and worked down the craggy and ice-girt coast of west Greenland as far as Cape Desolation, then stood southwest, across the Labrador Sea, and through a dense stream of "Storis," the river of ice that is carried down the east coast of Greenland and back up the west coast. It was a mixture of bergs and very heavy old sea ice, all rafted and tortured and very blue—definitely not a friendly sight. We saw our last ice on the southeast coast of Labrador, then made stops in Newfoundland, Nova Scotia, and Maine before reaching *Belvedere*'s home port in Massachusetts. As we entered the harbor I saw Romayne on the dock with a crowd of friends and well-wishers.

After a week spent sprucing up *Belvedere* we headed to New York City to conclude the voyage, docking at South Street Seaport to *The New York Times*'s headline: YACHTING EASTWARD INTO ARCTIC HISTORY.

The next day, July 26, 1989, we took a group of friends down to the Statue of Liberty. *Belvedere* had come more than twenty thousand miles on her voyage, and as I stood on the deck with Johnny, I realized that it had been almost exactly twenty years to the day since I had first flown to Bering Strait, and my own northwest passage had begun.

Index